PERFORMANCE MANAGEMENT

PERFORMANCE MANAGEMENT

FINDING THE MISSING PIECES
(TO CLOSE THE INTELLIGENCE GAP)

GARY COKINS

WILEY

John Wiley & Sons, Inc.

Published by John Wiley & Sons, Inc., Hoboken, New Jersey
Published simultaneously in Canada

Library of Congress Cataloging-in-Publication Data:

Cokins, Gary.
    Performance management : finding the missing pieces (to close the intelligence gap) /
Gary Cokins.
      p. cm.
    Includes bibliographical references and index.
    ISBN 0-471-57690-5
      1. Organizational effectiveness—Measurement. 2. Performance—Measurement.
    3. Industrial productivity—Measurement. I. Title.
HD58.9 .C643 2004
658.4'012—dc22
                                                                 2003021215

Printed in the United States of America

10 9 8 7 6 5 4 3 2 1

CONTENTS

ABOUT THE AUTHOR

Gary Cokins is a strategist in Performance Management Solutions with SAS (parent of the acquired ABC Technologies, Inc.), the world's largest privately owned software vendor. He is an internationally recognized expert, speaker, and author in advanced cost management and performance improvement systems. He received a B.S. in Industrial Engineering/Operations Research from Cornell University in 1971 and was a member of both the Tau Beta Pi and Alpha Pi Mu honor societies. He received his MBA from Northwestern University's Kellogg School of Management in 1974 and was a member of the Beta Gamma Sigma professional society.

He began his career as a strategic planner with FMC Corporation. With FMC's Link-Belt Division he served as Financial Controller and then Production Manager, which exposed Gary to the linkages between cost information, strategy, operations, performance measurements, and results. In 1981 Gary began his management consulting career with Deloitte & Touche. There he was trained by Eli Goldratt and Robert Fox and implemented Theory of Constraints (TOC) OPT software. Gary then joined KPMG Peat Marwick, where he implemented integrated business systems and ultimately focused on cost management systems, including activity-based costing (ABC). At KPMG Peat Marwick, Gary was trained in ABC by Professor Robert S. Kaplan of the Harvard Business School and Professor Robin Cooper. Next, Gary headed the National Cost Management Consulting Services for Electronic Data Systems (EDS). He joined ABC Technologies in 1996.

Gary was the lead author of the acclaimed *An ABC Manager's Primer* (1992, ISBN 0-86641-220-4), sponsored by the Institute of Management Accountants (IMA) and the Consortium for Advanced Manufacturers International (CAM-I). In 1993 Gary received CAM-I's Robert A. Bonsack Award for Distinguished Contributions in Advanced Cost Management. Gary's second book, *Activity-Based Cost Management: Making it Work* (New York: McGraw-Hill, 1996), was judged by the Harvard Business School Press as "read this book first." His 2001 book, *Activity-Based Cost Management: An Executive's Guide* (New York: John Wiley & Sons, 2001) regularly ranked as the #1 best-seller by book distributors of over 150 books on the topic.

Gary is Certified in Production and Inventory Management (CPIM) by the American Production and Inventory Control Society (APICS). Gary serves on several performance management committees, including CAM-I, APICS, the Supply Chain Council, the Council for Logistics Management (CLM), the Institute of Management Accountants (IMA), the American Society for Quality (ASQ), the Society of Manufacturing Engineers (SME), and the American Institute of CPAs (AICPA). Gary was the coeditor of CAM-I's 2001 *Glossary of ABC/M Terms* and is a member of the *Journal of Cost Management* Editorial Advisory Board. He is an instructor for the Institute of Industrial Engineers (IIE), the Purchasing Management Association of Canada (PMAC), and the American Society for Quality (ASQ). Gary can be contacted at garyfarms@aol.com or gary.cokins@sas.com.

ABOUT THE WEB SITE

As a purchaser of this book, *Performance Management: Finding the Missing Pieces (to Close the Intelligence Gap)*, you have access to the supporting Web site:

http://www.wiley.com/go/performance

The Web site contains files for:

Appendix A   Performance Management Process Cycle
Appendix B   Customer Value Measurement Using Customer Lifetime Value
Appendix C   Was the Total Quality Management Movement a Fad?
Appendix D   Categorizing Quality Costs: Key to Measuring Progress
Appendix E   Rank-Ordered Capital Efficiency of Product and Customer Combinations

These appendices expand on portions from the book for those who would like a little more depth on a topic. In the book there are references to the associated appendix at appropriate location.

Appendix A expands on Part Two. It describes a how-to-implement approach to strategy maps and balanced scorecards. Appendix B expands on a section from Chapter 17 on customer relationship management. It specifically describes the emerging measurement concept of customer lifetime value that treats each customer as if they are a financial investment. Appendixes C and D go into more detail on material in Chapter 19. Appendix C provides some historical background on how the "total quality management" movement progressed into six sigma methodologies. Appendix D describes how to measure the cost of quality. Finally, Appendix E expands on a more advanced methodology for measuring changes in economic value as was described in Chapter 20.

The password to enter this site is: management

PREFACE

In the preface of my earlier book, *Activity-Based Cost Management: An Executive Guide* (John Wiley & Sons, 2001), I stated: "Sometimes luck beats planning. I have been fortunate in my professional career—a career that began in 1973 as an accountant and continued into operations management and management consulting. Without realizing it—through this series of different jobs and management consulting assignments—I somehow earned a reputation as an internationally recognized expert in activity-based cost management (ABC/M). In truth, I am always learning new things about how to build and use managerial systems. I'm not sure that any expert in ABC/M exists. I'm just fortunate to have been formally working with ABC/M since 1988 when I was introduced to ABC/M."

My training was in industrial engineering and operations research, and I attribute that foundation to letting me think about how organizations work as a set of intermeshed systems—like linked drive gear teeth. In the 1990s my work assignments began to weave in strategy and nonfinancial performance measures. This book reflects my observations from these work experiences and from some exceptional people I have been fortunate to interact with.

ORGANIZATIONAL DIRECTION, TRACTION, AND SPEED

Direction, traction, and speed. When you are driving a car or riding a bicycle, you *directly* control all three. You can turn the steering wheel or handle bars to change direction. You can downshift the gears to go up a steep hill to get more traction. You can step on the gas pedal or pump your legs harder to gain more speed.

However, senior executives who manage organizations do not have *direct* control of their organization's traction, direction, and speed. Why not? Because they can only achieve improvements in these through influencing people—namely, their employees. And employees can sometimes act like children: They don't always do what they're told, and sometimes their behavior is just the opposite!

This book is about giving managers and employee teams of all levels the capability to improve their organization's direction, traction, and speed—and most importantly, to move it in the *right* direction. That direction should be as clear and focused as a laser beam, pointing toward its defined strategy.

THE RELENTLESS PRESSURE TO PERFORM

There are never-ending obstacles and challenges for managers seeking to line up and leverage an organization's energies, and these obstacles often surface as questions. In an unforgiving economy, executives from all functions are asking tough questions:

- Chief executive officers are asking, "How can we position the company for profitable growth by integrating our strategy with daily operations? How can we foster innovation without losing control? How do we win?"

- Chief financial officers are asking, "How can we move beyond the role of the cost-cutting police to be viewed as a strategic partner? How can we report reliable profit and cost data, rather than misleading information flawed with improper arbitrary cost allocations? How can we provide more visibility?"

- Senior human resource and information technology managers ask, "How can we appear to be a service provider and establish service level agreements with equitable charge-back reporting to our users? How do we prove our value to the organization?"

- Sales and marketing executives are asking, "How do we identify and retain our more profitable customers? How do we profitably add services to our increasingly commoditylike products and base service lines in order to differentiate ourselves from competitors?"

Each of these questions arises due, in part, to the complexity of today's organizations, but the questions are not really new. What is new is the pressure to get the correct answers from increasingly complex and interdependent processes. Furthermore, some problems are made more difficult to solve by information technology systems that were, ironically, implemented as solutions, not problems—such as diverse nonstandard software packages, legacy systems, and incompatible computing platforms.

To make matters worse, employees and managers who are tasked by these executives to improve performance are stymied by their own questions:

- How do I reduce my budget without sacrificing service or quality levels?

- How efficient do I have to become to support my expected future workload volume or a new program with my current budgeted resources?

- How do I get out of this pickle? I'm now a process owner and being held accountable—but I have minimal influence and control!

- Do I need to expand warehouse space to handle my expected volume? Or, alternatively, can I ship direct? Which choice is better?

- What will be the impact of discontinuing some products? of changing delivery frequency and routes? of changing packaging formats?

- Who in my supply chain is creating costly waste? Where is there redundant work among us?

The managers' dilemma is that they cannot get answers to these questions from their transaction-based operational systems. Their execution systems are adequate for processing and filling an order, but not for showing them where to improve or what to change in order to better align their employees' work with the organization's strategy. Enterprise resource planning systems (ERP) have become popular as a tool to fill orders and attempt to plan for future orders, but although ERP provides some cross-functional visibility of operations, ERP tools (or the planning and operation control systems) are not designed for producing the analytical intelligence that is central to managing performance. ERP systems deluge employees with data, but not necessarily with *business intelligence* for decision support.

ALIGNING EMPLOYEE BEHAVIOR WITH STRATEGY

"Alignment" is a key word I will frequently mention. Alignment boils down to the classic maxim, "First do the right things, and then do the right things well." That is, being effective is more important than being efficient. Organizations that are very, very good at doing things that are not important will never be market leaders. The concept of work alignment to the strategy, mission, and vision deals with focus. The economics then fall into place.

Another challenge involves how well executive management communicates its strategy. Figure A illustrates this. Most employees and managers, if asked to describe their organization's strategy, cannot adequately articulate it. Many employees are without a clue as to what their organization's strategy is. They sometimes operate as helpless reactors to day-to-day problems. In short, there is a communication gap between senior management's mission or vision and employees' daily actions.

Performance management can close this communication gap. Methodologies with supporting tools like *strategy mapping* and performance measurement

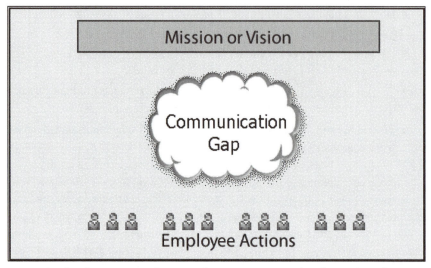

"Many leaders have personal visions that never get translated into shared visions that galvanize an organization. What is lacking is a discipline for translating individual vision into shared vision."

Peter Senge, *The Fifth Discipline*

Figure A   The Communication Challenge

scorecards (discussed in Part Two) aid in making strategy everyone's job. Performance management allows executives to translate their personal visions into collective visions that galvanize managers and employee teams to move in a value-creating direction. The traditional taskmaster/commander style of executives who attempt to control employees through rigid management systems is not a formula for superior performance. Performance management fosters a work environment in which managers and employees are genuinely engaged and behave as if they were the business owners. Destructive beliefs and unwritten rules that are commonly known in an organization's culture (such as "Always pad your first budget submission") are displaced by guiding principles.

But this gap is more than a communication gap. It is an intelligence gap as well. Even organizations that are enlightened enough to recognize the potential value of their business intelligence and assets often have difficulty in actually realizing that value as *economic value*. Most companies are still unable to get the business intelligence they need; and the intelligence they do get is not delivered quickly enough to be actionable. Methodologies like *activity-based management* (ABM), discussed in Part Three, provide a reliable, fact-based financial view of the costs of work processes and their products, services, and customers (service recipients and citizens for public sector organizations).

IMPACTS OF ACCELERATING INNOVATION AND INFORMATION TECHNOLOGY

Why have stock share prices plummeted for some of the world's most successful, market-leading companies? Why are companies experiencing wave after wave of employee layoffs in order to meet or beat their so-called target earnings projection, rather than achieving it with top-line sales growth? It is apparent that many companies are struggling with slimmer profit margins and less predictable financial results.

Part of this problem involves the increasing speed of change. The half-life of technologies, organizational structures, processes, policies, and procedures is shrinking all the time. For example, the annual budget quickly becomes obsolete before it is finalized and certainly after it is published, so it is typically replaced with quarterly rolling forecasts. Another example is the shortening of product and service line life cycles. Increasingly products are perceived as commodities that competitors can quickly copy and produce soon after new products are launched by others. Consequently, product differentiation is giving way to value-added service differentiation as a way to retain increasingly demanding customers. (And few companies adequately measure this increasingly important cost-to-serve for various customer segments, which means they don't know which customers are more or less profitable!)

Innovations in technology—particularly communication and computing advances—that spawned dramatic economic gains in the 1990s have also led to new types of organizations, such as third party logistics firms (3PLs) in physical distribution and contract manufacturers, that require tightly compressed business planning and decision-making cycles.

Trends that were once tracked by quarters now fluctuate from week to week. Yesterday quickly becomes ancient history, and it is often not a very good predictor of tomorrow. Without business intelligence, companies are swiftly punished. But the cost of incomplete or inefficiently generated intelligence can be huge—not only in missed revenue opportunities, but in real cash outlays wasted on niche software products and incompatible applications that are expensive to integrate and maintain. Worse yet, new software systems often do not provide one consistent version of the truth, and they can leave decision makers doubtful of their organization's outcomes and output. In short, poor business intelligence leads to uninformed decisions and misguided strategies.

BALANCED SCORECARD: MYTH OR REALITY?

This book will describe how *strategy maps* and *scorecards* enable leadership and motivate people by serving as a guide with signposts and guardrails. Strategy maps explain high-level causes and effects that facilitate making choices. With strategy maps and their resultant choices of strategic objectives and the action items to attain them, managers and employee teams easily see the priorities and adjust their plans accordingly. People don't have sufficient time to do everything everywhere, but some try to. Strategy maps and their companion scorecards rein in the use of peoples' time by bringing focus. Untested pet projects are discarded.

Scorecards are derived from strategy maps, contrary to a misconception that scorecards are simply a stand-alone reporting system. However, scorecards solve the problem of excessive emphasis on financial results as the measure of success. Consider that telephone calls are still "dialed" even though there are hardly any dial phones left. A car's glove compartment rarely stores gloves. Eventually, the motion picture "film" industry will rely on digital technology, not film. Similarly, "financial" results will likely be shared with more influential nonfinancial indicators, such as measures of customer service levels. Going forward, managers and employee teams will need to be much more empowered to make decisions, hopefully good ones, in rapidly reduced time frames. Scorecards, supported by business intelligence, improve decision making.

Commercial software plays an important enabling role in performance management (PM) by delivering an entire Web-based and closed-loop process from strategic planning to budgeting, forecasting, scorecarding, costing, financial consolidations, reporting, and analysis. Commercial software from leading vendors of statistics-supported analytics and business intelligence (BI), like SAS (www.sas.com), provide powerful forecasting tools.

LEADERSHIP RISES FROM TAKING CALCULATED RISKS

Organizations need to overturn decades of traditional business practices. They must now manage the total enterprise by aligning themselves, their customers, and their suppliers in one strategic direction. Leadership's role is to determine the direction and motivate people to go in that direction. After a strategic direction is defined or adjusted, then the senior executives are challenged with cascading it down through their organization and across to their trading partners.

There is a large distinction between managing and leading. Leadership is often characterized as directing, aligning, visioning, rewarding, energizing, or cheerleading. In contrast, managing is associated with doing. The border between the two, where management ends and leading begins, has to do with risk taking and being decisive. Management is characterized as avoiding risks, whereas leadership is characterized as taking risks. Improved leadership can result from removing risks, or at least minimizing them into *calculated* risks. Uncertainty and risk are never removed, but they can be diminished. Risk-avoiding managers can evolve into leaders by drawing on more courage to take calculated risks. My father once told me that life is ten percent what happens to you and ninety percent how you deal with it. Leading is always about courage and making choices.

POSITION STATEMENT

My basic beliefs are simple and few:

- The discipline of managing is embryonic. Unlike the fields of medicine or engineering, which through codification have advanced their learning decade by decade, managing is more comparable to an apprenticeship program. We learn from observing other managers, whether their habits are good or bad. The introduction of performance management, with an integrated suite of tools and solutions, can make managing a discipline on par with the other mature fields. And managing with reliably calculated risks converts managers into leaders.

- We substantially underestimate the importance of behavioral change management. Each year that I work, I increasingly appreciate the importance of change management—considering and altering people's attitudes and behavior.

- Strategy is of paramount importance. Strategy is all about choices and focus. Given limited resources, executives must get the most from them. However, the most exceptional business processes and organizational effectiveness will never overcome a poor strategy. Defining strategy is the responsibility of senior management, and it may indeed be their primary job, with everything else they do being secondary.

- Power is shifting irreversibly from suppliers to buyers due to the Internet. As the need to increase customer satisfaction increases, senior executives must make this central to formulating their strategies. With power shifting to the customer, pressure on suppliers and service providers will be relentless. Consolidations of businesses are predictably in the future.

- Intangible assets, like employees and branding, are becoming far more important than tangible assets.

- All decisions involve trade-offs that result from natural conflicts, such as customer service level objectives and budgeted cost (i.e., profit) objectives. It is essential to balance the overall enterprise's performance with better trade-off decision making, rather than allow political self-interests to preside.

- It is critical to operate with reliable, fact-based data. For example, organizations need visibility of accurate costs, but most receive flawed and misleading cost information from arbitrary cost allocation methods. They do not receive visibility to their hidden costs of marketing and sales channels. They also need increasing transparency of their trading partners' profit and cost structures and their operating data. With the facts comes a better understanding of what drives results and costs. Without agreed-on, reliable facts and an understanding of if-then causality, the organization can stumble, lacking the ability to build strong business cases for ideas.

I ask that the reader patiently absorb my description of the interdependencies of the various aspects of an organization. Learn from this book how methodologies like forecasting demand, measuring performance, measuring segmented profits and costs, and planning for resource levels can themselves be integrated.

My hope is that reading this book will instill an increased sense of confidence that complex organizations can finally see clearly—that employees within such organizations can find the pervasive fog lifted and see how they truly operate. There is hope. It *is* possible to tame an organization's dysfunctional behavior, despite how prevalent it seems.

WHERE DOES INFORMATION TECHNOLOGY FIT?

Before I conclude the preface and discussing my beliefs in greater depth, let me address the role of information technology (IT). Where do software and data management fit in? Software is a set of tools that serves as an enabler to the performance management solution suite of methodologies. However, in the big picture, performance management (PM) software is necessary but not sufficient. Software does not replace the thinking needed for the strategy and planning that is involved in PM—but it can surely enable the thinking process. Software and technology are not at center stage for making PM work. However, unlike the situation in the mid-1990s, software is no longer the impediment it was then. Back then you could dream of what the tools can do today, but the technical barriers were show-stopping obstacles. That is no longer the situation.

Today, advances in software and data management are well ahead of most organizations' abilities to harness what can be done with these tools. Today the impediment is not technology but rather the organization's thinking—its ability to conceptualize how the interdependencies can be modeled, to configure software, and to incorporate the right assumptions and rule-based logic. Commercial software has made great leaps in the ease with which it can be implemented, maintained, and, most importantly, used. Casual users, not just trained technicians and statisticians, can easily use statistical and analytical software programs.

Information technology can substantially aid leaders in managing risk and being more decisive. However, a fool with a tool is still a fool. When world-class commercial software is used by people who understand business, commerce, and government, then look out for high performance. They will collectively aid their companies in achieving that elusive competitive advantage—or, if they are a public sector or not-for-profit organization, they will optimize their service levels with their finite resources.

Executives are recognizing that computers and technology are much more than just information management. The larger picture involves knowledge management. What good is capturing data if people can't have access to it? What good is using data if you cannot use it wisely? Information technologies enable performance management, but performance management is much more. It forms the foundation to escalate managing into a formal discipline.

OVERVIEW OF THE BOOK

Chapter 1 expands on the six beliefs outlined earlier and builds the business case for what is driving the need for PM to evolve into a formal discipline. Part One then describes what *PM* is. Parts Two and Three explain two foundational pillars of PM: performance measurement (strategy mapping, balanced scorecards, and employee communications) and managerial accounting and economics (measuring profits and costs, including activity-based costing, and predicting future resource requirements and expenses).

Part Four describes five core business process solutions that are aided by the measurements derived from Parts Two and Three. Here transaction-based data that was converted into information is further transformed into higher forms of business intelligence for decision support. Part Five concludes with how data management and mining technologies operationalize PM.

This book does not need to be read cover to cover. I see it more as a reference guide or manual. I encourage readers to initially scan the outline and the many illustrations with the purpose of marking which sections are of greatest interest to read first. But remember that the main idea is not to examine business improvement methodologies in isolation but rather as an integrated solution set. Also remember that strategy-aligned performance measurement (Part Two) and measuring resource consuming costs (Part Three) are the underpinnings for the core solutions in Part Four.

I would like to thank my many coworkers in SAS and other individuals, in particular Eleanor Bloxham, who reviewed sections of this book and gave me valuable feedback. I'd like to thank those special people from whom I have learned a nugget of insight, distilled it, and synthesized it into this book. I'd also like to honor in memoriam Robert A. Bonsack—friend, mentor, and craftsman in the field of performance improvement, who twice hired me (Deloitte and EDS).

Finally, I am forever grateful to my wife, Pam Tower, who for the year I was writing this book allowed me to balance—and occasionally misbalance—my job and family.

Gary Cokins
garyfarms@aol.com (I welcome your e-mail.)

1

WHY THE NEED FOR PERFORMANCE MANAGEMENT AS A SYSTEM?

"A man's mind stretched by a new idea can never go back to its original dimensions."
—Oliver Wendell Holmes,
U.S. Supreme Court Justice, 1897[1]

Performance management (PM) is the process of managing the execution of an organization's strategy. It is how plans are translated into results. Think of PM as an umbrella concept that integrates familiar business improvement methodologies with technology. In short, the methodologies no longer need to be applied in isolation—they can be orchestrated.

PM is sometimes confused with human resources and personnel systems, but it is much more encompassing. PM comprises the methodologies, metrics, processes, software tools, and systems that manage the performance of an organization. PM is overarching, from the C-level executives cascading down through the organization and its processes. To sum up its benefit, it enhances broad cross-functional involvement in decision making and calculated risk taking by providing tremendously greater visibility with accurate, reliable, and relevant information—all aimed at executing an organization's strategy. But why is supporting strategy so key? Being operationally good is not enough. In the long run, good organizational effectiveness will never trump a mediocre or poor strategy.

But there is no single PM methodology, because PM spans the complete management planning and control cycle. Think of it as a broad, end-to-end union of solutions incorporating three major functions: collecting data, transforming and modeling the data into information, and Web-reporting it to users. Many of PM's component methodologies have existed for decades, while others have become recently popular, such as the balanced scorecard. Some of PM's components, such as activity-based management (ABM), are partially or crudely implemented in many organizations, and PM refines them so that they work in better harmony with its other components. Early adopters have deployed parts of PM, but few have deployed its full vision. This book describes the full vision.

The term "knowledge management" is frequently mentioned in business articles. It sounds like something an organization needs, but the term is somewhat vague and does not offer any direction for improving decisions. In contrast, the main thrust of PM is to make better decisions that will be evidenced, and ultimately measured, by outputs and outcomes.

Many organizations seem to jump from improvement program to program, hoping that each one might provide that big, elusive competitive edge. Most managers, however, would acknowledge that pulling one lever for improvement rarely results in a substantial change—particularly a long-term, sustained change. The key to improving is integrating and balancing multiple improvement methodologies. You cannot simply implement one improvement program and exclude the other programs and initiatives. It would be nice to have a management cockpit with one dial and a simple steering mechanism, but managing an organization, a process, or a function is not that easy.

Some believe that implementing a balanced scorecard (described in Part Two as blending nonfinancial and financial measures for balanced emphasis) is the ultimate solution. However, evidence demonstrates that a balanced scorecard will fail unless it is linked with other management processes. "Balanced scorecard implementations often fail to deliver anticipated benefits because they are not integrated with PM processes, particularly those used at an operational level," says Frank Buytendijk, research vice president of Stamford, Connecticut–based Gartner, Inc. "We believe that 80 percent of enterprises that fail to integrate the balanced scorecard into PM methods and tools will drop the balanced scorecard and return to a less organized and less effective set of metrics."[2]

SPOTLIGHT ON OBJECTIVES, OUTCOMES, CONFLICTS, CONSTRAINTS, AND TRADE-OFFS

Even with a clearly defined strategy, conflicts are a natural condition in organizations. For example, there will always be tension between competing customer service levels, process efficiencies, and budget or profit constraints. Managers and employee teams are constantly faced with conflicting objectives and no way to resolve them, so they tend to focus their energies on their close-in situation and their personal concerns for how they might be affected. PM escalates the visibility of quantified outputs and outcomes—in other words, results. PM provides explicit linkage between strategic, operational, and financial objectives. It communicates these linkages to managers and employee teams in a way they can comprehend, thereby empowering employees to act rather than cautiously hesitate or wait for instructions from their managers. PM also quantitatively measures the impact of planned spending, using key performance indicators born from the strategy map and balanced scorecard.

Knowing these strategic objectives and their relative importance, managers and employee teams then use tools from the PM suite, such as activity-based costing data and customer relationship management information, to objectively evaluate the trade-offs. Everyone recognizes that employee teams are very knowledgeable in their own space. When management communicates to them what is wanted, employees can reply with an understanding of what initiatives it will take and how much it will cost. Internal politics and gaming are replaced by the preferable behavior of employees taking responsibility like independent business owners.

As problems constantly surface, the context for making trade-off decisions is framed. This applies to the ultimate value creators, the executive management team, who struggle with short-term versus long-term trade-offs. The CEO and CFO also wrestle with those conflicting cost and customer service objectives governing financial earnings that investors and hand-wringing stock analysts anxiously anticipate each quarter. Differentiating customer value from shareholder value is a tricky exercise, and PM brings objectivity and balance to the process of making spending and investment decisions. Budgeting becomes a profit-fostering funding mechanism rather than an accounting police control weapon. Prioritizing and coordinating begin to displace control.[3]

The appeal of PM is that it realizes there is no sun around which lesser improvement programs, management methodologies, or core processes orbit. PM is about sense-and-respond balancing, always striving for better organizational direction, traction, and speed. PM involves constructing powerful combinations linking software, such as business intelligence analytics, with core processes enhanced by improvement initiatives (e.g., lean and/or six sigma) to prioritize efforts and align an organization's work activities with its corporate strategy. If PM is properly implemented, it can produce an epidemic of common sense within an organization—and also probably with the trading partners (e.g., suppliers and customers) with whom it interacts. Maximizing everywhere is not equivalent to optimizing—it is suboptimizing. Optimizing acknowledges constraints. PM facilitates balancing conflicts.

What issues and circumstances have created the need for PM now? Let's explore them next. There are several, some involving pain and others opportunity, and their combination is compelling organizations to pursue PM.

ACCELERATING TURNOVER AT THE TOP: WHY?

Surveys by the Chicago-based employee recruitment firm Challenger, Gray & Christmas, Inc., repeatedly reveal increasing rates of job turnover at the executive level compared to a decade ago.[4] It is almost as if when you accept a C-level job you also sign your undated resignation letter—what is omitted is your forced resignation date.

The primary cause for the executives' revolving door involves failed strategies. In my opinion, defining and adjusting strategy is the number one purpose of the CEO. However, despite their best formulated plans, when executives adjust their strategies, their major frustration is they cannot get their employees to execute the revised strategy. This is due in part to the fact that while new strategies may be planned, the performance measurement system is typically not changed to reflect the new emphasis on what is newly important or the reduced emphasis on what is less important. You get what you measure, so without changes in measurements, the organization's inertia keeps it plowing straight ahead in the same direction it had been going. In short, there is a big difference between formulating a strategy and executing it.

The balanced scorecard has been hailed by executives and management consultants as the new religion to resolve this frustration. It serves to communicate the executive strategy to employees and also to navigate direction by shaping alignment of people with strategy. The balanced scorecard resolves a nagging problem. There is a substantial gap between the raw data spewed out from business systems and the organization's strategy. Figure 1.1 illustrates an upside-down pyramid-shaped diagram with *strategy* located at the top and *operational and transaction-based systems and data* at the bottom. The systems at the bottom, such as enterprise resource planning (ERP) and general ledger accounting systems, are like plumbing—you need to have them, but they do not tell you what to do strategically or what risk-adjusted choices to make. The business intelligence of PM in the figure adds value on top of these operational systems that organizations have invested huge sums of money in. Ideally, daily operations should align with the strategy—but do they? That is, do the transactional systems consuming resources and spending at the bottom convert to value at the top? Not without a business and analytical intelligence layer. This is a senior management dilemma.

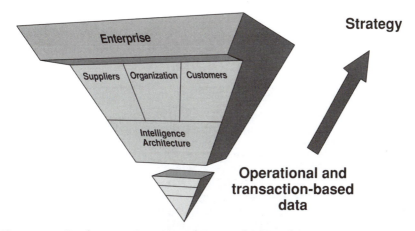

Figure 1.1   Gap between Strategy and Transaction-Based Systems

It is a tough time to be a chief executive. CEOs put out one fire, only to see another start to smolder. Top corporate officers have always been under intense pressure to meet earnings projections for Wall Street and improve profit margins in a turbulent economy. They are continually identifying and trying to realize cost-reduction opportunities. They are pressured to deliver short-term return on investment (ROI) without undermining long-term returns. They grapple with trading off responsibilities to increase shareholder wealth without compromising the spending and investments needed to respond to market forces. Unfortunately, the incessant drumbeat of security analysts and the capital markets, often too fixated on quarterly earnings per share (EPS) measures, pressures executives. Many of their executive compensation programs include EPS, as if it equates to adding economic value; so whether they want to or not, many executives discover they are running on a quarterly reporting earnings treadmill, and they do not know how to jump off.

FALSE PROMISES OF INFORMATION TECHNOLOGIES

Now turn your attention to the bottom of Figure 1.1. This is where expensive operational and transaction-based information technology (IT) systems reside. Figure 1.2 magnifies the tip of the pyramid at the bottom of Figure 1.1. In a simplistic way, it depicts the IT data center's three layers of software:

1. The *IT infrastructure* systems at the bottom, such as for security or backup/recovery, to control, manage, and route the hardware and communications.

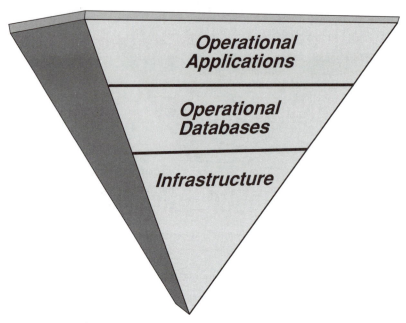

Figure 1.2   Database Core

2. The *operational databases* from which the operational software applications draw and deposit data.

3. The *operational applications* that process transactions and produce simple summary reports.

Regardless of what goes on near the bottom, value increases as this data is converted to support analysis and decisions. Organizations rely on operational and transaction-based IT systems, such as ERP or customer relationship management (CRM), to perform their day-to-day business functions. The improvement opportunity lies in analyzing the data from these systems.

Information technology (IT) continues to herald the next new wave of promise for organizations to allegedly drive execution and leapfrog competitors to leave them behind in a trail of dust. Application software vendors promote their systems as the keys that can open any lock. However, at best, these expensive IT systems have only helped maintain parity. At worst, they may have distracted resources. (And IT magazines and journals routinely chronicle failed implementations by large companies with lawsuits blaming the software vendors.) Few organizations have translated their IT system capabilities into sustained profit growth.

The truth is that ongoing improvements of IT systems are necessary but not sufficient. Without them, a company risks falling too far behind. Furthermore, as customers and service recipients enjoy an exceptional experience from a company, from its competitors, or from a different industry, their feel-good experience unforgettably raises a high-water-mark baseline for them. For example, once people have used an automated bank teller, they want similar self-service kiosks in other areas of business, such as to carry out hotel registrations. In the future, customers will judge and expect similarly exceptional experiences from the companies they patronize, and anything less will be a disappointment.

To complicate matters, in the 1990s an organization was happy if its business system simply recorded and reported transaction information. But today this is commonplace and expected. Transactional systems are effective at producing data but not at providing knowledge. So organizations may be deluged with data without necessarily getting any closer to what they need. They are data rich but information poor.

Figure 1.1 depicted a layer of software technology, described as intelligence architecture, that converts raw data from transactional systems into meaningful information for decision support. But technology simply supports the methodologies in which it operates.

Business systems should be more forward-looking. They should drive performance and operational excellence. They should provide predictive information. But do they? Or do our IT systems today simply report history and support existing methodologies?

Figure 1.3 displays the intelligence architecture on a timeline across which successful organizations will eventually pass. The vertical axis measures the power and ROI from leveraging data. Most organizations are mired in the lower left corner, hostage to standard reports and a little analytical capability provided by some tools selected for everyone by the IT department—sometimes as a compromise. The figure demonstrates that the upside potential is enormous to robustly analyze and understand one's own organization, its customers, suppliers, markets, competitors, and other external factors, from government regulators to the weather.

IT transactional systems may be good at reporting past outcomes, but they fall short on being predictive for good planning. Given a sound strategy, how does the organization know if its strategy is achievable? What if pursuing the strategy and its required new programs will cause negative cash flow or financial losses? Will resource requirements exceed the existing capacity?

Employees are creative, innovative, and driven if they know an objective or goal is obtainable. But too often, senior managers put forth unrealistic goals without having validated the fundamental financial, process, or resource

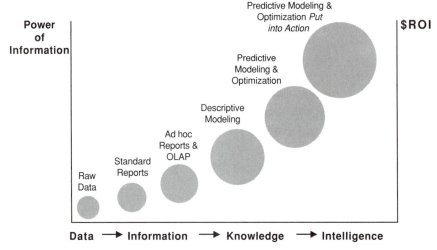

Figure 1.3   Evolution of the Intelligence Architecture

requirements needed to achieve them. Operational systems were designed with a different purpose thus contributing to their false promises as analytical solutions. In order to successfully set and reach goals, managers and employee teams must be able to create accurate, feasible plans and budgets that will support and drive goal achievement. (The large disconnect between the annual budget—a bookkeeping exercise administered by the accountants—and the strategic plan is discussed in Part Two.)

A MAJOR POWER SHIFT IN THE VALUE CHAIN

Power is shifting irreversibly from suppliers to buyers. The cause is the Internet. Customers and consumers, including purchasing agents and buyers in businesses, now have access to powerful search engines to seek and compare offerings from suppliers of products and services as well as to gain education for more informed decisions. And the suppliers, in effect, aid the buyer's learning and shopping experience by adding increasingly useful information in their own Web sites and through industry trade exchanges.

In the last half of the 20th century in the United States, economic prosperity conveniently generated customer demand for goods and services, which led to a fair amount of arrogance. Organizations took their customers for granted. Some companies held the attitude that, essentially, "If the customer doesn't like our solutions, then they have the wrong problems." Those days are over.

The World Wide Web has forever changed the velocity of business and changed everything about how organizations interact internally and externally. The volatility of a Web-time and Web-speed world forces any organization relying on traditional Industrial Age business models to operate in a catch-up mode. The Web compresses business planning and decision cycles. Trends that were once tracked by quarters are now revealed to fluctuate weekly and daily. Should you react or stay the course? There are both perils and promises in now having access to immediate, real-time data.

Presuming that most organizations always operate with scarce resources, then financial language like the "return on customer" (a variant of return on investment) and "customer lifetime value" creeps in from the CFO function of the enterprise. Phrases like "customer satisfaction" and "customer for life" permeate the popular sales and marketing literature. Yet customers are not created equal in terms of how they contribute to profits. Discoveries from activity-based cost management systems reveal that a company's largest customers may be hardly profitable due to their high demands, high maintenance requirements, and persistent requests for customization. This adds another dimension for how to segment and differentiate customers beyond the traditional ones like gender, income level, or purchase frequency. A customer's sales volume cannot be considered a substitute for the customer's level of profit contribution. As a result, the CFO is increasingly servicing the chief marketing officer (CMO) and chief logistics officer (CLO) by providing mission-critical information. (CRM with marketing automation tools and value chain analysis and management are discussed in Part Four.)

DISPLACEMENT OF TANGIBLE ASSETS BY INTANGIBLE ASSETS

PM is an effective way to understand value creation. *Value* is an ambiguous term. Does it refer to customer value or shareholder value? In the context of describing an organization's assets, I am referring to shareholder value—the monetary view. Sustained value creation is another task of the senior executives. But here again executives are running into a problem. The sources of value have been shifting. Ideas are taking the place of land and property in establishing value. Organizations are now much more knowledge-based. Working smart seems to beat working hard.

Statistics from the Balanced Scorecard Collaborative[5] provide evidence of this shift. In 1982, for every U.S. dollar of market capitalization (as measured by the Wall Street–like stock trade exchanges), 62 cents was attributed to tangible

assets. Tangible assets are buildings, machines, and inventories. A simple definition of long-term assets is things one purchases which *depreciate* as period expenses with time.

But in 2001, for every U.S. dollar of market capitalization, only 15 cents represented tangible assets. This means that 85 cents of investor-valued worth came
in the form of brands, relationships, and employees. Employees are intangible
assets. The knowledge of workers who go home each night and return in the
morning is what produces value in many organizations today. A simple definition
of this type of intangible asset, in contrast to a tangible asset, is something with
potential that *grows* with time, rather than depreciates.

The sources of value creation are in people's know-how and their passion to
perform. You don't supervise a product development engineer or advertising editor to create a better product or ad copy. Rather, they do it, given the right environment. PM powers an organization as an economic engine by recognizing that
social systems are the fuel. This is not to say that the organization's mission is
not fundamental—it is. It simply means that performance requires cooperation,
teamwork, and people giving effort for the benefit of the whole. Value creation is
central to the purpose of an organization. (Economic value management, aimed
at decisions and actions to increase shareholder wealth rather than destroy it, is
discussed in Part Four.)

Some publicly-traded corporations feel investor pressure to cut costs to meet
earnings expectations, which usually translates into laying off employees. But
right-sizing decisions based solely on head count and cost reductions can rob an
organization of its key talent. Human resource systems need to acknowledge employees as valued intangible assets, each with unique skills and experiences.
(Human capital management, with a focus on retaining better-performing employees, is also discussed in Part Four.) Inevitably management must come to
grips with increasing bottom-line by getting more from its existing resources
rather than removing them with layoffs. This imperative adds to the interest in
performance management.

Despite this substantial shift toward valuing intangible assets, current accounting and performance measurement systems still reflect outdated industrial models. Recent accounting scandals, like Enron's sudden collapse, have
alerted the general public that accounting practices have failed as early warn-
ing signals. The trio of accounting watchdogs—external auditing firms,
boards of directors, and stock analysts—are failing to detect or report impending disasters. The solution is not to meddle with more accounting regulations. Rather than tweak the status quo, where each party likely has vested
interests in preservation, the accounting industry should take an investor's

perspective. It should provide disclosure and financial transparency of operating processes. The performance of processes does not suddenly improve or degrade—it changes gradually.

GENERATING INCREASING SHAREHOLDER VALUE INVOLVES TRADE-OFFS

A few paragraphs back it was stated that *value* is an ambiguous term. Customer value or shareholder value? There are always trade-offs because of natural conflicts, such as with higher costs for greater service; and a cornerstone of PM is providing the capability to make better trade-off decisions. For example, if products, features, and services for customers were expanded, would the additional spending increase or decrease shareholder wealth? It depends on many factors, but there can be a scenario where customers receive higher value while shareholder wealth declines.

As mentioned previously, taking an investor's perspective of value is a good course of action. A forward-looking value reporting system would reveal and quantify management decisions and expectations. Management and investors should be provided a better picture of how their companies are doing and what their prospects are. They both deserve reports on indicators about the company's business and intangible assets. Examples of such indicators are employee retention rates, customer turnover rates, product development cycle time, employee and customer acquisition costs, new product success rates, customer service levels by type of customer, and reject rates.

Forward-looking projections, where estimating capabilities are judged for accountability, should be greatly emphasized. To accomplish this, there is a need for a commonly accepted method to understand value, and changes in an organization's value, stated in financial terms. No rational businessperson would buy or sell a business solely on the basis of looking at historical financial statements. Determining value involves a lot more than EPS reporting. Economic value creation involves understanding the generation of free cash flow above one's cost of capital, not just historical revenues, costs, and accounting profits. It involves measuring economic profit.

An economy with intangible assets as its primary source of economic value creation requires new forms of strategic direction, measurement, decision analysis, and organization. The formalization of PM as a discipline is central to these new forms.

WHAT IS MISSING? PERFORMANCE MANAGEMENT AS THE INTELLIGENCE BRIDGE

There has been too large a gap between high-end strategy and tactical operational systems to effectively achieve an organization's strategy, mission, and ultimate vision. In complex and overhead-intensive organizations, where constant redirection to a changing landscape is essential, the linkages between strategy and execution have been coming up short.

Michael Hammer, an early thought leader of the 1990s business process reengineering (BPR) movement, gives evidence to these problems of gaps and misalignment of goals with actions:

> In the real world, a company's measurement systems typically deliver a blizzard of nearly meaningless data that quantifies practically everything in sight, no matter how unimportant; that is devoid of any particular rhyme or reason; that is so voluminous as to be unusable; that is delivered so late as to be virtually useless; and that then languishes in printouts and briefing books without being put to any significant purpose.... In short, measurement is a mess.
>
> We use two percent of what we measure. The rest is CYA... We are masters of the micro. We measure paper clip acquisition times ... The appearance of precision substitutes for substance ... We measure far too much and get far too little for what we measure because we never articulated what we need to get better at, and our measures aren't tied together to support higher-level decision making.[6]

What is the answer for executives who need to expand their focus beyond cost control, into economic value creation, and toward more strategic directives? What's the answer for business strategists trying to navigate a more profitable course in turbulent seas? How do they regain control of the direction, traction, and speed for their enterprise?

More than ever, organizations need to align their customers, service recipients, suppliers, contractors, and their own organizations in one strategic direction. That direction must be based on a holistic view of interdependent variables and trade-offs across functions and organizational boundaries. Decision makers at all levels of the organization must be empowered to make effective decisions in rapidly reduced time frames. They need at-a-glance reporting to quickly key in on areas of their business operations in urgent need of attention. They need the equivalent of real-time bells or whistles in the form of "alert" messages to let them know if something is likely to happen that will exceed a threshold—before it happens. PM resolves these issues.

As mentioned earlier, there is a gap between the raw data that is spewed from transaction-intensive production and operating systems and the required business information needed for making decisions. Unfortunately, most companies don't recognize this intelligence gap. ERP tools, for example, report raw data, but they do not enable workers to *actively* manage business drivers that result in outcomes. This gap or missing piece was depicted in Figure 1.1 as the arrow highlighting the linkage between operations and strategy—the PM suite of systems. Earlier it was noted that this gap is being filled with software tools collectively called the intelligence architecture. Examples of these tools are data management, data mining, analytics, forecasters, and optimizers.

An integrated suite of methodologies and tools—the PM solutions suite—provides the mechanism to bridge the intelligence gap. When orchestrated, this integrated tool suite supports executive management's strategy. By pulling together multiple management systems with a common strategic direction, PM provides the power to dig deeper and understand how to act, wherever the market takes you. PM correlates disparate information in a meaningful way and allows drill-down queries directly on hidden problem areas. It helps assess which strategies are yielding desired results without the need to wade through a mountain of raw data. Executives and employee teams need to be alerted to problems before they become "unfavorable variances" reported in financial statements and requiring explanation. PM aids employees and managers to *actively* manage change—and in the right direction. PM converts intangible assets—such as your brand, relationships, and knowledge—into your company's long-term success.

In summary, PM integrates operational and financial information into a single decision support and planning framework. What makes today's PM systems so effective is that *work activities*—what people, equipment, and assets do—are foundational to PM reporting, analysis, and planning. Work activities pursue the actions and projects essential to meet the strategic objectives constructed in strategy maps and the outcomes measured in scorecards. Work activities are central to ABM systems used to accurately measure output costs and customer profitability.

ABM also aids in understanding the drivers of work activities and their consumption of resource capacity (e.g., expenses). With that knowledge, organizations can test and validate future outcomes given different events (including a varying mix and volume of product/service demand). This helps managers and employee teams understand capacity constraints and see that cost behavior is rarely linear but is a complex blend of step-fixed input expenses relative to changes in outputs. Workloads are predicted in resource planning systems to select the best plans. PM combines the increasingly accepted strategic frameworks, such as the balanced scorecard, with intelligent software systems that span the enterprise to provide immediate feedback, in terms of alerts and traffic-lighting signals to unplanned deviations from plans. PM provides managers and employee teams with the ability to act proactively, before events occur or proceed so far that they demand a reaction.

The purpose of this book is to present PM not just as an integrated set of decision support tools but also as a discipline intended to maintain a view of the larger picture and to understand how an organization is working as a whole. PM applies to managing any organization, whether a business, a hospital, a university, a government agency, or a military body—any entity that has employees and partners with a purpose, profit-driven or not. In short, PM is universally applicable.

MANAGEMENT AS A "DISCIPLINE" IS AT AN EARLY EMBRYONIC STAGE

Have organizations neglected a formal approach to PM? To answer this question, recall that I defined PM as translating plans into results—execution. In this manner the important domain of strategy formulation is left outside of PM. It is actually a fuzzy boundary dividing strategy from execution, and there has been much already written on strategy.[7] PM is the process of managing the strategy.

Getting from the drawing board to value realization with high certainty involves execution. However, translating plans into results is no simple task. Execution may not be pretty and may not involve the highest paid employees. Execution is not a matter of following an instruction manual. It requires knowledge, reasoning, and prudence by all employees.

It may be helpful to step back and think about what managing an organization is all about. Of course, the existence of business schools, executive education programs, and MBA degrees implies that managing is a formal profession, but it is not nearly as formalized as fields such as engineering, law, or medicine. In those fields, there are well-documented bodies of knowledge and rules so that in successive decades those professions continually improve upon themselves. For example, bloodletting is, fortunately, a medical practice of the past, and great progress has been made since then. However, the development of how to manage organizations has not followed such a well-lit path of refinement. New management fads routinely surface, and managers quickly purchase the latest popular books heralding the newest fad as *the* solution.

We need better PM because we need better organizations. However, organizations are pretty well taken for granted because they just seem to happen. It wasn't always that way. Not long ago, people simply exchanged goods at the local market—cobblers could offer the shoes they had made in exchange for agricultural produce from the farmers. Societal organizations for earning a living emerged from guilds and village craftspeople, based on economies of scale and specialization. Organizations evolved as a better way than an individual going it alone. Organizations are created to accomplish things that individuals cannot do on their own. Management makes organizations work—however, more effective management makes them work better. That is where we are today: trying to manage organizations more effectively.

The current dilemma is that not all managers are good managers. Some in fact are pretty poor. Ever work for one? Many managers get it wrong, not because they are incompetent but because they often simply do not have a complete grasp of what they are doing and how whatever they are doing aligns with their organization's objectives. Many workers have a false impression of what managing is, formed by their experiences of being managed by others. This is hardly the way to understand the true discipline of managing. By default, managing is learned through on-the-job apprenticeship and trial by fire. If you have a poor manager, you learn the wrong lessons.

There have been some popular thinkers about the discipline of managing, such as Peter Drucker, but I view their books and articles as only the beginning. There have also been popular thinkers in *specific* areas of management. Examples are Philip Kotler on marketing, Michael Porter on competitive strategy, and Robert S. Kaplan on managerial accounting and performance measurement. I view these popular contributors as the framers of the big ideas. But I keep returning to the observation that the ideas presented by such visionaries must be used and executed in an organizational context in order to be fully realized. This is what managing is about—and I contend that managing has yet to become a formal practice with a discipline or an organized body of knowledge.

Management today remains mostly silo-based and functional, despite all the business literature about process-based thinking. A physician would never take a component view of a patient when diagnosing an illness the way managers do of their businesses. Physicians recognize that a patient's lungs, heart, circulatory system, and other organs work as system. Organizations should similarly view organizational management as a system. In fact, I advocate that PM ups the ante to further transition from process-based thinking to an even higher level: systems thinking. By viewing an organization as a system—comparable to a living organism—its managers can comprehensively consider as manageable variables its strategies, measures, organization charts, processes, reward incentives, employee competencies, culture, and technologies.[8]

Do not misinterpret my stance as extremist or alarmist. I am not suggesting that people need a license of certification, like a CPA or an MD, to be a manager. Experience is more important than being book-smart or trained in education courses. Managing is important to do, but difficult to do well. Further, there is no university degree in PM that I know of. It embraces many of the methods and techniques that are so fundamental: strategy, value creation, decision making, and performance monitoring. However, there are many unwritten rules, and PM, as described in this book, provides an overarching framework with badly needed rigor.

My intent is that readers of this book come to recognize PM as an important branch of general management. This book is intended as a way to appreciate how some of the big ideas of management thinking, like business process reengineering and customer relationship management, relate to one another. This book is not another set of broad platitudes or sloganeering. Rather, I describe with some rigor managerial techniques, such as strategy mapping, scorecarding, ABM, and customer relationship management, without overcomplicating them—keeping it simple but not simplistic. Some believe the KISS rule (keep it simple stupid) is mandatory, but there is the corollary LOVE rule (leave out virtually everything). The message is you must dig in a little bit.

PERFORMANCE MANAGEMENT— MANAGING COMPLEXITIES OF PEOPLE, PROCESSES, PRODUCTS, AND CUSTOMERS

As organizations flatten and tilt 90 degrees from being hierarchical to more process-based and customer-focused, core processes replace the artificial boundaries of functional silos. Things get more complicated. Many employees multitask in two or more processes. This increases the need for matrixed management, implying that employees have at least two types of managers—one for the function and the other for the process. In addition, while process management is no longer a new concept, the definition and scope of process continues to broaden, in some cases extending across business-to-business supply chains.

Organizational charts divide the organization into work units. Although these organizational lines are drawn and constantly redrawn, the hierarchy will never disappear because individuals continue to need mentoring, coaching, career development counseling, and direction. *Functional managers* typically perform those roles. The emergence of process owners—such as one for sales order fulfillment, which can cover a spectrum from customer order placement to receipt of cash payments and many other functions—involves giving *process managers* fewer people but the all-important responsibility for the purse strings. That is, providing the process owner control over the functional managers' allocated resources resolves the thorny issue of matrixing employees with two or more bosses. Hierarchical lines of authority are one matter; what is less visible but equally important is who gets to decide what.

A less obvious twist to managing with a flattened hierarchical chain of command involves the virtual worker. Employee teams are no longer working at a common physical location. Many on the team may work from remote home offices or field offices. There may be fewer managers, but this does not mean there will be less managing. In fact, it is just the opposite. PM is all about converting formulated strategies into execution, outcomes, and results. Executive managers may appear to be in charge, but they are finding that their direct control of employee performance is decreasing. This is why everyone needs to understand what defines achievement, how their work and decisions contribute toward it, and what is required to accomplish it.

As organizations experience an increasing diversity of products, service lines, types of channels, and types of customers, the level of complexity will only grow. As product differentiation shifts to service differentiation in order to seek competitive advantage, then expenses will likely increase. Organizations can try their best to standardize product and service line offerings, but this is against a strong head wind of mass customization to satisfy increasingly segmented customers. The increase in complexity and value-adding services is a driving force for the need for the discipline of PM.

In addition, not all customers are profitable. At some point shareholder value is destroyed due to inaction by management to deal with this situation. Optimizing value for both customers and shareholders involves a delicate balance between goals that can be in conflict. These conflicts require decisions with trade-offs that affect work activities. PM's wide span of information enables better trade-off analysis and deployment of resources (i.e., expenses).

An additional factor driving the need for PM is an increasing requirement for specially skilled workers and equipment. The presence of more skilled workers may give the illusion that workers are more self-directed without requiring supervision, but their breadth of skill in no way removes the interdependencies that collectively lead to productive organizational performance. Managers must harness the power and genius of people who ultimately are behaving as individuals.

In summary, rising specialization, complexity, and value-adding services cause the need for more, not less, PM. Despite the impact that technology and more flexible work practices and policies have on continuously changing organizational structures, without ongoing adaptation the correct work at acceptable service levels will not get done. It is true that so-called knowledge workers, not their supervisors, increasingly take charge of their own careers. All employees must have some grasp of managing for results. However, despite each worker's responsibility to self-manage, somehow the collective performance must be co-ordinated. The organization's strategic objectives must be clearly communicated so that everyone pulls in the same direction, not opposite and conflicting ones, and so that their combined efforts produce success. A united and sustained performance is a challenging part of management. PM aids in accomplishing the necessary coordination.

NOTES

1. Oliver Wendell Holmes, "The Path of Law" (1897), as quoted in George Seldes, *The Great Thoughts* (New York: Ballantine Books, 1985).

2. Tad Leahy, "The Balanced Scorecard Meets BPM." *Business Finance*, June 2003, 33.

3. Dean Sorensen, "The Value Market," *Strategic Finance*, July, 2003, 43–49.

4. Alan Webber, "CEO Bashing Has Gone too Far," *USA Today*, June 3, 2003, 15A.

5. See www.bscol.com.

6. Michael Hammer, *Agenda* (Three Rivers Press, 2003), p. 101.

7. Michael Porter, *Competitive Advantage* (Free Press, 1998).

8. Brache, Alan, *How Organizations Work* (John Wiley & Sons, 2002), p. 11.

PART ONE

Performance Management Process

"Nothing else in the world . . . not all the armies . . . is so powerful as an idea whose time has come."
—Victor Hugo, *The Future of Man* (1861)

Change in people results from the presence of two items needed in great abundance: dissatisfaction with their current state, and a vision of what a better state looks like. This book is about the latter, but I suspect many readers are experiencing some of the former. This book describes a vision of an integrated suite of enterprise-wide methodologies and tools that comprehensively link strategy objectives with planning, budgeting, processes, costing, performance measures—and, more importantly, people. Organizations that can make this vision their reality will profitably create value at accelerated rates plus have opportunity for competitive advantage, presuming their competitors don't get there before them.

The need for applicable technology is no longer an impediment for organizations to realize this vision. The technology already exists. The impediment is in the thinking and the willingness of an organization's executive leaders to do it.

2

INTEGRATING A SUITE OF
PROVEN METHODOLOGIES

Performance management (PM)[1] is translating plans into results—execution. It is the process of *managing your strategy*. Strategy is of paramount importance and is senior management's number one responsibility. For commercial companies, strategy can be reduced to three major choices:[2]

1. What products or service-lines should we offer or not offer?
2. What markets should we serve or not serve?
3. How are we going to win?

Although PM provides insights to improve all three choices, its power is in achieving number three—winning—by adjusting and executing strategies. PM does this by aiding managers to sense earlier and respond more quickly to uncertain changes. It does this by driving accountability for executing the organization's strategy to the lowest possible organization levels.

In contrast to the popular 1990s *business process reengineering* (BPR) approaches, where after radical redesign every single step and task were explicitly mapped, PM relies on the power of focusing on the pertinent and relevant. After determining the strategic objectives and the supporting projects, measures, and appropriate (not old-style) budgets to achieve these strategic objectives, the rest will naturally follow. That is, the work activities align to pursue strategy, often intensely customer-focused, as job number one. Do not confuse PM with *business process management* (BPM) or workflow tools and their software vendors. PM is inclusive of BPM tools and much more. PM includes the thinking as well as the number crunching.

So if PM includes much more, then what is it comprised of? PM is an umbrella-like concept covering the tightly integrated and universally applicable methodologies of strategic planning, scorecard measurements, budgeting, costing (including activity-based management [ABM]), forecasting resource requirements, and financial consolidations. PM also includes the important adjacent neighboring methodologies that are independent of any industry: customer intelligence systems (e.g., customer relationship management [CRM]); supplier intelligence systems; shareholder intelligence systems (e.g., cost of capital, economic profit and value); human capital management (HCM) systems; and six sigma and lean operations. These are core process solutions and are described in Part Four (see in particular Chapters 17, 18, and 19).

Similar to the popular plan-do-check-act (PDCA) iterative cycle made popular by W. Edwards Deming, the famous quality improvement expert, PM also has an iterative cycle. As Figure 2.1 illustrates, imagine PM as a wheel with

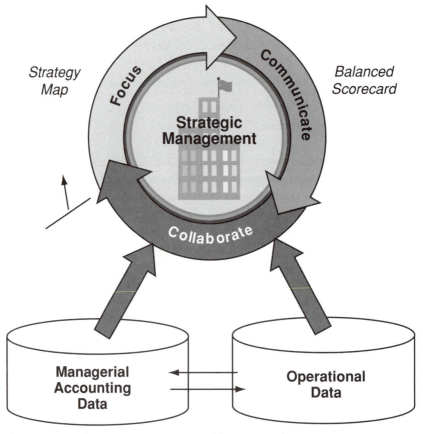

Figure 2.1   Performance Management with Fact-Based Data

three elements or arcs: focus, communicate with feedback, and collaborate. The figure also shows how fact-based managerial accounting data and operational data provide input to the PM wheel.

The basic premise of the wheel is this: Employees can effectively implement a strategy only when they clearly understand the strategy and when they clearly *see* how they contribute to its achievement. That sentence encompasses a lot. It also supports why a mantra of the middle arc ("communicate") is the powerful question that all employees and managers should be able to quickly answer: "How am I doing on what is important?"

One can think of strategy maps and scorecards similarly to how financial analysts rely on balance sheets and income statements to describe an organization's financial health. Strategy maps and the feedback from their companion scorecards describe an organization's strategic health and consequently its chances for increasing prosperity. Many organizations report measures, but they are without depth. Users can view a result, but whether it is good or bad, they are unable to investigate the underlying cause. Scorecards with data management systems resolve this. Scorecards express the strategy in measurable terms, communicating what must be done and how everyone is progressing.

In summary, employees and managers should be provided with the tools to align their work with the strategy and to be recognized for their contribution to the organization's success. A strategy-focused organization enables targeted feedback on strategic performance to specific employee teams, in order to effect continual strategy implementation. An organization must be vigilant and look for potholes on even the best roads. PM involves people knowing that all members of their organization are focusing, communicating, and collaborating on strategy from a single vantage point. It aids in everyone's understanding of how one performance measure affects another. It also involves digging deeper to see causal relationships and manage work activities across the entire enterprise so that everyone is on the same page.

Part Two of this book will delve deeper into the elements, or arcs, of this iterative cycle, but for now let's briefly look at each one:

1. Focus. The process of managing strategy begins with making choices and *focus*. There is never enough money or resources to chase every opportunity or market on the planet. We are continually limited by scarce and precious resources and time, so focus is key—and strategy yields focus.

In this important initial step, senior management defines and continuously adjusts its strategy. Next, by mapping cause-and-effect relationships, it selects and defines strategic objectives and higher-impact action steps and projects that will achieve those objectives. *Strategy maps* are the key tools for developing focus.

Do not underestimate the importance of strategy maps. They have been over-shadowed by the popular scorecard that stars in arc number two; but those in the know place far greater respect and emphasis on strategy maps compared to scorecards as the key to successfully executing strategy.

Companies can ideally turn big goals into small, manageable projects that can be accomplished. This can happen! The first step in this translation is to create a set of strategic themes that will bridge the gap between the existing state of operations and the desired state. These themes then organize the work of the company and can be used to subdivide work among various operating divisions, departments, and em-ployees. Whether you base your strategy on a balanced scorecard, the Malcolm Baldrige Award criteria, six sigma, total quality management (TQM), or lean man-agement framework, an organization should define and use clear, concise perfor-mance indicators that help its workers see the causes and effects of its strategy. Strategy maps begin that process. By focusing on critical areas, everyone can iden-tify the true sources of business failure as well as the best practices that lead to fu-ture success. This is also a logical place to link the strategy to the budgeting process.

2. Communicate with Feedback. The process of managing strategy contin-ues with *communication*. This context is reserved for senior management articu-lating to its employees its strategy. Along with articulating strategy comes the all-important feedback to employee teams. Remember the mantra, "How am I doing on what is important?" A *scorecard* is the key tool for reinforcing commu-nication of the strategy. Think of scorecards as the drive gears of the strategy map. Think of a scorecard as having carefully selected and defined indicators and measures, each weighted to reflect its relative level of importance that are weighted in the strategy map. Think of a scorecard as a set of chain links of the strategy map's strategic objectives, where each chain link uses if-then relation-ships with leading and lagging measures to drive work efforts to align with the organization's mission and vision.

By integrating, distributing, and analyzing enterprise-wide information, an organization gains the power to act on this information—ahead of its competi-tors. The goal is to communicate a strategic vision to the entire workforce and empower employees to execute its strategy proactively, before events occur that demand a reaction. To stay ahead, individuals must draw on their organization's business intelligence to make decisions based on hard facts that are timely, not on assumptions and late news. And when it is too late, sufficient enterprise intel-ligence should be accessible to conduct root-cause analysis to fix the situation and get back on track.

3. Collaborate. The process cycle of managing strategy ends with *collabo-ration*. (The cycle never actually ends; it is a continuous iterative loop.) By aligning various strategies among business units, the organization taps into the collective knowledge of its employees and unleashes each person's potential. From the "top desk" to the desktop, e-mail-based discussion threads, based on feedback from key performance indicator (KPI) scores from the scorecard, can be created for faster problem solving and consensus. The PM process truly makes executing strategy everyone's job. Collaboration in this sense is all about collective dialogue. Management is not equivalent to control—management is coaching people for continuous improvements

A simple way to think about this PM cycle is that it embraces both planning and executing. However, PM is greatly aided when managers and employee teams have access to and visibility of fact-based intelligence, such as the rich information from an ABM system. With fact-based intelligence, correct strategies are more likely to be formulated, and employee teams can analyze what is happening and what might happen (e.g., what-if scenarios) in order to make better decisions.

PM also links the annual budget process, usually performed by the finance function, with the strategic planning process. If executives approve the projects and initiatives to meet strategic objectives, then they also need to give employee teams the commensurate resource levels. But the budget is typically exposed only in general ledger accounts. In contrast, strategies are expressed in terms of programs and performance measures. What is missing is the mechanism to explicitly link them. PM does that. When all is said and done, much is often said and little is done. PM inspires actions based on calculated risks to support the best or right decisions.

Chapter 5 discusses strategy maps and scorecards. These are the tools that help define strategy and then facilitate the navigational guidance to assure that the organization is keeping on track, altering its direction and speed as shifts in strategy necessitate new courses. Part Three describes ABM as an important category of data, some of which can serve as a source of KPI measures in a scorecard as well to aid in the understanding of drivers of work activities and capacity (i.e., expense) consumption.

PEOPLE AND CULTURE MATTER

Business schools tend to divide their curriculums between hard quantitative-oriented courses, such as operations management and finance, and soft behavioral courses, such as change management, ethics, and leadership. The former relies on a run-by-the-numbers management approach. The latter recognizes that people matter most.

The *quantitative* approach applies Newtonian mechanical thinking as if the world and every thing in it is a big machine. This approach speaks in terms of production, power, efficiency, and control, where employees are hired to be used and periodically replaced, somewhat as if they were robots. In contrast, the *behavioral* approach views an organization as a living organism that is ever changing and responding to its environment. This Darwinian way of thinking speaks in terms of evolution, continuous learning, natural responding, and adapting to changing conditions.[3]

The trick to general management is integrating and balancing the quantitative and behavioral approaches. Today command-and-control style executives who prefer to leverage their workers' muscles but not their brains run into trouble. Ultimately things get done through people, not via the computers or machines that are simply conduits for arriving at results. Most employees are not thrilled by being micro-managed. The good performers are people and teams who manage themselves, given some direction and timely feedback. Management creates value and produces results by leveraging people.

THEORY VERSUS PRACTICE

Executives need to provide a clear vision and set the direction for their organization. Further, they need to put in place the culture, communication habits, and incentives that *align* with and move the organization toward their strategy. Executives also need to secure people and equipment with the right skills and capabilities, which is itself a capital-versus-spend balancing act. In the never-ending end, the strategy must be tied to customer preferences and needs, but it must also satisfy the shareholders (i.e., owners) entitlement to wealth creation, not destruction. In the end, the organization needs top-down guidance with bottom-up execution. From the shop floor to the top floor—and back again. PM bidirectionally converts plans into results.

PM is not a theory, and it does not require a graduate degree to figure out how to get an organization to perform. However, without a set of tools and principles, it is difficult to see what is going on, interpret what it means, and prescribe what to do. Things change quickly today and constant change is now the norm. A consequence is that proven methods of the past may not solve today's problems because the problems have changed. This makes understanding fundamental principles, such as matching the level of resources and their type with demand, more critical than ever before. What PM provides is a way to make sense of what matters and, more importantly, a way to ask better questions.

The output of performance management is not briefing books and endless meetings, but rather, when properly practiced, it provides robust and practical insights. PM informs an organization about where it is located, which direction it is going, which direction it should be headed, and what it will require to get there. When budgets are approved or spending and investment decisions are made, the funding involves hard cash.

Although this cash outflow is certain, the future cash inflow can often be characterized as a hope and a guess. There is no guarantee that a net positive return will materialize. PM, rooted in business modeling, decreases those risks. It increases the likelihood that a solution to a problem will not become the *next* problem. With PM, acceptable returns on investments (ROIs) are more predictable and risk management becomes real, not just a buzzword. Exposing and reconciling the trade-offs between customer value and shareholder economic value, in quantitative financial terms, is one of the potentially large benefits of practicing PM. (The topic of economic value management is discussed in Chapter 20.)

PERFORMANCE MANAGEMENT IS BASED ON BUSINESS MODELING

In the past, visionary managers dreamed of using tools to plan, but the technology was the impediment. Programmers were busy coding the transaction-based operational systems rather than preparing analytical reports from them. And when management made any programming request, it usually took months to receive results—results that did not always match the original request.

But today, with advances in software modeling tools and data warehousing and mining, technology is no longer the obstacle—the thinking is! How can we best model for business decisions? The answer may seem trite, but modeling is best done with business modeling principles and tools. Business modeling has been defined as "the representation or model of how an organization works and functions, created in a way that it can productively be used as a means to simulate the real world."[4] Business modeling is central to the PM solution suite.

It is senior management's primary role to define and continuously adjust the strategy. That is why they are paid huge salaries and have large corner offices. With effective business modeling, organizations can now test the executive's proposed strategic initiatives against a model to replace uncertainty with a range of calculated risks. Make uncertainty your friend, and learn to understand it. When using PM business modeling, senior managers can verify the feasibility of their proposed new programs in the computer rather than in the school of hard knocks.

The business models from PM provide for the basics that every manager wants:

- To identify business problems.
- To uncover opportunities to improve, and then to size their impact if successfully improved.

Senior managers can rely on these same systems to foster communications *among* managers and employee teams. Employees can *actively* manage with an increased confidence that what they choose to work on aligns with the organization's strategy and goals.

Business modeling is an effective way to understand value creation. *Value*, again, is an ambiguous term. Whose value are we referring to, customers or shareholders (i.e., owners)? With customers you may be able to *create* value, but the question shareholders ask is whether you *capture* it. In this context I do not mean value in terms of product features and customer preferences but more in

---

Reflections from College Days

I must confess that I believe in modeling. My first true experience with modeling was my senior year in college, 1971 at Cornell University. I was taking an elective course from my engineering curriculum. The course was titled "Game Theory" and was taught by a professor who had written a chess game computer program that competed with the computer chess game programs of world class Russian academics. In short, I modeled a simulation of the 1969 National Baseball League using random number generators based on probabilities linked to each player's batting average profiles—including differentiating power hitters from singles hitters. The program also adjusted for each pitcher's strength and dominance by reducing batting average-based probabilities of the hitters they faced at the plate. I amazed myself when the model darn near replicated the team's actual rankings; and it selected the actual MVP award winner, based on a weighted formula. I received an A+ in the course, and I was sold on modeling as a valid basis for predicting future outcomes.

terms of wealth creation. In Chapter 20 this ambiguity and its trade-offs are described. A customer-focused strategy sounds appealing as a silver bullet solution, but advocates of the *take an investor's perspective* approach have countered with a *shareholder returns-driven strategy* way of thinking.[5]

Business modeling is instrumental for predictive planning. It assists in balancing short- with long-term performance. Managers must acquire resources, understanding there is uncertainty that will inevitably affect their plans, to create future value. By definition, the future is uncertain. They must know which resources are required on varying and frequently changing priorities.

IS PERFORMANCE MANAGEMENT OLD WINE IN A NEW BOTTLE?

Some view the successful coordination and integration of the suite of PM methods and tools as simply old wine in a new bottle, meaning we are no longer inventing radically new solutions. Instead, managers may have already been exposed to these concepts in an MBA curriculum or a year of paging through popular business magazines. Many of these solutions or methods concentrate on a single topic with great intensity but also in isolation and out of context with other aspects of managing. Some solutions and methods cause confusion with competing theories.

In short, people who view PM as old wine are fed up with alleged *breakthrough* programs and lists with to-do steps. They view such breakthrough programs as merely a repackaging of existing ideas. They simply desire to harvest improvement from the pretty good new ideas and methods that already exist and that ideally are described as a coherent view of the whole.

In contrast, others view PM as new wine in an old bottle. That is, not only do PM systems provide all employees and managers with more visible, relevant, accurate, and timely information, but the interpretation and information from this layer of intelligence can be much more quickly communicated. How? Think e-mail, cell phones, and phone voice-mail mixed with the automated "alert" messaging and traffic lighting. More importantly, these communications need no longer start with senior managers barking from the top of the organizational hierarchy. Rather, PM system-generated communications can be targeted directly to those specific employees who are accountable for results and can take actions. Employees and managers can now directly communicate with those individuals who can quickly take actions—and they can do so *from* PM software (i.e., to the hypertext individual's name e-mail address) rather than waiting until they meet that person in the hallway or get around to composing an e-mail later in the day or week.

I am not sure I want to choose a side on this old versus new wine debate. I like the idea of using well thought out methods that simply haven't been adequately tested or integrated (i.e., old wine). But I also strongly believe in team communications where trust exists. So I like *both* sides of the debate.

Although it is not obvious, it is becoming intuitive to an increasing number of IT research analyst firms that combining the components of PM as a unified approach makes more sense than treating individual methods in isolation.

NOTES

1. There are several variants of PM, including business performance management (BPM), enterprise performance management (EPM), corporate performance management (CPM), and strategic performance management (SPM). Consider them all as synonymous.

2. Alan Brache, *How Organizations Work* (New York: John Wiley & Sons, 2002), 10.

3. Stephan H. Haekel, *Adaptive Enterprise: Creating and Leading Sense and Respond Organizations.* (Boston: Harvard Business School Press, 1999).

4. Bill Rosser, "Strategic Planning," *The Gartner Group Research Note*, October 31, 2000.

5. Mark L. Frigo and Joel Litman, "What Is Return Driven Strategy?" *Strategic Finance*, February 2002, 11.

3

SUPPORT FROM
FACT-BASED DATA AND
INFORMATION TECHNOLOGY

In the absence of facts, anyone's opinion is a good one. A major benefit of PM is that when everyone gets the same facts, they generally come up with the same conclusions. Therefore, it is not enough to define strategies and plan. With reliable and timely fact-based data that brings far broader visibility to managers and employee teams, actions are taken rather than pondered. This is represented by the operational and managerial accounting data that were depicted in Figure 2.1.

ROLE OF RELIABLE FACT-BASED DATA—
PRIMARILY COST MEASUREMENTS

Organizations need to understand their cost structure and how it behaves relative to changes in volume, by customer, and by market influences. Despite 500-plus years since the birth of accounting,[1] accountants have yet to get it (i.e., calculating costs) totally right! The activity-based cost management (ABC/M) methodology,[2] which throughout this book will be referred to as activity-based management (ABM), has become the accepted proven solution. Activity-based management (ABM)—acting on the ABC data—drives the PM wheel by providing it with high-octane information.

ABM is more than just an accounting system. It is also much more than a managerial information system. ABM lifts managerial accounting into the realm of managerial economics. It should be considered a change management tool.

31

Many ABM project managers have been slow to recognize the behavioral change management aspects of the ABM data. ABM is a socio-technical tool, and the emphasis should be on the social side. Many managers and ABM project teams see ABM as simply a better measuring scheme or cost allocator. However, its real value lies in introducing undebatable, fact-based information that can be used by employees and managers to build business cases, quickly recognize business problems or opportunities, and test hypotheses.

Here is a strongly encouraged suggestion: As the ABM model and system are being constructed, do not omit performing value analysis with ABM attributes. Costs are not the be-all and end-all. In addition to understanding what causes costs using driver analysis, it is important to classify the relative value that activities have in meeting the organization's goals. Attributes are scores and tags that are attached to the calculated costs. Alone, attributes are not sufficient for making decisions, but the visibility and insight they provide are suggestive of which way to act.

When historians of organizational management in the 21st century look back at the 20th century, they will likely observe that most organizations were operated more on intuition, instinct, and gut feeling than on facts. Many organizations are a bit unwieldy. Some have gone through various rounds of serial slash-and-burn cost reductions in which they certainly took out the bodies, but perhaps not the work. The end result often was a newly reconstructed organization that was merely a cut-down stovepipe, still trying to operate the fragmented pieces of what in reality was always an end-to-end business process that transcends organizational boundaries. Even after downsizing, there still was no clear visibility of their costs or effective control.

Gifted and talented managers recognized that the real problem lay with insufficient or flawed data. They still could not compute costs or measure performance with any degree of accuracy or confidence. However, they muddled through the best they could. Everyone recognizes that today the margin for error is slimmer, such that the availability of reliable, timely, fact-based data has become essential. Simplistic cost management practices, like cost allocations, may be acceptable when a company is far away from optimum performance, but you need ABM when you get closer.

It may be safe to begin questioning much of the traditional management theory that has been taught and unchallenged for years. Put simply, we must question whether much of what organizations measure as management and control information is really like the *emperor's new clothes*. If middle managers cannot find a useful outlet for the data they receive, then aren't they living a myth? Business school professors and popular business gurus write articles and books proposing their principles. But are we not possibly like the early astronomers who defended the idea that the Earth was the center of the universe? We create and maintain elegant theories, but the underlying logic and concepts are flawed.

ABM has many of the characteristics of an organizational methodology. Many managers are frustrated by the difficulties in bringing about change within their organizations. Behavioral change management is receiving wider attention, and ABM data will continue to play an important role in transforming organizations.

ROLE OF INFORMATION TECHNOLOGY AND DATA WAREHOUSING

A few of the commercial database and application software vendors are integrating all the components of the PM suite of methodologies. They are able to automatically manage end-to-end processes, including allowance for manual intervention; and they are able to extract, analyze, and forecast information.

The convergence of the integrated solution components of PM by leveraging data warehousing technology provides valuable advantages:

- **Single version of the truth.** The financial, costing, and PM components can all draw their data from a central data warehouse. A world-class data warehouse technology can read data (formally referred to as extract, transform, and load [ETL]) from virtually any source, in virtually any form, off of any platform, while assuring data quality. It can consolidate operational data from disparate systems into a powerful, consistent information resource.

- **Data quality and integrity.** A data warehouse does more than collect data. It prevents problems that are hazardous to a business intelligence system by cleansing data of such problems as duplicate data, illogical combinations, or missing values. It helps users make sense of it by translating it into useful information, storing it, and then delivering it in a consumable format where the quality and data integrity are never in question.

- **Information sharing.** Through integration housed in a data warehouse, disparate employee teams and their local systems can automatically share information from multiple locations in ways that were once cumbersome and time wasting.

- **Knowledge sharing.** By applying business rules, assumptions, and evaluation criteria against the data warehouse, users can analyze and drill into data bent on performing "root cause" or filtering analysis to reveal understandings that could have been overlooked when relying on only one solution set.

Spreadsheet—An Infectious Disease?

Disjointed spreadsheets are becoming an issue. Spreadsheet-itis, once a nuisance, has become a serious problem, not only because it involves cumbersome and untimely reporting, but because it denies people a single, unified view of vital data—one version of the truth. There may be good spreadsheet reports within a given department, but generally the rest of the organization is not aware of them. Additional pain results when others recreate their own version of the same report—a wasteful duplication of effort. With multiple spreadsheets, when data differs, which are the right numbers? Linked spreadsheets, some perhaps a decade old, and disjointed legacy systems are just not dynamic enough, nor are they flexible. Finally, problems with maintaining undocumented or documented spreadsheets surface when the employee who personally developed the spreadsheet transfers to elsewhere in the organization or departs it altogether.

When data is stored on clients' computers (e.g., a laptop or personal computer) rather than on a server or a Web-accessible source, this means the data is not stored centrally, making dissemination and analysis difficult. Nonintegrated data means that assumptions in one person's plans will likely not include the most recent version from someone else's assumptions and plans. Most spreadsheet users have a widely held misconception that their spreadsheet application is some sort of database. It's not. It is a calculator effective at manipulating and viewing data, but it is not particularly good at storing and managing it in a reliable, secure, scalable way. (Spreadsheets are also poor at handling *sparcity* where a substantial number of cells are blank. You drag around the deadweight of a lot of "0s" with only a few cells populated with real data—not a very efficient use of computer memory or processing power.)

Organizations cannot continue to spend eighty percent of their time collecting, copying, pasting, and reformatting data, ten percent weeding out errors, and then realize in the remaining ten percent that the resulting data is not structured in a way that allows it to be analyzed. They cannot rely on undocumented macros and formulas when no one remembers how to maintain them—or the business policy they were invented to support. The hard truth is that most organizations are not equipped with managerial information that is properly structured to make prudent business decisions.

So-called end-to-end processes are beginning to spill over into the processes of an organization's trading partners. Organizations increasingly need greater access to their own and their partners' information sources for a 360-degree view of their suppliers, customers, and internal resources.

A data warehouse does not replace the thinking that typically goes with data analysis, but it sure makes the analysis proceed more easily. Chapter 22 will expand on these points.

SHIFT IN POWER FROM CHIEF INFORMATION OFFICER TO THE BUSINESS FUNCTIONS

As a factor in so many other changes in business, the Information Revolution is also the catalyst for PM. The timing is right for PM. Why? There is a parallel between the Industrial Revolution of two centuries ago and today's Information Revolution. The more visible impacts of each revolution appear to surface about a half-century after each revolution began. For example, in North America, James Watt's steam engine was invented in the late 1770s, but it wasn't until the 1820s that society was reshaped from being rural agrarian to one with a sizable factory working class drawn into cities. Today, following the development of the computer in the 1950s, we are currently witnessing near-universal application of information computing and storage power.

Underlying the Information Revolution is actually the harnessing of knowledge. This revolution is much less about electronics and semiconductors than about codifying logic, systems, and economic analysis. The rise in PM as a discipline may not be heralded as comparable to the discipline of biotechnology, but both share common heritages: smart, knowledgeable workers leveraging the convergence of IT computing power and compelling problems. For biotechnology, the problem is improving the health of humanity and animals. For PM, the problem is improving the organization's navigation—traction, direction, and speed—with real-time response to turbulence and unforeseen obstacles.

Professor Robert S. Kaplan of the Harvard Business School has consistently demonstrated an astute sense for identifying and researching the next popular management method. In his 1987 book, *Relevance Lost: The Decline of Managerial Accounting*,[3] Kaplan and his coauthor, H. Thomas Johnson, introduced the topic of ABM. I was personally fortunate to have been trained by him and his colleague Dr. Robin Cooper when they partnered with KPMG Peat Marwick to deliver ABM consulting services. In 1996 Professor Kaplan coauthored *The Balanced Scorecard*,[4] and more recently he authored *The Strategy-Focused Organization*.[5]

Kaplan's reasoning is that two major forces draw companies to focus on customers:

1. As products become commodities, the importance of services rises. That is, as differentiation from product advantages is reduced or neutralized, the customer relationship grows in importance, and the cost-to-serve component of each customer's profit contribution requires measurement and visibility.

2. The Internet is irreversibly shifting power from sellers to buyers.

The more you know about your external customers' habits and preferences, the more likely you are to retain them and gain their repeat business.

The sense of urgency to better manage customer relationships, together with the entry of new IT-literate managers, is creating a titanic shift in how information technology is purchased. Investments in technology are no longer under the primary control of IT departments and the chief information officer (CIO). The power is shifting out into the business functions—to the leaders in sales, marketing, procurement, customer service, logistics, and human resources. They are uncomfortable relying on the IT function. It is these IT-savvy business managers who feel the heat and sense of urgency to meet customer needs. They have bigger problems than the CFO and CIO, so they are taking control of their own destiny and driving the IT strategy for their portion of the business. They realize that if you are not the lead dog of the dogsled, the view never changes. As a result, they now have substantial influence in IT buying decisions.

So let's begin our journey with Part Two by learning about what are likely the premier components of the PM suite of tools: strategy maps and scorecards.

NOTES

1. Luca Pacioli, an Italian Franciscan friar from Sansepolcro, Italy, invented double entry bookkeeping in 1492.

2. The confusion with semantics around activity-based costing is large. My last three books were titled "activity-based cost management," but I have accepted the shortened ABM, without the "cost" term, as being more universal and less threatening.

3. H. Thomas Johnson and Robert S. Kaplan, *Relevance Lost: The Rise and Fall of Management Accounting* (Boston: Harvard Business School Press, 1987)

4. Robert S. Kaplan and David P. Norton, *The Balanced Scorecard: Translating Strategy into Action* (Boston: Harvard Business School Press, 1996).

5. Robert S. Kaplan and David Norton, *The Strategy Focused Organization* (Harvard Business School Press, 2001).

Strategy Maps and Balanced Scorecards

The Link between Strategy and Successful Execution by Operations

"A new scientific truth does not triumph by convincing its opponents and making them see the light, but rather because its opponents eventually die out, and a new generation grows up that is familiar with it."
—Max Planck, physicist and originator of the Quantum Theory, in *The Philosophy of Physics* (1936)

In the opening paragraphs of Chapter 2, the performance management (PM) process was depicted as a wheel comprised of three arcs: focus, communicate, and collaborate. The PM process is all about formulating strategy and then executing it by aligning resources and their focused behavior on the execution. Part Two covers strategy maps, scorecards, and how to use their results. It describes how to make a strategy operational—without excessive reliance on quarterly financial measures as the primary evidence demonstrating whether a strategy is successful.

4

MEASUREMENT PROBLEMS AND SOLUTIONS

One of the mysteries of the workplace continues to be how to support a manager's claim that "We did well last quarter." The normal follow-up question is, "How do you know?" Despite a sea of collected data, organizations struggle with making sense of it all. Organizations are generally data rich and information poor. Attempts are being made to fix this with data warehouses and number crunching software. But are those technologies simply Band-Aids and medications or a real cure?

HOW DO YOU KNOW IF YOU ARE PERFORMING WELL?

When a manager states that "we did well," how can anyone detect if the *entire* organization benefited overall from whatever that department did when it supposedly "did well"? How does management know how much of that department's work and outcomes advanced their organization toward realizing their strategy, and how much was errant work on less relevant pursuits?

One way to answer these questions is to improve the organization's measurement system itself. Strategy maps and scorecards are excellent tools in the quest for a strategy-supporting measurement system that links to operations and tactics. These are management tools that establish strong relations between the vital areas of the strategy and the organization's measures. They do so by:

- Making crystal clear the vital few strategic objectives (the strategic focus areas) of the strategy plan;
- Establishing the cause-and-effect relations *between* strategic objectives;

41

- *Cascading* strategic measures to employee teams whose performance is being monitored; and thus

- Aligning employee behavior with a common focus on the strategic objectives typically defined in the boardroom or by the governing body.

Strategy maps are like geographical maps that visually aid in understanding how one gets from point A (the present capability, organization, and focus of the enterprise) to destination B (the future desired state of capabilities, organization, and focus, as laid out in the enterprise vision, mission, and strategy plan). *Scorecards* are like a cockpit enabling managers and employee teams to navigate and steer. Scorecards without strategy maps may lead to failure. When scorecards are built and reported in isolation, there is no direct linkage to strategy.

As its name suggests, a scorecard contains the key and relevant performance measures. A scorecard is like the coxswain of a racing boat crew who periodically shouts critical information to the rowers. The scorecard's critical role is that it puts the measures (key performance indicators, or KPIs) in the context of the strategy. The concept of *context* is important. It elevates this methodology well above management by objectives (MBO) and spreadsheet performance reports. With strategy-linked measures reported through scorecards, the scorecard immediately explains not only what happened but also where that leads to and why it is important.

Performance measures that are related to the strategic objectives defined in the strategy map are usually referred to as *strategic measures*. Strategic measures are gathered in what has become popularly known as a balanced scorecard—*balanced* because it is comprised of both financial and nonfinancial as well as leading and lagging measures. Lower-level measures can optionally be derived from the strategic measures in a top-down measurement cascading process that will soon be described, as a way to create a common focus on an awareness of the strategy. These lower-level measures are typically referred to as *tactical* and/or *operational measures*. Tactical and/or operational measures are gathered in *functional* scorecards that are understandably not balanced in the way that measures at the enterprise level are. (See the discussion of functional scorecards in the sidebar "Enterprise-Wide versus Functional (Local) Scorecards" in Chapter 6.) As a result, the term scorecard—not the balanced scorecard—is reserved for the functional level, not the enterprise level. For the remainder of Part Two, I will use the generic term *scorecard* as synonymous for both balanced scorecards and functional scorecards.

Strategy maps and scorecards go hand in hand. Once created, they embody the strategic intent of the organization and communicate to all both the strategic objectives the organization intends to meet as well as the critical measures of success for attaining those objectives—be they strategic, tactical, or operational measures. A way to think of this is how the organization's vision and mission statement answer the questions, "Where do we want to go?" and "Why are we here?" whereas and how the strategy map and scorecard answer, "How are we going to get there?" Through continuous reporting of the actual scores against the KPI targets, they then keep the organization on track as part of PM. The organization's values are an additional concept that shapes the vision and mission. Values should be thought of as timeless, deeply held beliefs of the organization, which are applied as guiding principles to assure the organization retains what initially made it successful.

Typically this endeavor to manage the strategy is performed separately from the annual *budgeting* process, which is done without linkage and usually by the finance department. The budgeting process needs to be much more than managing the next year-end financial results; it must link to executing the strategy. Now there is a great opportunity for the budget to be an extension of the strategy. Think of these interrelationships as a perpetual cycle:

- *Strategy maps* tell where are we going and why.
- *Scorecards* explain how well and provide guidance for what can be next.
- *Budgets* tell how.

How do you know if your organization's measures are driving the right behavior? Correctly developed strategy maps and scorecards dramatically increase the likelihood that they are. Strategy maps and scorecards provide a framework for literally keeping score of the functions and processes that are most important to the success of an organization. Focusing on the vital few measures for different employee teams is a key. What you measure you can likely control, and what you control you can improve. With the strategy map–derived scorecard, performance is monitored based on weighted measures reflective of their importance to achieving the strategy. Typical organization measures are haphazard, excessively emphasizing after-the-fact financial measures, and consequently the entire measurement system is imbalanced and usually fragmented across multiple computers.

Just like at a sports event, a scorecard quickly conveys how teams are doing at what matters most. However, unlike with a sports event, an enterprise scorecard system allows managers and employees to keep digging deeper for explanations, to view trends, and to get answers, particularly for unexpected results. With scorecards, measures have measures within measures—as briefly explained earlier, high-level measures for executive and senior managers (strategic measures) and derived lower-level tactical and operational measures for employee teams or even individuals.

EXECUTIVE HEADACHES WITH EMPLOYEES

What reasons have led to interest in scorecards? High on the list of major frustrations of executives is their inability to get their employees to carry out the executive's strategies they have so carefully formulated. More specifically, when executives adjust and shift their strategy, they find that their employees continue to perform without much change. Failing to execute the strategy is a major disappointment in the boardroom and to the governing body.

The massive inertia of the existing and typically unchanging measures forces employees to continue to do what they have been doing in the past. A change in direction may not happen despite the executives' proclamations and appeals to managers. The executives are not particularly interested in employees just getting better at what they have been doing. They want employees to change their priorities. Getting people to focus on the right things is much more important than improving on things that don't matter. Everyone recognize the saying "What you measure is what you get." Scorecards make it a reality. Measures drive behavior!

Another explanation as to why employees do not automatically align their work with strategy is that today's employees are *empowered workers*. Unlike many years ago, when employees dutifully obeyed a snap-to-attention command-and-control senior management style, things are different now. Employees are empowered. But empowerment is a two-edged sword. Empowerment means employees can now choose what they believe they should do but also reject what they think they should not do—regardless of their marching orders. So when today's executives announce new changes in direction for their organizations, today's knowledge-worker employees ask themselves, "Am I persuaded? If not, I will continue with my current ways."

To the executives, this is like driving a car with excessive play in the steering wheel. When they turn the steering wheel left or right, the car barely turns. Scorecards are intended to provide precision steering—and speed. Strategy maps clearly display the destination as well as the guideposts along the way. Like a good golf swing or tennis stroke, scorecards give the follow-through that separates the novices from the professionals. Continuing with the golf analogy, do not confuse the golf club with the golf swing. The scorecard is like the golf club—it is a tool, but only by using it often and properly do you improve your skill.

WHAT IMPEDES ORGANIZATIONAL PERFORMANCE?

Why is it that so many organizations exhibit so much energy but never seem to get much traction? And why is it that those few organizations that get traction seem to drift off course from their strategy? Some people believe this dysfunctional behavior is due to the fact that, while traditional hierarchical command-and-control management structures have changed, the core processes, such as the customer order fulfillment system, have not adequately improved. Their premise is that the *business process reengineering* rage of the 1990s successfully replaced an outdated organizational structure with process-based management— but without adequate planning and execution systems. Other people believe that managers and employee teams do not know the correct priorities and what they should be doing to drive toward the organization's strategy. Perhaps these are both valid explanations. But isn't the answer deeper?

Increasingly the blame for poor organizational performance is pointed directly at senior management—their lack of leadership skills. However, senior executives quietly counter that poor performance is not entirely their fault. They believe they do a good job at formulating and continuously redefining their organizational strategies, but they simply cannot get their organizations to execute in alignment with their strategies. They do not view the problem as being solely related to planning and execution systems, such as enterprise resource planning (ERP) systems, but rather as being people-related—a problem of communications and culture.

What do the middle managers and employee teams believe causes the drag on and misdirection of their organizations? The cynical ones think the strategies may be wrong, so their hearts are not in it; but the majority of them see three problems with separate but related explanations:

1. Lots of energy, but poor traction. Employees often spin their wheels without much to show for their work. I genuinely believe that most employees do show up at work to put in a good day's effort. But it is not usually clear to them what the more important priorities are to work on. They often work on pet projects.

To complicate matters, frequently there are too many disconnected improvement initiatives going on in parallel (as well as conflicting process improvement initiatives going on). Employees are often participating on numerous improvement project teams at the same time. This can dilute their focus, thus retarding the organization's progress.

2. Poor alignment. Few if any employees truly know and understand what their organization's strategies are as defined by their senior management. Can you succinctly summarize your organization's strategies? If you can, can your coworkers? Most managers and employees, if asked, cannot articulate them. As a result, increasingly empowered employee teams may be selecting the wrong projects to work on, despite their good intentions.

Often we judge employees by monitoring their results with too many measures. Is it fair to measure people on, let's say, ten measures, particularly if several of them are outside the employees' influence and control? How fair is it for you or your team to be judged by measures that are affected by the performance of others? Management may think that this type of conflict will motivate teams to pull together and help each other out, but is that practical? And when we assign people too many measures, isn't it likely that an employee will concentrate on only those measures they know they can accomplish? I believe we should minimize people's measures to roughly a maximum of three or four—only the vital few measures. You cannot just dump a hundred measures like children's blocks on a table and instruct employees to perform well on *all* of them. Some measures have more impact than others do on overall results. Without some weightings to reflect the relative importance of each measure, the organization can roam without a compass. When an organization focuses on fewer, more vital measures, it gets better traction.

In some instances, there can be competing measures—for example, if my department does well, it adversely results in another department performing poorly. This is classic suboptimization. Some tension among measures is unavoidable, but it should be minimized.

Organizations also can be monitoring the *wrong* measures. Selecting the correct measures is critical and is likely the single most impactive factor in making a PM system work successfully.

3. A focus on historical financial measures. Performance information is typically reported too late, is too financially weighted, and is not predictive. Is your organization reactive or proactive? Most PM systems are reactive.

Employees and managers are swamped with too many after-the-fact measures that inadequately summarize too much information. A good example of this is the emphasis on financial results as the primary measure of success. If the month-end reported profits are below expectations, it is too late to do anything about it. It already happened.

The evolving management philosophy of the *balanced scorecard*,[1] evokes immediate appeal because of its fundamental message: Excessive focus on financial results is unbalanced because nonfinancial measures influence eventual outcomes. However, many organizations monitor and analyze their financial results with much more energy than they put into understanding the influencing metrics that lead to those financial results. Nonfinancial measures, such as customer satisfaction or service levels, deserve more attention.

Organizations need more nonfinancial measures reported *during* the period, not *at the end* of the period. This type of measure, popularly called a *leading indicator* measure, if reacted to can provide enough time to favorably change the outcome of the strategic objective(s) it influences and, eventually, the financial results. In this sense, these leading indicator measures are predictive measures of imminent results.

In summary, many factors impede organizational performance. The impediments can be removed if employees better understand their organization's strategy and the key initiatives chosen to achieve it; and by selecting the correct performance measures. In these ways, employees can more clearly view how the work they do contributes to their organization's results. Measure things that people can influence.

I think of strategy maps and scorecards as enabling employees to soar like a flock of birds or school of fish. It is amazing how Mother Nature provides the instinctive navigation so that hundreds of birds in a flock or fish in a school can fly or swim in formation with such synchrony. Up, down, left, right—all together as if they were one. But I imagine an organization in motion as birds, I see some of them as colliding and others straying away from the pack as if they lost their bearings. Imagine how strategy maps and scorecards can keep all employees in formation. They can.

Let's explore further why strategy mapping and scorecarding are becoming popular, what issues are involved that differentiate success from failure in implementing scorecards, and how to construct strategy maps and scorecards.

NOTE

1. Robert S. Kaplan and David P. Norton, *The Balanced Scorecard: Translating Strategy into Action* (Boston: Harvard Business School Press, 1996).

5

STRATEGY MAPS AND SCORECARDS AS A SOLUTION

Strategy maps and their associated scorecards can trigger a substantial advance in performance metrics and management that address the problems with work misalignment and with confusing or conflicting priorities. Strategy maps help organizations define and subdivide broad strategic objectives into manageable projects and action plans that can likely be accomplished. Scorecards communicate strategic objectives to the workforce in terms that are meaningful to them. Scorecards can assure that the vision and mission created at the boardroom level are *achieved* by the organization. Combining these two methodologies aligns the behavior of employees to focus their work efforts on the strategic issues. Most organizations have managers engaged in tug-of-war contests of ego display and persuasion, but a good strategy map places everyone on one side of the rope. Further, they establish sufficient ownership and accountability that responsibility for results is not ignored.

The overriding goal of a strategy map and scorecard system is to make strategy everyone's job. In short, strategy maps and scorecards are leadership tools that help translate strategies into actions and actions into results. Scorecards are tools that help remove confusion for employees and aid them to better understand priorities. The executive team's strategy is all about focus—in themselves and the employees.

Progress toward attaining the vision and mission via the strategic objectives always involves work efforts with typically scarce resources. For important initiatives, what things people work on is highly dependent on well-reasoned action plans—otherwise people find other personal priorities and pet projects to work on.

- *Strategy maps* provide the guardrails such that budgets and resources are deployed based on a clear understanding of the strategy *before* the budget planning and resource allocation process begins.

48

- *Scorecard* systems assist in managing these initiatives by tracking each initiative, project, and business process, and then linking them to the strategic objectives that they have an impact upon. The intent, benefits, resources, budget, and ownership are tracked, allowing the scorecard users to easily document their efforts in making major performance gains.

A primary purpose of strategy maps and scorecards is to determine action plans and projects that will achieve the strategic objectives to meet the overarching strategy that supports the organization's vision and mission. Some projects may already be in progress, but some needed new projects are also identified. The actual measurements that will be scored are also important, but they are of secondary importance compared to selecting the correct things to work on. A true test that has proven the validity of scorecards is testimonials that when the initial scorecard is constructed, many existing improvement projects and initiatives are terminated because they do not support the strategic intent. Articulating which key strategic objectives to focus on acts as a filter to point out costly projects that should be abandoned or postponed because they obviously don't fit with the strategy map and are thus not relevant.

POOR ALIGNMENT OF STRATEGIES AND MEASURES

The mantra for using scorecards is a simple question: "How am I doing on what is important?" This question should ideally be answerable at every level of the organization—from the operational teams to managers to directors up to the governing bodies in the boardroom. The question has two components:

1. "How am I doing" guides people with feedback on what work to do more or do less of.
2. ". . . on what is important" points toward what matters in order to attain the strategy.

One of today's organizational problems is the disconnection and absence of alignment between *local* measurements of things a manager, team, or employee can control or influence and the subsequent *organizational* results. Figure 5.1 reveals how dysfunctional measures create undesirable behavior and results. It illustrates the problem with a symbolic "wall of disconnects" that prevents the existing measures from aligning with the strategy. Strategy maps and a scorecard

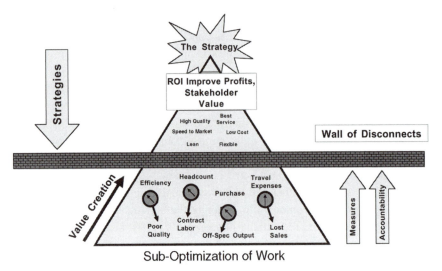

Figure 5.1　Goal Noncongruency, Conflict, and Misalignment

system remove this wall and then provide paths to achieve the organization's vision and mission.

The original idea for the balanced scorecard, introduced by Professor Robert S. Kaplan and Dr. David Norton, recognized the problems and issues just described. However, their thinking introduced additional order and structure to this procedure when they described dependencies among broad groupings of strategic objectives. They called these groupings "perspectives" and described a hierarchy where accomplishing strategic objectives in one perspective contributed to the success of accomplishing the strategic objectives in the dependent perspectives.

Four popular perspectives are often selected, as illustrated in Figure 5.2:

1. **Financial**—profit and investment return results
2. **Customer**—customer satisfaction and needs attainment
3. **Internal core business process**—efficient and effective execution
4. **Innovation, learning, and growth**—the "soft" side measures describing new product and service development as well as people development and learning. Another way to think of this perspective is as enabling assets, including not only people but also equipment, technologies, and brand power.

The first perspective, financial, inherently contains lagging measures. The other three perspectives, which collectively are the horsepower for value cre-

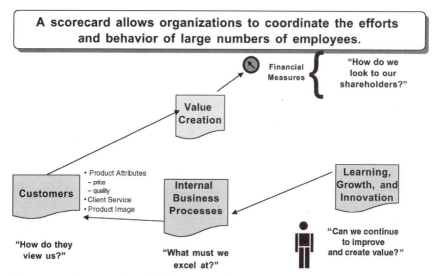

A scorecard allows organizations to coordinate the efforts and behavior of large numbers of employees.

Figure 5.2   Scorecards: Multiple Perspectives

ation, are each individually comprised of both lagging and leading indicators. The differences between them will soon be clarified, but the brief definition of a leading indicator is a measure that has a causal effect on time-lagging indicators. Leading indicators are valuable to track because merely sanctioning and reporting them serves to drive behavior—which is the intent.

Do not make the mistake of assuming that lagging indicators appear only near the upper perspectives of the strategy map. Lagging indicators exist for every single strategic objective. As lagging indicators are improved at the lower perspectives, think of them as cumulatively adding power to the alignment and achievement of the overarching strategic objective. That is, a lagging indicator often becomes (or directly influences) a leading indicator for a next-in-line strategic objective. They are cause-effect connected. However, when initially constructing a scorecard, push the pedal on identifying leading indicators to begin the shift away from years, perhaps decades, of focus on the ultimate lagging indicators—usually financial measures. By placing greater emphasis on leading indicators, lagging indicators will eventually benefit.

Some organizations have added other perspectives, such as quality, environment, safety, health or community. For example, a chemical manufacturer may choose a fifth perspective because of its huge responsibility for the surroundings of its facilities. The number of perspectives is not as important as the recognition that financial results are not effective in guiding the organization; they only tell the organization how earlier efforts, including external factors, have contributed to the bottom line. Additional perspectives, if desired, facilitate construction of the organization's strategy map and elevate the importance of strategic objectives related to these topics. The sequential position or layer of a fifth perspective depends on whether its strategic objectives are a driver or are driven by the other strategic objectives.

A good set of measures will balance competing forces such as short-term versus long-term priorities or internal needs versus external (customer and supplier) needs. When the measures are related based on their dependencies, I refer to the collection of measures as *cascading measures*.

The next chapter discusses how cascading measures connect the interdependencies of the strategic objectives and maintain a common focus on the strategy.

6

STRATEGIC OBJECTIVES' DRIVE GEARS

Cascading Measures

Monitoring too many indistinguishable measures that are outside people's control dilutes the impact of bothering to measure anything. It is my opinion that managers and employee teams can handle at most only three measures—perhaps three to five, but ultimately only a vital few. Further, the managers and employee teams must be able to significantly influence and control the results of those measures. When this approach is used, the emphasis shifts to the selection of the correct measures.

After initiatives and projects have been identified, local measures are selected, and the measures can be cascaded downward for the employee teams. These linkages maintain a common focus on the strategy, and the results can then be rolled up and aligned with the organization's strategy. These cascaded measures act like drive gears to the strategy map's connecting paths, which will soon be described. That is, the strategy maps define strategic objectives and associated initiatives and action plans that support the organization's vision and mission, and the key performance indicator (KPI) measures, when scored, signal whether the action plans are succeeding. Some bottom-level measures lend themselves to monitoring from an activity-based management (ABM) system. ABM as a supplement to populate scorecards with measures will be discussed shortly.

Figure 6.1 illustrates the overall idea that operational indicators at the employee team level should be measured frequently. The higher-level indicator results, measured less frequently, should respond in synchronization, presuming there is a reasonable level of correlation among the measures. Selecting

Enterprise-Wide versus Functional (Local) Scorecards

Strategy map and scorecard projects do not necessarily need to begin at an enterprise-wide (or strategic business unit) level. They can be first designed for a specific function or process—at the warehouse first, for example, and then for the top of the house. As described earlier, these variations should be referred to simply as a scorecard. The term *balanced scorecard* applies to the enterprise-wide measurements. An enterprise-wide balanced scorecard is intended to balance the emphasis of four or more perspectives, and it is constructed to assist in achieving the organization's vision and mission. The functional or departmental scorecard is less strategic and more tactical. However, it may not be balanced in the same sense as the enterprise-wide balanced scorecard. Functional scorecards will have mini-strategic objectives and break them down into smaller, more detailed projects, processes, and actions for more intense monitoring.

Carrying the performance measurement methodology throughout an organization eventually requires adoption of the principles of scorecarding at *all* levels. Commercial business analytic software enables the creation and management of strategy maps and scorecards at *any* level in the organization. The proliferation of local scorecards throughout the organization results in a top-down cascade of performance measures that links the highest-level vision, mission, and strategy in the balanced scorecard with the actions at the tactical level where strategic objectives are actually implemented and realized by the day-to-day activities of individuals on projects or in processes.

A modeling software environment allows for customized scorecards with an unlimited number of strategies, objectives, key performance indicators (KPIs), critical success factors, perspectives, or themes. Both numeric and text-based or subjective measures are supported by commercial software,[a] thus providing the greatest possible flexibility in designing a performance tracking system.

---

[a]Refer to www.sas.com for an example of commercial strategy map and scorecard software.

KPI measures is more art than science. Associating KPI measures with action plans is key. Strategy maps, described soon, bring science to the art of selecting measures.

An organization can have many layers of leading/lagging indicators. A lagging indicator typically becomes a leading indicator in the next higher level perspective, and so on.

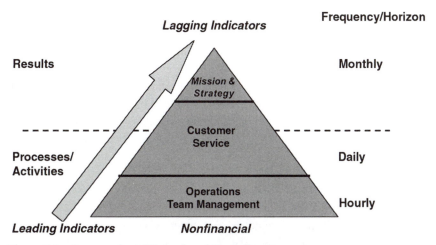

Figure 6.1   Scorecards: A Hierarchy of Cascading Measures

Figure 6.2 visually reveals the decomposition and cascading of a top-level strategy to a front-line action. This ensures that managers and employees share a common focus on the strategy. The top of the figure is humorously referred to as the "O-zone." This is because these are the measures for the CEO, COO, CFO, and other so-called C-level executives. The figure has teams at the bottom with their own operational measures. (Ideally, the separate, functional scorecard

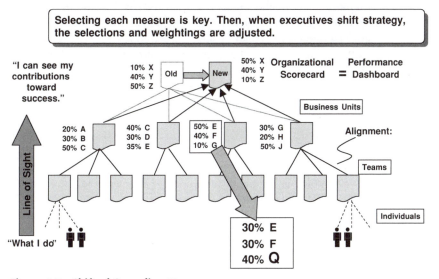

Figure 6.2   Shift of Cascading Measures

decomposed from the enterprise's balanced scorecard.) Presuming these lower-level measures align with the high-level measures, then if they are scoring high, the collective work efforts will be achieving the overall strategy.

With a properly cascaded strategy map, changes in strategy can quickly be mirrored in the measurement system. That is, leading and lagging measures are ideally selected by the employee team, configured among themselves, and weighted in parallel to the levels of importance of the strategic objectives and corresponding action plans or business processes that they support. Remember that the KPIs serve as the drive gears to the strategy map's strategic objectives and its action plans or processes.

Note in Figure 6.2 how an employee can have a line of sight on how what he or she does can affect other performances that eventually affect the achievement of the strategic objectives. Employees can therefore see how what they do contributes to the organization's success. If management is bold, it will allow the employee teams to see how coworkers are also contributing to success.

Figure 6.2 also illustrates that when the senior managers shift strategy, they can replace one or more of an employee team's vital few measures with different and more applicable measures, and/or rebalance the weightings of emphasis for

---

Driving a Scorecard System with Fact-Based Data

Scorecards require data. Without reliable and single-view data, the credibility of the scorecard's signals is lowered. It is important to feed fact-based data information to the scorecard system. A subset of the KPI measures can come from an ABM system. That is, ABM data can populate the scorecard framework with robust and high-octane information to be used as *scores* in the scorecard systems. For example, unit cost trends (e.g., the processing cost per invoice), customer profit margin levels, or cost of quality levels may be strategy-relevant. Each of these is reported by an ABM system.

In short, the outputs of an ABM system are excellent inputs to a weighted scorecard system. But let's not confuse ABM and performance measures. ABM is not the performance measurement system. As previously mentioned, the output of ABM can be an important input to performance measures. And the presence of ABM data can lead to actions and decisions, not just emotional sighs or an "oh my." Also, ABM is not a prerequisite for designing and using a scorecarding system. Scorecards can certainly operate without ABM data, but scorecards can work better when managerial accounting data is a subset of the KPIs.

the measures. That is, when senior management shifts to the new strategy, not only do the high-level weightings change, but also in one case measure Q replaces measure G. This does not mean that measure G is now unimportant. It simply means that measure Q has now become important and the desire is to have the vital few measures.

Rebalancing the weightings by modifying the coefficient percentages that reflect importance is comparable to an airline pilot slightly adjusting the ailerons on the airplane's wings to slightly alter the airplane's course. But replacing an old measure with a new one is more intense—like banking the airplane left or right.

What are the sequential steps to implement a scorecard? These steps are discussed in much greater detail at www.wiley.com/go/performance.

7

A RECIPE FOR IMPLEMENTATION

The steps for implementing a strategy map and its scorecards are like a recipe. The initial steps to build the strategy map are primarily performed by the executive team. After that, the managers and employee teams get involved identifying the projects and initiatives intended to achieve the strategic objectives and identifying the KPIs. The steps are as follows.

1. AGREE ON THE VISION, MISSION, AND STRATEGIC INTENT OF THE ENTERPRISE, AND DEFINE THE STRATEGIES.

The initial exercise is to define the organization's vision and mission statements. These two statements are not the same, and their definition must precede the construction of strategy maps or scorecards because they serve as signposts.

The vision statement answers the question, "Where do we want to go?" in terms that describe a highly desirable future state for the organization. It says it all, as these examples demonstrate:

- President John F. Kennedy: "We will put a man on the moon."
- Microsoft Corporation (1990s): "A computer on every desk top."
- Microsoft Corporation (21st century): "Information anywhere, anytime."

The mission statement provides to all employees the answer to the question, "Why are we here?" in terms of desirable impacts to gain a competitive edge. Here are some examples:

- To exceed *customer needs* well ahead of their realization that they even have the need (e.g., 24 hour automated bank teller [ATM])
- To leverage *technology capabilities* in fulfilling customer needs
- To leverage *employee capabilities* for whatever we excel at

Now the construction of the strategy map begins. Its initial purpose is to serve as a framework in the form of a network connecting strategic objectives—hence the name *strategy map*.

2. DEFINE THE STRATEGIC OBJECTIVES THAT SUPPORT STEP 1.

Strategy maps (sometimes referred to as *value driver trees*) are used to communicate a unified view of the overarching strategy to the organization. A strategy map defines corporate direction and aligns internal processes, strategic objectives, initiatives, key performance indicator (KPI) measures, and target scores.

The balanced scorecard has received substantial attention, as if the scorecard were the answer, when in fact it is the strategy maps that serve like a builder's blueprint for the scorecard. The strategy maps are like the secret sauce in this recipe because their straightforward logic becomes so compelling. A study by Hewitt Associates estimated that companies who use strategy maps and scorecards perform with forty percent better results compared to companies that do not.[1]

However at this point, the themes that blossom into strategic objectives, have yet to be organized or positioned among themselves. That comes in Step 3.

3. MAP THE INTERRELATED STRATEGIC OBJECTIVES WITH THEIR CAUSE-AND-EFFECT LINKAGES.

The strategic objectives are interrelated. Kaplan and Norton originally proposed four perspectives—financial (or stakeholder), customer, internal process, and learning and growth—that are very useful in simplifying what otherwise would be a difficult task. That task is to take all of the strategic objectives (congealed from a workshop where the executives identify the strengths, weaknesses, opportunities, and threats from the popular SWOT analysis, and then cluster them into themes) and slot each one into the perspective it best fits.

The sequence of the four perspectives makes very good sense. The top perspective (i.e., the *financial* perspective for commercial companies and the *customer/stakeholder* view for the public sector company) is the beneficiary of the strategic objectives in the three perspectives beneath it. The bottom perspective, the *learning and growth* (or *enabling assets*) perspective, is the most foundational, not unlike the foundation for a house.

An effective way to understand a strategy map is to visualize a hypothetical example. Figure 7.1 illustrates a strategy map of a hypothetical XYZ Corporation. Each node in the network represents a strategic objective. The figure includes if-then linkages where the paths drive, or at least contribute to, the outcome of the strategic objectives above them.

An interesting question routinely asked is "Where is the organization's *strategy* defined and located on the strategy map?" The simple answer is it does not appear. Why not? The reason is that the connected network of the strategic objectives is equivalent to the strategy! Strategic objectives are the actions that an organization must complete—or at least make much progress toward—to

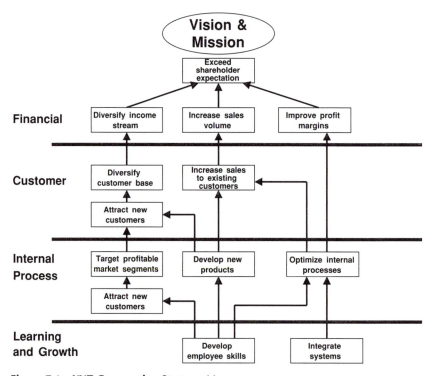

Figure 7.1   XYZ Corporation Strategy Map

Source: Ralph Smith, Orion Development Group, 2003, www.odgroup.com, permission to reprint granted.

achieve the organization's *mission*, which in turn would realize its *vision*. The role of the strategy map is to tell employees and managers what the organization is looking for, rather than have the executives state what they want the employees to do. In short, *the strategic objectives collectively are the strategy!*

4. DEFINE INITIATIVES TO CLOSE THE PERFORMANCE GAP FOR EACH STRATEGIC OBJECTIVE, AND SCALE BACK NONSUPPORTIVE PROJECTS.

Strategic objectives are oblique. You cannot go out there and "do" an objective. But you can perform projects, programs, and actions or manage business processes that drive to *accomplish* the strategic objectives. In short, an effective PM system demystifies the oblique strategic objectives by articulating how every action program or business process—by teams and even individuals—contributes to the achievement of the higher-level enterprise strategic objectives and, subsequently, the vision and mission.

5. SELECT APPROPRIATE STRATEGIC MEASURES AND CASCADE THEM TO RELEVANT PARTS OF THE ORGANIZATION.

A key in this step is to allow the different parts of the enterprise to define their own KPIs (tactical and operational measures), aimed at supporting the strategic KPIs and maintaining a shared focus on the strategy.

Up to this point there have been no defined measures—specific or general. Now they are defined. This is the most influential step for the success of the scorecard, yet it is arguably the trickiest to do.

Each strategic objective should be restricted to the KPI measures for the action programs or business processes. A KPI should answer the question "What is an excellent quantitative measure that would communicate how well the strategic objective is being met?" by considering the action step or business process aimed at the strategic objective. Do not confuse this step with *choosing* the specific *target* score for the KPI measure. That comes in Step 7.

Figure 7.2 is the scorecard for our hypothetical XYZ Company. Note that strategic objectives are identical.

Although all of the columns are completed in Figure 7.2, in reality we would only have the first column filled in after completing this step—the remaining ones are described in Steps 6, 7, and 8.

XYZ Corporation Balanced Scorecard					
Vision: To be the premier provider of our products in specific global markets.					
Mission: To delight target customers through innovative products and application of leading-edge technology of our processes.					
			2Q, 200X		
PERSPECTIVE /	Lagging KPI Measures <---	KPI	KPI	KPI	Comments /
Strategic Objectives	<--- Leading KPI Measures	Target	Actual	Score"	Explanation
				>1 good	
FINANCIAL				<1 poor	
Exceed shareholder expectations	Share price	72.0	71.0	0.975	
	ROI	25.0%	21.5%		
40% Increase sales volume	Revenue ($ mil)	$6.000	$5.482		
35% Improve profit margins	Gross margin %	35.0%	31.6%		
	Operating expense % sales	20.0%	24.2%		
25% Diversify income stream	% $ from top 20% of customers	50%	48%		
	# products > 5% of revenues	6	7		
CUSTOMER					
Increase sales to existing cusomers	Cross-sell ratio %	30%	13%		
	Customer retention rate	95%	90%		
	% preferred supplier to customer	35%	20%		
Diversify customer base	# sales call to new markets	90	84		
Attract new customers	Revenues from new customers ($ mil)	$0.500	$0.800		
	advertising $ spent	$ 25.0 K	$ 23.4 K		
PROCESS					
Target profitable customer segments	# segments identified	3	0		
Develop new products	Revenues from new products	$ 40.0 K	$ 55.5 K		
	New product intro time (# days)	60 days	95 days		
Streamline order fullfillment process	Fulfillment cycle time (#days)	7.5 days	8.8 days		
	On-time delivery %	95%	51%		
LEARNING & GROWTH					
Develop employee skills	Profit per employee	$ 50.0 K	$ 32.5 K		
	Employee satisfaction index	80%	82%		
	# training days / employee	2.00	1.25		
	Retention rate	95%	99%		
Integrate systems	% IT plan integration	80%	90%		
	% orders received via Internet	10%	4%		
		hi:	92		
*Score equation example	share price	lo:	52		
		score = 1 + [(actual-target) / (hi - lo)]			
		where hi/lo range has target as midpoint			

(From Strategy Map — arrows pointing to Exceed shareholder expectations, Increase sales volume, Improve profit margins, Diversify income stream)

Figure 7.2   XYZ Corporation Balanced Scorecard

Source: Ralph Smith, Orion Development Group, 2003, www.odgroup.com, permission to reprint granted.

KPIs do not always need to be quantitative measures. Measurement data can come in all types. They can be text-based, as in "yes" or "no" for a discrete event, or as "above/below"; or they can be described as an estimated degree-of-completion (either as a percentage or even as basic as "started, midway, or complete"). It is totally acceptable with scorecards to use subjective measures or measures scored with employee estimates rather than facts; these may be the most economical form of input data.

Figure 7.3 describes the differences between leading and lagging indicators. The simplest way to think of this is by asking and answering the question, "*When* is the actual score reported against the KPI—during the time period, or at the end of the time period?" (Of course, this begs the question of "For which time period—the past quarter, month, week, day, or hour?") Figure 7.3 displays a two-dimensional view useful in understanding how leading and lagging KPIs relate to one another. The horizontal axis displays the time *during* the period, with the extreme right being the end of the period. The vertical axis displays how deep measures describe root causes of the behavior of the most upper-right measure. The latter is referred to as the *benefiting* KPI, because this measure is a receiver of all the efforts of the actions reflected in the *contributing* KPIs.

At this step in the performance management process, the leading and lagging measures will have been selected by the employee team, configured among

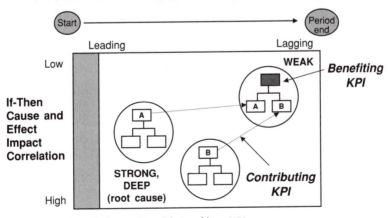

Figure 7.3   Relating If-Then KPIs with Lead/Lag KPIs

themselves, and weighted in parallel to the levels of importance of the strategic objectives and corresponding action plans or business processes that they support. That is, with a properly cascaded scorecard hierarchy strategy, changes in strategy should result in new initiatives (or old ones escalated in importance) and quickly be mirrored in the measurement system. At this point, and not before it, the scorecard as a mechanism is finally completed, but it is not yet being used to measure and score *actual* data.

After this step in the PM process cycle, the correct KPI measures have been defined, weighted, and related. So let's proceed with the next set of steps to build and assemble the PM process wheel. These steps are in the second arc of the PM process wheel as it was depicted in Chapter 2. These next steps insert each KPI *target* score (and their meter ranges) into the scorecard.

6. SELECT THE TARGET LEVELS[2] FOR EACH KPI FOR RELEVANT TIME PERIODS AND IDENTIFY THE PERFORMANCE DEFICIENCY GAP.

With this step, we finally get to the point where a specific metric level or amount, or a text description, is agreed on. A target measure level or amount should pass the test of "If we were doing well in accomplishing the associated strategic objective, this would be the level or amount of this metric."

7. COLLECT THE ACTUAL KPIS, DISPLAY THE SCORES, AND COMPARE TO THE TARGETS.

This step is mechanical. Actual KPI measures are collected and inserted into the scorecard. Figure 7.4 displays a screenshot of meters from one of the leading analytical software vendors, the SAS Institute Inc. (www.sas.com).

The differences between the *actual* KPI scores and the *target* KPI scores are calculated and displayed, usually with a meter. Regardless of which side of the KPI meter a score difference lands on, it is implicit that a favorable score positively contributes to accomplishing the strategic objectives that, when achieved, guide and speed the organization toward realizing its vision and mission.

Web-enabled scorecards with traffic-light and alert messages as visual aids add timely communications and discussion threads among managers and employees. That is, Web-enabled scorecards allow employees to *actively* write e-mails and record notes to investigate problems, to focus on key needs, and to *actively* take corrective actions to improve their scores. These types of signals

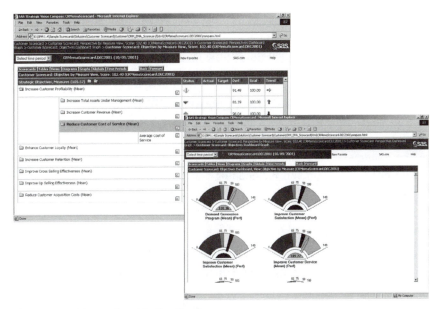

Figure 7.4   Meters Provide Feedback

and alert messages that monitor real-time trends assure managers and employee teams that if something is likely to happen that will exceed a pain threshold, they will be notified before it happens.

8. MANAGE PERFORMANCE GAPS TO STEER THE ORGANIZATION BY INTERPRETING AND REACTING TO THE SCORE, THEN REVISING THE ACTION PLANS.

If the strategy map and scorecard construction has been properly developed, what is now left is for human nature and good leadership to take over. At this stage of maturity in using the scorecard, managers and employee teams are receiving continuous feedback on how they are performing (they know the score). They also more clearly know what they all are trying to attain—the strategic objectives that satisfy the vision and mission statements.

Unlike most internal e-mail messages, with scorecard feedback that is now Web-enabled for e-mail and discussion threads, the dialogues are focused and associated in the *context* of the strategy. The metaphor used earlier was that the scorecard is like a racing boat coxswain shouting to the crew. Here the crew are dialoging among themselves, and the scorecard's measures (KPIs) have been selected in the *context* of the strategy. This ensures behavioral alignment. The concept of context is important. It elevates this methodology well above management by objectives (MBO) and spreadsheet performance reports.

PERFORMANCE MANAGEMENT
PROCESS WHEEL IN ACTION

Focus, communication, and collaborate—iteratively. It does work. This is not theory but rather a proven methodology supported by commercial software technology.[3]

Scorecard Software Systems:
Technology Is No Longer the Impediment

Organizations can fine-tune the selection of their measures with an ongoing scorecard system that allows the flexibility to remove, add, substitute, and reconfigure how the key performance indicators (KPIs) relate to strategies. Unfortunately, most organizations are usually so preoccupied with trying to steer the organizational ship through the high seas, they have not implemented the platform—the navigational system and compass—to facilitate steerage, let alone fine-tuning.

Despite huge investments in time (and perhaps in consultants) to define the corporate strategy, the executive team typically asks a young spreadsheet whiz in the accounting department to automate it all. This usually results in an overly complex and incomprehensible set of disconnected scorecards that are difficult to maintain and update, and, worse yet, problematic to adjust for new strategies. This defeats the benefits of effective learning, communications, and feedback. Commercial strategy mapping and scorecard software solves this problem.

In complex environments, it is no simple task to identify owners of strategic objectives, to select the correct measures, to give each measure the right level of emphasis for balance, to assign a reasonable level of performance, and then to monitor the results. In the past, to complicate matters, there was little in software technology to support this methodology that links dependent performance measurements. Some organizations advocated chalkboards prominently displayed in the cafeteria for employees to see, while others harnessed mainframe computers to generate reams of paper stuffed through the mail to people who may not see it for a week.

Scorecard Software Systems *(Continued)*

But now times have changed. Information technology is no longer the impediment—the thinking becomes the main problem. Software and communication platforms now ease the selection, configuration, data collection, and distribution of measurements. Data warehouses store the data. Internet delivery via Web browsers to individual personal computers is now very practical (this is discussed in the Chapter 9, under "Reporting and Distributing Scorecard Information: Internet-Based Architecture").

Scorecard software systems can also support widely accepted measurement methodologies such as for criteria laid out in the United States' Malcolm Baldrige Award or the European Foundation for Quality Management (EFQM). Regardless of the number of views or perspectives measured (e.g., customer, internal processes, innovation, etc.), scorecard software provides a multidimensional framework for describing, implementing, and managing strategy at *all levels* of an enterprise. Scorecards integrate financial measures with other key performance indicators around whatever perspectives are deemed important for an enterprise.

But, as earlier cautioned, poor measure selection can lead to unintended and poor results.

NOTES

1. "Building Your Balanced Scorecard in Just Five Days" presentation by Brett Knowles, December 13, 2003 on *Better Management Live* in Mexico City on July 15, 2003.

2. To keep this concept simple, I will not differentiate between indicators and measures. However, I prefer indicators over measures because the word *measure* implies precision, whereas for scorecards, indicators based on approximations or subjective estimates of trusted employees are more than adequate for communicating direction.

3. Visit www.sas.com or www.bettermanagement.com for industry case studies.

8

THE HUMAN SIDE
OF COLLABORATION

Management's attitude is key to successfully sustaining strategy maps and score-cards. It is inevitable that the executives acknowledge that traditional management styles must change. Strategic learning among the workforce must replace control. Management reviews will need to shift from interrogations about "Why did you miss your target?" to "What did we learn to explain why we have a performance gap?"

WHO SHOULD DEFINE AND CONSTRUCT— EXECUTIVES OR EMPLOYEES?

There are two schools of thought for implementation:

1. A somewhat dictatorial approach, in which a top-down strategy map is cascaded down and deployed at all levels of the organization with little modification, to ensure strategy-aligned behavior and make everyone aware of the larger picture.
2. A decentralized approach in which each business group or function can adapt to encourage buy-in and foster in employees a sense of belonging and involvement.

The culture of an organization should influence which approach the implementation should go toward; but the best approach lies in between these two extremes. Figure 8.1 shows who should be responsible for which components of constructing and operating the strategy map and scorecard system. Do not get

1st Quarter						
	Strategic Objective	Identify Projects, Initiatives, or Processes	Measure	KPI Target	KPI Actual	Comments/ Explanation
Executive Team	X			X		
Managers and Employees			X		*Their Score*	X
					<----- *Period Results* ------->	

Figure 8.1   Who Is Responsible for What?

the impression this is an us-versus-them game. A key determinant of successful scorecard implementations is employee involvement.

In short, the executives must initially construct the strategy map in order to derive the themes (ultimately the strategic objectives) and their interconnections. The employees then select the appropriate measures they believe will best report progress toward achieving the strategic objective. The executives' next role is to approve the measures and, more importantly, assign a target. The target should be set with a Goldilocks spirit of not too high or too low—both are demoralizing—but just right and achievable so that measurable progress can be made. During each reporting period, the employee teams try their best to achieve the key performance indicator (KPI) target. Finally, the employee team, or alternatively the KPI owner accountable for the measure, explains why the score hit, exceeded, or fell short of the KPI target and whether the difference was within typical and acceptable variation (to prevent unnecessary and often wasteful over-steering) or truly an outlier worthy of corrective action.

ACCOUNTABILITY, RESPONSIBILITY, AND OWNERSHIP

Communicating the intent of strategic objectives is as important to achieving their success as is tracking the performance indicators. Educating the entire organization on the full meaning of each strategic objective allows an individual to internalize the strategic objectives and adopt as his or her own the high-level strategy formulated by the executive managers. However, in the end, performance measures are intangibles that themselves cannot push the buttons or pull the levers. The utility of performance measures is proportional to how well they influence people to do the right things. That may sound profound, but it is true.

Strategy maps and scorecards have tremendous analytical capability, but their real power is as a management application that can coordinate the efforts of large numbers of people. Scorecard software allows each manager and employee team to customize their local scorecards—both those of the individuals and those of the team. Subject to security and policy, managers and employees can have access to and visibility of to the scorecards of other employee teams as well as those of higher-level managers located above the teams, and even all the way up to the CEO's scorecard. Ideally, easy access to visibility of scorecards fosters discussion about common or shared interests and problems. In addition, within any and each scorecard, multiple custom views can be constructed to track many different measurable objects.

Ultimately a single employee should be held accountable for progress and results. As organizations become increasingly matrixed to support cross-department processes, projects, and initiatives, identifying and locating that person who is ultimately responsible for a strategic objective and its measure becomes tricky. Commercial scorecard software solves this by assigning discrete ownership of strategic objectives and KPI measurements with scores throughout the strategy map and eventually into the organization's culture.

MOTIVATING EMPLOYEES TO TALK TO EACH OTHER

In the supply and value chain management discipline, a popular term is *seller-and-buyer collaboration*. Observers note, however, that in practice collaboration has been much more talk than action. Its lack of widespread acceptance is partly due to long-term adversarial relationships, where external suppliers and customers have been wary and mistrustful of each other. But aren't there also similar *internal* issues within an organization due to poor communication and lack of collaboration among employees? These are behavioral issues.

As described in the previous chapter's Step 8 discussion about reacting to the score, commercial scorecard software resolves problems related to inadequate collaboration and poor cooperation by adding rigor to what has traditionally been a very informal process that is broadly affected by human nature. Trust and suspicion are large factors that affect how people interact with and influence one another.

The brass ring in the PM arena is in fostering a cooperative and collaborative culture where strategy implementation is managed not by senior executives but by the middle-level managers and employee teams that actually perform the work. To support this cultural development, scorecard systems create an environment where the various participants can conveniently communicate about strategic objectives and performance issues. This enables them to coordinate their actions in striving toward improved performance and subsequent align-ment of work efforts with strategy. This collaborative environment, using com-mercial scorecard system software, enables the various players to share all aspects of performance, and it captures a chronology of commentary on each strategic objective.

OPENNESS VERSUS SECRECY: SHARE THE SCORES?

With any apparently good managerial improvement method, there are also dark sides. One way to explore the dark side of applying scorecards is to imagine that you are an IT security manager, the person who controls passwords and determines who has access to which data. Pretend that you control the switches for all of your organization's employees' access to potentially all of the scorecards—the enterprise as well as the local scorecards. Let's assume that all employee teams have unpro-tected visibility to all of the scorecards above them—that is, access to their more se-nior managers' scorecards with strategy-mapped paths and linkages, all the way to the chief executive officer's scorecard that sits on top of the enterprise scorecard.

Here is your situation: You can choose to remove all the security switches that block every team from seeing *across* to view scorecard results of the other em-ployee teams and also their managers' KPI scores reported above your cowork-ers' scores. Or you can keep all the current security in place, thus preventing workers and managers from seeing their coworkers' scores and how coworkers are performing relative to their KPI targets and their managers' KPI targets at higher levels.

Which option would you choose and what might be the consequences? In training workshops, the majority of the responses are to unblock the security switches, giving full access and visibility to all employee teams. The reasoning is that by seeing which target scores owned by other teams are not being achieved, perhaps there is some recommendation or at least insight that people can share with one another. This interpretation supports an altruistic optimism that all employees are on the same team with no internal politics. Those who choose the option to retain tight security, thus blocking workers' view of their coworkers' scorecards, worry about the blame game. That is, workers who wished their KPI scores were better and higher will search for low performance elsewhere and may rationalize an explanation as to why they did not score better, claiming it was caused by low performance elsewhere.

What is a lesson from this mind game exercise? It implies that the attitude with which executive management introduces strategy mapping and scorecards to employees is very important. Ideally, a strategy map and scorecard system should be used to improve that direction, traction, and speed I referred to in the Preface. Scorecards should foster internal communications for solutions rather than heat up internal politics and needless backstabbing. A value on strategic learning by employees must replace an emphasis on operational control. Let's now further discuss executive management's attitude when implementing a scorecard system.

SCORECARD OR REPORT CARD?

Who do scorecards help more—senior management or the workers? The answer is a moot point if there is a win-win result for both groups. Management and employees equally benefit from scorecards. But a note of caution: There are organizational obstacles that can hamper a successful application of strategy maps and scorecards. For example, is the intent that it be a scorecard or a report card? Will it be used for punishment, or for remedy and root cause analysis and corrective action collectively?

Regardless of which particular KPI measurements are selected, the resulting tool should be a *scorecard*, not a report card. There is a distinction. Scorecards are not about accounting police work. They are not about who has been good and who has been bad. Scorecard systems are about uniting the organizational muscle to get much more traction. It is true that responsibility and accountability are important. However, for many employee teams, much of what they strive for is influenced by the priorities and performance of their coworkers. Therefore, as was described in Step 5 in Chapter 7, executive teams should allow their managers and employee teams to select their own measures that support the strategic objectives. They should try less to simply monitor performance with the sole purpose of making harsh judgments, but rather monitor performance to generate feedback communications about what needs to be adjusted. In other words, managers and employee teams should contribute to the selection of the measures. They usually know their surroundings better than anyone else does.

An online survey by Pepperdine University[1] from scorecard teams who volunteered information has helped in understanding differences between successful and unsuccessful scorecard implementations. A prominent differentiator is the attitude of senior management. Once again, will KPI scores be used by executive management for punishment or to foster remedies? Will management view its benefit from a scorecard system as a return of power over employees and a chance to reclaim the command-and-control style of management from the past? Or will it view the scorecard as a tool to benefit employee teams and collectively aid in improving the organization's direction, traction, and speed?

Will it be a scorecard or a report card? What is the difference?

- A *scorecard* is an individual's personal resource for monitoring his or her own performance.
- A *report card* is a measure of someone else's standard imposed on others.

What emotional response did you just feel when you read those descriptions? Many readers might revert back to grade school memories of anxiously awaiting their grades—the teacher's assessment of their classroom performance. Fear and anxiety prevail with report cards. If management can wisely introduce scorecards as an instrument for navigating direction and priorities rather than as a search for the guilty, then a scorecard system will be more effective.

The difference between a scorecard and a report card can be seen by considering the differences between a scorecard and a scoreboard at a baseball game. Think of the scoreboard as the report card. With a scoreboard we only view the outcome—which team has more runs. Similar to a report card, a scoreboard tells very little as to why the results occurred. With a scorecard, every play is recorded, which enables one to go back and analyze what events influenced the outcome. Should the batter have bunted to advance an on-base runner, or was it wiser to allow the batter to swing away? Scorecard users can review these events with an eye to potentially do things differently in the future. Some baseball fans record substantial detail in their scorecard, including the number of balls and strikes for each batter's trip to home plate. The level of detail depends on what will be useful for interpreting and analyzing the results. The lesson here is to measure what matters for relevance in the context of improving things.

Role of Consequences and Financial Incentives

A counterview advocating scoreboard thinking suggests that reporting actual scores be not simply for the pleasure and curiosity of workers and managers. A key principle must be considered: *Measurements without consequences won't impact behavior.*[a] What should be the reaction when actual KPI scores significantly deviate from KPI target levels or amounts? An altruistic view would be that the organization should quickly shift its focus to the underachieved strategic objectives—the red traffic lights—and marshal its energies to identify and remedy the problems.

The counterview, which considers the nuances of human behavior, is that

(Continued)

Role of Consequences and Financial Incentives *(Continued)*

a single individual (or at least a small number of employees) should own the strategic objective and its measures, and be held accountable for its performance. The consequence from a reported unfavorable score variance does not automatically mean some form of adverse judgment or punishment should be made. Rewards can be applied for positive reinforcement to encourage good performance, rather than discouraging workers with penalties. But some form of consequence should periodically happen when KPI scores are reported.

Does this mean we should link scorecard performance with employee compensation? Has "pay for performance" finally discovered a truly valid and equitable method with scorecarding for effectively managing a variable compensation incentive program? I have yet to take a position on this, but there seem to be two schools of thought:

1. Do not mix scorecards and pay. This opinion holds that a formal linkage of scorecards and salary adjustments (up or down) is the fastest way to ruin the sustained use of a scorecard system.

2. Financial rewards are the most effective way to focus employee energies. People with this opinion believe that adding financial rewards creates the fine gear wheels to assure essential organizational traction for the scorecard system, aligning people's work and accomplishments with the strategic objectives, vision, and mission.

Both positions have strong supporting arguments. What may be true is that simply rewarding pay raises based only on the most lagging high-level (and likely financial) KPIs, such as profits and return on equity (ROE), merely adds costs to the detriment of shareholders! The levers that contribute to profits are beyond the influence and control of the vast majority of employees. If an organization were to apply a pay-for-performance compensation program, the pay should be linked to the employee's scorecard, not to the scorecards of others, or some weighted combination should be considered.

[a]Bill Abernathy, Abernathy & Associates, Memphis, Tennessee at a CPA Manufacturing Services Association (MSA) workshop, January 8, 1998.

NOTE

1. Bill Stratton and Raef Lawson, "The Use and Adoption of Scorecarding in North America: Who Is Doing What?" preliminary findings; presentation to Consortium for Advanced Manufacturing International, Portland, Oregon, September 10, 2002.

9

FACT-BASED MANAGEMENT ACCOUNTING DATA

Ideally organizations benefit from strategy maps and scorecards when they communicate strategic direction and priorities, but also provide a supporting decision-making framework. Scorecard initiatives benefit greatly by linking with other analytical applications, such as those tools that provide the bottom-up analysis that enables managers to drill down to determine the true causes of performance problems.

The notion of managing leading indicator processes to achieve desirable lagging indicator results and outputs is a central idea behind PM. One of the pillars of evaluation and decision analysis is managerial accounting data. While period-end reported sales, profits, and spending are the ultimate in after-the-fact *lagging* indicators, the price and computed cost data are useful and popular *leading* indicators in scorecards—particularly per-unit cost data. Activity-based management (ABM) systems are a perfect source for this kind of data.

One of the primary ways in which ABM will accelerate information-enabled productivity is by providing fact-based data. ABM's reliable data can be used to both assess past progress and support future decisions. In its most basic form, ABM is simply data that are a means to an end. ABM should not be considered as an *improvement program* because then it may be perceived as a temporary fad or a project of the month. In reality ABM simply reflects the economics of how an organization behaves and spends and consumes expenses, and the output of the ABM calculation engine is always the input to something else. More specifically, the output of ABM is an excellent input for PM systems.

The outputs of ABM are excellent inputs to a scorecard system. Let's not confuse ABM and performance measures. ABM is *not* the measurement system. The *output* of ABM can be an important *input* to PM in a scorecard system. The presence of ABM data can stimulate a greater number of actions and decisions.

ABM is not a prerequisite for designing and using a scorecard system. Scorecards are much more about communicating strategies to employees and increasing alignment of execution of the work to stay focused on the strategies. But the existence of ABM data can populate the scorecard framework with robust and high-octane information. Furthermore, ABM becomes an essential tool to move from an annual budget to continuous *rolling* forecasts to allow for faster reactions to external events, revised strategic objectives, and changes in resource allocations.

Focus on Outputs and Outcomes

With fact-based and relevant cost data, managers and teams can see things they had never seen before—and some of it might not be pretty. They really find out, for example, what the true cost is to process an individual customer return. They can differentiate profitable from unprofitable customers. They can isolate the location, amount, and cost of unused and available processing capacity.

It is important to treat activity-based management (ABM) data responsibly. Often leaders in organizations are surprised when they see the truth about the consumption patterns from their cost structure. But, as with scorecards, finding someone to blame is not the point of having ABM data. The key is to use the ABM data as a guide for making better decisions, and use the data for performance measures as a valuable benefit.

Most organization leaders have very little insight about their *internal* outputs. I'm not referring to the obvious products and standard service lines that they deliver to end-customers and service recipients. Rather, most leaders lack a minimal understanding of the internal outputs of work, such as knowing what the work effort and cost are to generate any of the following:

- A new enrolled account.
- A processed invoice.
- A returned and put-away product.
- A completed engineering change.
- A completed new customer sign-up.
- A completed executive report.
- A registered student.

Focus on Outputs and Outcomes *(Continued)*

- A sales call.
- A setup or changeover of equipment.

These are not simply the *work activities* that people perform but the descriptions of the results after the activities have been performed; they are the outputs of work. A collection of outputs leads to *outcomes*, a more macro result for which cost can also be calculated. ABM does a great job of tracing resource expenses to all sorts of outputs. This does not mean that the work processes that produce the outputs are unimportant. It simply means that many people react more to the visibility of output costs relative to the process costs, even though they are essentially the same costs, just reported differently.

In short, when unit costs are trended, employees and managers gain more insight. They can use benchmarks to deduce whether they might have a best or worst practice. Per-unit costs should not be included only in the scorecard's *financial* perspective but should appear in the other perspectives as well. They may have a currency sign attached, but they are a representation of the equivalent resources consumed by the unit measure, stated in terms of money.

Whether the ABM data measure the work activity costs, the processes that the activities belong to, or the outputs, ABM makes scorecards easier to populate. This is because ABM already has accurate numbers in place, and in a format designed for decision support. Some organizations have initially designed their scorecards without cost data. This leaves gaps or incorrect *allocations* that corrupt the result measurements. Adding ABM fills in the weak spots.

With the visibility created by ABM, organizations can identify where to remove waste, low-value-adding costs, and unused capacity, as well as understand what drives their costs. With ABM, businesses can measure where they are and are not profitable, and also understand why.

Some perceive ABM as just another way to spin financial data rather than as useful, mission-critical managerial information. However, practitioners view ABM as essential for good decision making. Also, in the past, an ABM project was just that, a project, and not viewed as a repeatable and reliable reporting system. As a project, ABM helps fix the problem and then the project is done. In contrast, for those who recognize its value, maintaining and regularly reporting scorecards quickly becomes essential. By combining ABM with scorecarding, there is an imperative to maintain the ABM system because ABM becomes an important feeder system of data into the scorecarding system.

Reporting and Distributing Scorecard Information:
Internet-Based Architecture

One reason that performance measurement systems have failed in the past has been the inability to easily disseminate the published scorecard data to large masses, if not to all the managers and employees. Scorecard software systems resolve the mechanics of reporting and distributing the data in several ways:

- **Internet delivery via Web browser.** The minimum threshold to truly sustain a scorecard system is to structure it as an Internet-based architecture that delivers the scorecard directly to each user's desktop via their Web browser. The state-of-the-art interface design is achieved without requiring the user to install any software on their local computer. The *zero footprint* design of scorecard systems allows the widest possible deployment of scorecard information with the least possible impact on the organization's IT resources. The goal is to maximize the number of potential participants in the scorecard initiative and thus to have the best possible impact on the success of the organization's strategy implementation.

- **Key performance indicator measure meters.** Evaluating the performance of the many different types of measures that are included in a typical scorecard can result in a confusing collection of metrics that defies easy understanding. Scorecard software systems display performance measures as a meter gauge, like on an automobile dashboard that compares each KPI and its score across a range. The range is anchored with a feasible high and desirable score and an under-performing undesirable score. The result is a scoring system that allows performance levels of vastly different measures to be compared on a common (sometimes called *normalized*) scoring scale.

- **Custom views to focus efforts.** Scorecard Web interfaces allow users to create custom views of the scorecard in order to isolate the strategic objectives that apply to a particular department, initiative, or individual. By using this capability, managers can influence the behavior of employees by isolating key metrics in custom views.

- **Quick recognition of performance levels.** A key benefit of the development of a scorecard reporting system is the ability to leverage visual indicators, such as traffic lights and alert messages, to quickly recognize performance levels. Many *nanosecond* managers need fast access to performance information in order to quickly identify problem areas and take action. Dashboard views provide this quick evaluation of performance as well as the ability to drill down further to see the contributing factors.

Reporting and Distributing Scorecard Information *(Continued)*

There have been remarkable advances in data warehousing and data mining retrieval systems relative to only a few years ago. With these capabilities, every byte of information that flows through an enterprise can be managed and, where relevant for scorecards, put to use.

By definition, strategic PM requires sharing of information across multiple solutions—and raises this function to a broader level when integrated into a business performance intelligence way of thinking. Access to a data warehouse provides a level of cohesion, consistency, and communication that could not be achieved with traditional approaches that only offer limited sharing of information from application to application.

10

SCORECARDS
AND STRATEGY MAPS
Enablers for
Performance Management

In today's environment, a business's road is no longer long and straight. It winds around bends and hills that don't allow much visibility or certainty about the future. Organizations must be agile and continuously transform their cost structure and work activities. This is difficult to do when employees and managers do not understand their strategies, the relevant performance measures, their cost structure, and the economics of their environment. It is much easier for organizations to transform themselves when their performance measurement system links and communicates their strategies to the behavior of their employees. The following are some reinforcing observations about scorecards:

- Scorecards help organizations move from being financially driven to mission-driven.
- If you fail to tie measures to strategy, you miss the chief benefit of the scorecard: alignment.
- The scorecard's purpose is to translate strategy into measures that uniquely communicate the senior executive's vision and mission to the organization.
- Scorecard software systems, where scorecards are routinely populated and published, promote e-mail dialogues for rapid messaging and note-taking documentation to prevent an organizational amnesia that plagues everybody.

In short, failing to link measures to strategies will cause misalignment of the cost structure and priorities with the strategy. Because monitoring strategy attainment usually relies on output or results measures, lagging measures need to be translated into more process-operational leading measures reported *during* the period. Competing measures need to be minimized.

Unlike a trickle-down-the-ranks method of management, scorecarding is more of a trickle-up phenomenon. In order to produce good results, the expected performance measures should reflect solid top-down planning, but the results— good or bad—will come from bottom-up performance. As an analogy, think of the organization as an orchestra. You do not want to motivate all the musicians to play very loudly. The balance comes from the correct decibel output from each of the instruments.

If the measures selected are those that align employee behavior to desired outcomes (e.g., meeting strategic objectives), then the near-attained target measures will be met. And since the target measures, popularly called the key performance indicators (KPIs), are derived from the strategy planning, this means the strategy itself is being achieved.

In sum, the need for reforms with organizational measures reflects the inability of senior management to communicate strategy changes and get their organizations to execute in alignment with revised strategies.

Performance management creates a shared vision that spans an organization's value chain upstream and downstream—with its suppliers and customers. An enterprise can effectively manage its strategic objectives and performance metrics in a way that maximizes value to all stakeholders and constituents, not just individual operating groups. By focusing on one version of the truth, a scorecard system optimizes organizational efficiency, supports continuous quality improvement, and maximizes the value of human and capital assets.

Scorecards provide a comprehensive tool that can coordinate and propel large numbers of employees. In the end, if the organization is performing well, then the rewards go to the employees, to the investors in the form of financial returns, or to the governing boards of not-for-profit organizations in the form of mission accomplishment.

Are strategy maps and scorecards going to be a management fad? Management consultants who have transitioned into these services repeatedly say this methodology has a higher "stick rate" than the improvement programs they have consulted on in the past. Strategy maps and scorecards do make sense, address a true need, and will likely be a keeper for organizations that are willing to try new ideas.

Leveraging Financial Analytical Facts and Truths[1]

"It is a common criticism of cost accountants that they spend too much time in working out elaborate distributions of expenses which are unimportant in themselves and which do not permit an accurate distribution. Undoubtedly some of that criticism is deserved, but it should also be remembered that once the basis for distribution has been worked out, it can generally continue in use for some time."[2]

—H. G. Crockett

Chapter 8 described how cost data from an activity-based management (ABM) calculation engine—namely process costs, output costs, and profit margins—provides good inputs to a scorecard system. Part Three now goes into depth about what ABM is, why it has grown in popularity, and how it works.

NOTES

1. Portions of Part Three are revisions of chapters from Gary Cokins' *Activity-Based Cost Management: An Executive Guide* (New York: John Wiley & Sons, 2001).

2. H. G. Crockett, "Some Problems in the Actual Installation of Cost Systems," *National Association of Cost Accountants (NACA) Bulletin*, vol. 1, no. 8 (February 1921).

11

IF ACTIVITY-BASED MANAGEMENT IS THE ANSWER, WHAT IS THE QUESTION?

There is a growing desire among organizations to understand their costs and the behavior of factors that drive their costs. However, there is also confusion over how to understand costs and how to distinguish competing cost measurement methodologies (e.g., activity-based costing, standard costing, throughput accounting, project accounting, target costing). The result is that managers and employees are confused by mixed messages about which costs are the correct costs. Upon closer inspection, various costing methods do not necessarily compete; they can be reconciled and combined. They are all cut from the same cloth: They measure the consumption of economic resources.

There is a need for an overarching framework to describe how expenses are measured as costs and used in decision making. An understandable framework is not rocket science; it can be simply constructed and articulated. A candidate framework is presented here. Figure 11.1 displays an overarching framework for the world of accounting with a tree, branch, and leaf structure. The figure is similar to taxonomies that biologists use to understand plant and animal kingdoms. A taxonomy defines the components that make up of a body of knowledge.

Note that at the top part of the figure the broad discipline of accounting immediately branches into managerial accounting and financial accounting. Make no mistake about the focus of this book—it is on managerial accounting, not financial accounting. Financial accounting addresses external reporting used as com-

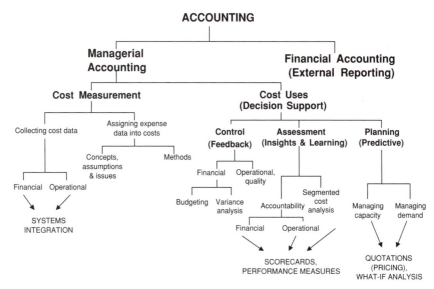

Figure 11.1   Accounting Taxonomy

pliance reporting for banks, owners, publicly owned companies, and government regulators. In contrast, managerial accounting is used internally by managers and employee teams for decision making. If you violate financial accounting laws, you may go to jail. However, you don't risk going to jail if you have poor managerial accounting, but you run the risk of making bad decisions. And, as frequently noted in this book, the margin for error is getting slimmer as the pressure grows for better organizational performance.

At the highest level of managerial accounting in Figure 11.1 are two broad elements: *measuring* the costs and *using* the cost data. In this framework, each branch can be further separated into the following key components:

- **Cost Measurement.** Measuring costs comprises two functions—collecting data and assigning the source expenses—in a way that is meaningful for the organization.

  1. **Collecting data.** These procedures are mature, dating back centuries.

  2. **Assigning expenses into costs.** This is an important branch because it displays the alternative methods, usually blended, for translating an organization's spending into its calculated costs. What the meth-

ods have in common is that they start with the cash outlay *source expenses* that were captured in the transaction-based systems, such as payroll and purchasing systems. The expenses are then causally traced and converted into the cost objects. Activity-based management (ABM) has emerged as the accepted costing method that assures accuracy.[1]

- **Cost Uses.** The first chapter of many managerial accounting textbooks usually states that there are three broad uses for cost data: operational control, assessment and evaluation, and predictive planning.

    1. **Operational control.** There is a growing belief that the emphasis in collecting and assigning cost data should shift away from control and toward the other two uses of cost data, assessment (learning) and predictive planning. The reasoning for this shift is that it is usually too late to control a process after the fact with historical expense and cost data. Furthermore, cost variances do not reflect quality or service levels—they are an incomplete message.

    2. **Assessment and evaluation.** The second purpose for cost data is to assess what is happening and evaluate why. This answers the question, "What does something cost now?" The emphasis here is on gaining insights and learning to better achieve the organization's goals.

    3. **Predictive planning.** Predictive planning, budgeting, and forecasting are increasingly becoming of great interest as ways of using cost data. This branch involves marginal expense analysis, often called incremental costing or relevant costing. Examples include what-if analysis, trade-off analysis, outsourcing decisions, investment decisions, and, more fundamentally, determining the costs associated with a customer quote to estimate the profit margin if that price quote were to be accepted. This branch of the managerial accounting framework can be described as expense forecasting. Some might argue that this does not qualify as cost accounting but rather is about economic analysis. This is in part due to its inclusion of capacity requirement analysis and adjustments to an organization's existing capacity.

In Part One, when I introduced the performance management (PM) wheel, I mentioned that ABM can generate important performance management data, some of which can serve as a source of inputs to the PM process wheel. Let's now understand what ABM is.

REMOVING THE BLINDFOLD
WITH ACTIVITY-BASED MANAGEMENT

Imagine that you and three friends go to a restaurant. You order a cheeseburger and they each order an expensive prime rib. When the waiter brings the bill they say, "Let's split the check evenly." How would you feel?

This is similar to the effect on many products and service lines when the accountants take a large amount of indirect and support overhead expenses and allocate them as costs without any logic. There is minimal or no link that reflects a true relative use of the expenses by the individual products, service lines, or end-users. This is unfair. It is somewhat like taxation without representation. ABM gets it right—it more fairly splits the bill.

Many ABM practitioners wish the word *allocation* never existed. It implies inequity to many people because of past abuses in their organization's accounting practices. Standard cost systems with bad cost allocations are the moldy basement of accounting. We need ABM to be the stepladder that lets us climb out and smell the roses. In my mind, the word *allocation* effectively means *misallocation* because that is usually the result. ABM practitioners will often say that they do not *allocate* expenses; instead they *trace* and *assign* them to costs based on cause-and-effect relationships.

ABM can do much more than simply trace expenses and costs. It provides a tremendous amount of visibility for people to draw insights from and also use for predicting the possible outcomes of decisions. Many operations people cynically believe that accountants count what is easily counted, but not what counts. Outdated, traditional accounting blocks managers and employees from seeing the more relevant costs.

As a lesson from past problems with implementing ABM, it is a mistake for project teams to refer to ABM as an improvement, project, program, or a change initiative. ABM merely creates data. The ABM data are simply used as a means to an end. As mentioned in Part Two, but worth repeating here, if ABM is described as an improvement program, it might be regarded by managers and employees as a fad, fashion, or project of the month. ABM data make visible the economics of the organization and its consumption of resource expenses. Money is continuously being spent on organizational resources whether ABM measuring is present or not. ABM is not just about supporting other initiatives but rather *driving* some of those initiatives—putting teeth into them.

OVERHEAD EXPENSES ARE DISPLACING DIRECT COSTS

So why has ABM become popular? A primary reason has been a significant shift in most organizations' cost structure, which I'll explain next. However, a secondary reason has been a mindset shift on the part of accountants to be a business partner to the users of the information they provide. Consider the remarks of Kim Wallin, president of the Institute of Management Accountants, at its annual conference:

> "From the beginning of double entry bookkeeping the role of accountants was to record, validate, and report information. This continued since 1492, when an Italian monk documented bookkeeping for merchants in Venice, until the 1980s. For almost five hundred years, the accounting profession hardly changed. In the early 1980s when electronic spreadsheets came out, this started a drastic change in the accounting profession. Things that accountants spent hours of time on were significantly reduced because of technology. These changes meant that accountants would have a very different occupation.
>
> "In the beginning the accountants were isolated. They did not interact with any other staff, and they had no personality. Their job was to just to record and report historical data.
>
> "Their jobs changed in the 1980s as a result of the information technology revolution to become the center of teams—executive and operational. They are now looked at as being impartial because they don't have an agenda such as an engineer or marketing manager might have. Accountants now interact with others. They can no longer hide behind their number crunching duties. They have become business advisors, and their involvement with supporting the organization has taught them to be more sensitive to what is relevant for their organizations to make better decisions."[2]

What do I mean when I say a shift has occurred in most organizations' cost structures? The direct laborers in organizations are the employees who perform the frontline, continually repeated work that is closest to the products and customers. However, numerous other employees behind the front line also do recurring work on a daily or weekly basis. The work of these employees is highly repetitive at some level. An example is a teller in a bank. Figure 11.2 is a chart that includes this type of expense plus the other two major expense components of any organization's cost structure: its purchased materials and its overhead.

Most organizations are experienced at monitoring and measuring the work of the laborers who do recurring work; cost rates and standard costs are reported. In the bottom layer of the chart is cost information that also reveals performance-related costs other than the period's spending, such as labor variance reporting. It is in this area of the chart, for example, that manufacturers use labor routings and

A key to understanding ABC is to understand how cost behavior varies in relation to other factors.

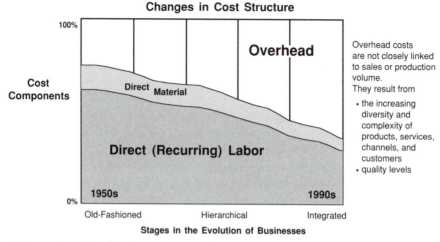

Figure 11.2   Overhead Costs Are Displacing Direct Costs

process sheets to measure efficiency. These costs are well known by the name *standard costs*. Service organizations also measure this type of output-related information. For example, many banks know their standard cost for each type of deposit, wire transfer, and so forth.

Problems occur in the overhead expense area, depicted by the top portion of the figure. The chart reveals that over the last few decades, the support overhead[3] expenses have been displacing the recurring costs. The organization already has substantial visibility of its recurring costs, but it does not have much insight for understanding its overhead or what is causing the level of spending there. ABM helps provide insights and learning.

In a bank, for example, managers and employee teams do not get the same robustness of financial information about the vice presidents working on the second floor and higher up in the building as they do about tellers performing the recurring work. The only financial information available to analyze the expenses of the vice presidents and other support overhead is the annual financial budget data. These levels of expenses are annually negotiated. The focus is on spending levels, not on the various cost rates to perform work. The expense spending is monitored after the budget is published. Spending is only monitored for each department or function for each period to see if the managers' spending performance is under or over their budget or plan.

ABM merely extends to the overhead the same type of understanding and visibility of spending that is already applied to the recurring laborers. It is not complicated. Basically ABM becomes an organization-wide method of understanding work activity costs as well as the standard costs of outputs.

IMPACT OF DIVERSITY IN PRODUCTS, SERVICE LINES, CHANNELS, AND CUSTOMERS

When you ask people why they believe indirect and overhead expenses are displacing direct costs, most answer that it is because of technology, equipment, automation, or computers. In other words, organizations are automating what previously were manual jobs. However, this is only a secondary factor for explaining the shift in organizational expense components.

The primary cause for the shift is the gradual proliferation in products and service lines. Over the last few decades organizations have been increasingly offering a greater variety of products and services as well as using more types of distribution and sales channels. In addition, organizations have been servicing more and different types of customers. Introducing greater variation and diversity (i.e., heterogeneity) into an organization creates complexity, and increasing complexity results in more overhead expenses to manage it. So the fact that the overhead component of expense is displacing the recurring labor expense does not automatically mean that an organization is becoming inefficient or bureaucratic. It simply means that the company is offering more variety to different types of customers.

Why do managers shake their heads in disbelief when they think about their company's cost accounting system? I once heard an operations manager complain, "You know what we think of our cost accounting system? It is a bunch of fictitious lies—but we all agree to them." It is a sad thing to see the users of the accounting data resign themselves to lack of hope. Unfortunately, some accountants are comfortable when the numbers all reconcile and exactly balance in total and could care less if the parts making up the total are incorrect. The total is all that matters, and any arbitrary cost allocation can tie out to the total.

The sad truth is that when employees and managers are provided with reports that have misleading accounting data in them, they have little choice but to use that information regardless of its validity or their skepticism as to its integrity. Mind you, they are using the data to draw conclusions and make decisions. This is risky.

In summary, the shift to overhead displacing direct labor reveals the cost of complexity, typically customer-driven. ABM does not fix or simplify complexity; the complexity is a result of other things. But ABM does point out where the complexity is and where it comes from. How long can organizations go on making decisions with the misinformation reported by their accounting systems?

EXPENSES ARE NOT THE SAME THING AS COSTS!

This is a critical concept in understanding ABM. *Expenses* are not the same thing as *costs*. What are the differences? *Expenses* are defined as when an organization exchanges money with another party, such as paying suppliers, or paying its employees' salaries. (Expenses may also be *near-cash* to reflect the obligation to pay cash in the near future.) In short, currency exits the treasury. In contrast, costs are always *calculated* costs. Costs reflect the use of the spending of the expenses.

It is important to recognize that assumptions are always involved in the conversion and translation of expenses into costs. The assumptions and business rules stipulate the basis for the calculation. Expenses occur at the point of acquisition with the other party, including paying employee wages. At that special moment, *value* does not fluctuate; it is permanently recorded as part of a legal exchange. From the expenses, all costs follow; they are calculated representations of how those expenses flow through work activities and into outputs of work.

ACTIVITY-BASED MANAGEMENT'S ACTIVITIES ARE EXPRESSED WITH ACTION VERBS

A key difference between ABM and the general ledger and traditional techniques of cost allocation (i.e., absorption costing) is that ABM describes activities using an "action verb, adjective, noun" grammar convention, such as "inspect defective products," "open new customer accounts," or "process customer claims." This gives ABM its flexibility. Such wording is powerful because managers and employee teams can better relate to these phrases, and the wording implies that the work activities can be favorably affected, changed, improved, or eliminated. Note in Figure 11.3 how ABM translates the ledger's expenses into calculated costs.

When each of the work activities in the ABM view is traced to its product or customer (i.e., final cost object) using the unique activity driver for each activity, ABM would pile up the entire $914,500 into each type of product, service, channel, or customer. This reassignment of the resource expenses would be much

In addition to seeing the content of work, the activity view gives insights to what drives each activity's cost magnitude to fluctuate.

From: General Ledger

To: ABC Data Base

Chart-of-Accounts View			
Claims Processing Department			
	Actual	Plan	Favorable/ (unfavorable)
Salaries	$621,400	$600,000	$(21,400)
Equipment	161,200	150,000	(11,200)
Travel expense	58,000	60,000	2,000
Supplies	43,900	40,000	(3,900)
Use and occupancy	30,000	30,000	—
Total	$914,500	$880,000	$(34,500)

Activity-Based View		Activity drivers
Claims Processing Dept		
Key/scan claims	$ 31,500	← # of __
Analyze claims	121,000	← # of __
Suspend claims	32,500	← # of __
Receive provider inquiries	101,500	← # of __
Resolve member problems	83,400	← # of __
Process batches	45,000	← # of __
Determine eligibility	119,000	← # of __
Make copies	145,500	← # of __
Write correspondence	77,100	← # of __
Attend training	158,000	← # of __
Total	$914,500	

Products/customers

Fixed versus variable classifications get redefined with ABC/M.

Figure 11.3   Each Activity Has Its Own Activity Driver

more accurate than any broad-brush cost allocation applied in traditional costing procedures and their broad averages. This cost assignment network is one of the major reasons that ABM calculates more accurate costs of outputs. As earlier mentioned, the terms *tracing* or *assigning* are preferable to the term *cost allocation*. This is because many people associate *allocation* with a redistribution of costs that have little to no correlation between source and destinations; hence to some organizations overhead cost allocations are rejected by users as arbitrary and are viewed cynically.

The assignment of the resource expenses demonstrates that all costs actually originate with the customer or beneficiary of the work, not with the general ledger. This is at the opposite pole from where accountants who perform *cost allocations* think about costs. Cost allocations are structured as a one-source-to-many-destinations redistribution of cost. But the destinations are actually the origin for the expenses. The destinations, usually outputs or people, place demands on work, and the costs then *measure the effect* by reflecting backward through an ABM cost assignment network.

The general ledger uses a chart of accounts, whereas ABM uses a chart of activities. In translating general ledger data to work activities and processes, ABM preserves the total reported revenues and costs but allows the revenues, budgeted funding, and costs to be viewed differently—and better. The data in the *chart of accounts* view are inadequate for reporting business process costs that run cross-functionally, penetrating the vertical and artificial boundaries of the organization chart. The general ledger is organized around separate departments or cost centers, thus preventing a view of process costs. Many organizations have been flattened and delayered to the extent that employees from different departments or cost centers frequently perform similar activities and multitask in two or more core business processes. Only by reassembling and aligning the work activity costs *across* the business processes, such as "process engineering change notices (ECNs)" or "open new customer accounts," can the end-to-end process costs be seen, measured, and eventually managed.

Two Views of Costs: Assignment View versus Process View

There are two ways to organize and analyze ABM work activity cost data. The *horizontal* process view sequences and additively builds up costs, whereas the *vertical* cost assignment view, governed by the variation and diversity of cost objects, transforms resource expenses into output costs by continuously reassigning costs based on causal-based tracing (i.e., cost allocations).

Vertical Axis
The vertical axis reflects costs as they are sensitive to demands from all forms of product, channel, and customer diversity and variety. The work activities consume the resources, and the products and customer services consume the work activities. The ABM cost assignment view is a cost-consumption chain. When each cost is traced based on its unique quantity or proportion of its driver, *all* the resource expenses are eventually reaggregated into the final cost objects. This method provides much more accurate measures of product, channel, and customer costs than the traditional and arbitrary "peanut-butter spreading" cost allocation method.

Horizontal Axis
The horizontal view of activity costs represents the business process view. A business process can be defined as two or more activities or a network of activities with a common purpose. Activity costs belong to the business processes. Across each process, the activity costs are sequential and additive. In this orientation, activity costs satisfy the requirements for popular flow-charting and process mapping and modeling techniques. Business process–based thinking, which can be visualized as tipping the organization

---

Two Views of Costs *(Continued)*

chart 90 degrees, is now dominating managerial thinking. ABM provides the cost elements for process costing that are not available from the general ledger.

In effect, think of the vertical ABM cost assignment view as being *time-blind* within the period. The ABM process costing view, at the activity stage, is output *mix-blind*. The cost assignment and business process costing are two different views of the same resource expenses and activity costs. They are equivalent in amount, but the display of the information is radically different in each view. In summary, the vertical cost assignment view explains *what specific things cost*, whereas the horizontal process view demonstrates *why things have a cost*, which provides insights into *what causes costs* and *how much processes cost*.

The primary focus in this book is the vertical view, popularly called *absorption accounting*. Activity-based costing is more closely associated with this latter view.

I am often asked to explain Figure 11.3 in the simplest terms. I humorously reply, "The right side is good because the left side is bad!" Now I did not say the general ledger is a bad thing. In fact, just the opposite; the general ledger is a wonderful instrument for what it was designed to do—to capture and bucketize or accumulate spending transactions into their accounts. But the data in that format is structurally deficient for decision support other than the most primitive form of control, budget variances. Translating it into calculated costs corrects this deficiency.

When managers receive the left-side responsibility center report from Figure 11.3, they are either happy or sad, *but rarely any smarter*. That is why I often humorously ask "What is another name for GL?" The answer is "good luck." It doesn't help much for decision support.

In summary, the general ledger view describes what was spent, whereas the activity-based view describes what it was spent for. The ledger records the expenses, and the activity view calculates the costs of work activities, processes, and all outputs, such as products. Intermediate output costs, such as the unit cost to process a transaction, are also calculated in the activity view. When employees have reliable and relevant information, managers can manage less and lead more.

Easy-to-Implement and Sustainable Activity-Based Management Using Technology and Rapid Prototyping

For years, activity-based management (ABM) was considered an expensive project that only large organizations with extensive resources could undertake. But today, with the proliferation of computers for gathering data and computing, the cost of data collection and measurement has fallen at the same time that information processing has improved. Today, not only are such activity measurement systems affordable, but much of the information already exists in some form within the organization. For example, quality management systems of ISO 9000–registered organizations have an abundance of data, usually not connected to the accounting system. Information technology has dramatically improved the deployment of ABM data for viewing, planning, and decision making. Powerful database management systems and computing engines make data processing no longer an impediment to understanding costs.

Furthermore, a technique for implementing ABM based on rapid prototyping scale models assures implementation success. In contrast to the long, multimonth, one-chance, single-design approach, the ABM rapid prototyping technique follows the quick build of the initial model, built roughly in two days, by iterative remodeling of increasingly larger scale ABM models. Eventually the larger scale ABM model becomes the organization's repeatable and reliable production system. (ABM rapid prototyping is discussed in Chapter 12.)

STRATEGIC VERSUS OPERATIONAL ACTIVITY-BASED MANAGEMENT

There is a common misconception that organizations use only a single enterprise-wide ABM system. There can actually be multiple ABM systems constructed for a single organization. The right side of Figure 11.3 suggests there are two broad types of users and decision makers viewing ABM data: *strategic and operational*. In fact, there are two types of ABM model designs that serve each type of user, but they both follow the same cost assignment principles. The difference between them is the scope of expenses included plus the inclusion or exclusion of pricing or revenue data for calculating profit margins.

Strategic ABM, also referred to here as "enterprise-wide ABM," is about first doing the right things. That is, selling profitable products to customers that are profitable. Strategic ABM is about enhancing revenues and assuring higher profits, based on the product's value to draw good prices and considering varying levels of demanding behavior of different types of customers. *Operational ABM*, also referred to here as local ABM, is not enterprise-wide, but rather addresses individual functions, departments, or business processes. Its intent is not about analyzing profit contribution margins, but rather focuses on improving process, managing activity costs more efficiently, and optimizing asset utilization.

In short, these are the differences in ABM model design:

- *Strategic ABM* includes all of the enterprise expenses and then subtracts the traceable costs (to products, channels, and customers) from sold line items to compute the profit contribution margins.
- *Operational ABM* restricts the expenses included to those mainly involved in the function, department, or process. It focuses on analyzing the work to remove waste, manage unused capacity, improve productivity, and improve asset utilization.

One of the values of commercial ABM software is it can consolidate multiple *operational* ABM models into the parent, enterprise-wide *strategic* ABM model.

NOTES

1. "The State of Management Accounting: The Ernst & Young and IMA Survey (2003)," www.imanet.org.
2. Kim Wallin, opening remarks at annual conference of Institute of Management Accountants, Nashville, Tennessee, June 24, 2003.
3. Organizations often refer to this support-related work as overhead. Overhead is also referred to as indirect costs. The term *overhead* can be misleading and often has a negative connotation. In many cases overhead is a crucial and very positive thing to have. In this book, *indirect* and *overhead* are used interchangeably or together to refer to this type of expenses and costs. Regardless of which term is used, the objective of calculating costs is to properly trace them, not arbitrarily allocate them, to what is causing them—and in the proper proportions.

12

ACTIVITY-BASED MANAGEMENT MODEL DESIGN AND PRINCIPLES
Key to Success

Figure 12.1 displays a generic activity-based management (ABM) cost assignment network that consists of the three modules connected by cost assignment paths. It initially appears to be overly complicated, but with just a few minutes consideration it is seen to be a logical representation of how input expenses are translated into calculated costs of work and ultimately outputs.

Imagine the cost assignment paths as pipes and straws where the diameter of each path reflects the amount of cost flowing. The power of an ABM model lies in the fact that the cost assignment paths and destinations provide *traceability* to segment costs from beginning to end, from resource expenditures to each type of (or each specific) customer—the origin for all costs and expenses.

ABM uses multiple stages to trace and segment all the resource expenses as calculated costs through a network of cost assignments into the final cost objects. ABM facilitates more accurate reporting because it honors the costing property of proportional *traceability*, not broad averages. In complex, support-intensive organizations, there can be a substantial chain of indirect activities prior to the direct work activities that eventually trace into the *final cost objects*. These chains result in activity-to-activity assignments, and they rely on *intermediate* activity drivers in the same way that final cost objects rely on activity drivers to reassign costs into them based on their diversity and variation.

The *direct costing* of indirect costs is no longer, as it was in the past, an insurmountable problem, given the existence of integrated ABM software. ABM allows *intermediate* direct costing to a local process, an internal customer, or a

98

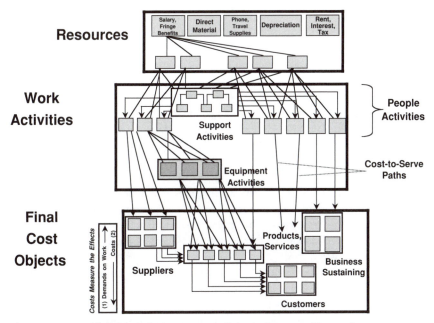

Figure 12.1   Activity-Based Management Cost Assignment Network

required component that is causing the demand for work. In short, ABM connects customers to the unique resources they consume—and in proportion to their consumption—as if ABM were an optical fiber network. Visibility to costs is provided everywhere throughout the cost assignment network.

With ABM the demands-on-work are communicated via activity drivers and their driver cost rates. Activity driver cost rates can be thought of as *very local burden rates* (VLBRs). They reassign expenses into costs at a more local, granular level than in traditional systems, and with arterial flow streams, not with the

---

Activity-Based Management Cost Assignment Network: A Tour

It may be useful to mentally reverse all the arrowheads in Figure 12.1. This polar switch reveals that all expenses originate with a demand-pull from customers—and the calculated costs simply measure the effect. The ABM network is basically a snapshot view of the business conducted during a specific time period. (Life-cycle costing will be described in Chapter 17's section on customer intelligence as "customer lifetime value.")

(Continued)

Activity-Based Management Cost Assignment Network *(Continued)*

Resources, at the top of the cost assignment network in Figure 12.1, are in sum the capacity to perform work because they represent all the available means that work activities can draw on. Resources are where all the period's expenditure transactions are accumulated into buckets of spending. Examples of resources are salaries, operating supplies, and electrical power. A popular basis for tracing or assigning resource expenses is the amount of time (e.g., number of minutes) that people or equipment spend performing activities. Percentage splits of time among activities are also popular.

The *activities* located in the middle module are where work is performed. This is where resources are converted into some type of output. The activity cost assignment step contains the structure to assign activity costs to cost objects (or to other activities), utilizing activity drivers as the mechanism to accomplish this assignment.

Cost objects, at the bottom of the cost assignment network, represent the broad variety of outputs and services where costs accumulate. The customers are the *final-final cost objects;* their existence ultimately creates the need for a cost structure in the first place. Cost objects are the persons or things that benefit from incurring work activities. Examples of cost objects are products, service lines, distribution channels, customers, and outputs of internal processes. Cost objects can be thought of as *for what* or *for whom* work is done.

This final cost object module is much more important than the resource and activity cost modules. That is because the inherently diverse and varied outputs that ABM segments and reflects so well with cost data originate as final cost objects. Unfortunately many ABM project teams spend much more of their energy worrying about the resource and activity modules, believing that the definition and design of resources and activities is what will influence accurate and useful results. They are misguided by misconceptions. The wiser ABM project teams realize it is best to begin designing their ABM model structure backward from the final cost objects. When the diversity and variation of what things draw on the workload are first modeled, it increases the likelihood that the consumed resource expenses will pile up in proper proportions into the final cost objects that uniquely used (i.e., caused) the resources.

What Are Drivers?

The term *drivers* can be confusing. A *cost driver* is something that can be described in words but not necessarily in numbers. For example, a storm would be a cost driver that results in much clean-up work and the resulting costs. In contrast, the *activity drivers* in ABM's cost assignments must be quantitative, using measures that apportion costs to cost objects. Activity drivers have their

Activity-Based Management Cost Assignment Network *(Continued)*

own higher order cost drivers. Cost drivers and activity drivers serve different purposes. *Activity drivers* are output measures that reflect the usage of each work activity, and they must be quantitatively measurable. An activity driver, which relates a work activity to cost objects, *meters out* the work activity based on the unique diversity and variation of the cost objects that are consuming that activity. A *cost driver* is that driver of a higher order than activity drivers. One cost driver can affect multiple activities. A cost driver need not be measurable but can simply be described as a triggering event.

The *cost object driver* applies to cost objects after all activity costs have already been logically assigned. Note that cost objects can be consumed or used by other cost objects. For example, when a specific customer purchases a mix of products, similar to you placing different items in your grocery cart than another shopper, the quantities purchased are a cost object driver.

Business Sustaining Expenses

Some activities in an organization do not directly contribute to customer value, responsiveness, and quality. That does not mean those activities can be eliminated or even reduced without doing harm to the business entity. For example, preparing required regulatory reports certainly does not add to the value of any cost object or to the satisfaction of the customer. However, that type of work activity does have value to the organization because it enables it to function in a legal manner. These types of activity costs are usually traced to a *sustaining cost object* group, popularly called *business sustaining costs.*

Business (or infrastructure) sustaining costs are those costs *not* caused by products or customer service needs. The consumption of these costs cannot be logically traced to products, services, customers, or service recipients. Another example is the accounting department's closing of the books each month. How can one measure which product caused more or less of that work? One cannot. Recovering these costs via pricing or funding may eventually be required, but that is a different issue; the issue here is fairly charging cost objects when no causal relationship exists.

Other categories of expenses that may be included as business sustaining costs are idle but available capacity costs or research and development (R&D). R&D expenses might be optionally assigned into the business sustaining costs so that the timing of the recognition of expenses is reasonably matched with revenue recognition for sales of the products or service lines. Because activity-based costing is management accounting, not regulated financial reporting, strict rules of GAAP (generally accepted accounting principles) do not need to be followed; however, they can be borrowed.

traditional accountant's rigid *step-down cost allocation method* that reduces costing accuracy.

The key to a good ABM system is the design and architecture of its cost assignment network. The *nodes* are the sources and destinations through which all the expenses are reassigned into costs. Their configuration helps deliver the utility and value of the data for decision making.

HOW DOES ACTIVITY-BASED COSTING COMPUTE BETTER ACCURACIES?

When people who are first exposed to ABM hear the phrase, "It is better to be approximately correct than precisely inaccurate," they smile because they know exactly what that means in their organization. But they usually do not know what causes ABM to produce substantially better accuracy relative to their existing legacy costing system despite its abundant use of estimates and approximations. The explanation, which is counterintuitive to many, is that the initial errors from estimates in an ABM assignment system cancel out. This is due, in part, because allocating (i.e., reassigning expenses into costs) is a *closed system* with a zero sum total error in the total costs of the final cost objects.

The starting amount of expenses to be allocated can be assumed to be one-hundred percent accurate because they come from the general ledger accounting system, which is specially designed to accumulate and summarize the spending transactions. However, subsequently, as we reassign expenses into calculated costs, imprecise inputs do not automatically result in inaccurate outputs. That is, precision is not synonymous with accuracy. In ABM's cost assignment view, estimating error does not compound, it dampens out. These are properties of statistics found in equilibrium networks (i.e., the amount of expenses and costs remains constant). And ABM is a cost reassignment network much more than it is an accounting system.

In ABM, poor model design leads to poor results. A well known and painful lesson about activity-based costing is that when an ABM implementation falls short of its expectations, it is often because the system was overengineered in size and detail. The ABM system usually quickly reached diminishing returns in extra accuracy for incremental levels of effort, but this effect was not recognized by the ABM project team. The system was built so large that the administrative effort to collect the data and maintain the system was ultimately judged to be not worth the perceived benefits. This results in a *death by details* ABM project; it is unsustainable. In short, overdesigned ABM systems are too detailed relative to their intended use.

As the designers construct their ABM information system, they usually suffer from a terrible case of lack of depth perception. There is no perspective from which they can judge how high or low or summarized or detailed they are. The implementation of an ABM system is usually influenced by accountants, and an accountant's natural instincts include a lowest-denominator mentality. Accountants usually assume a detailed and comprehensive level of data collection, based on the premise that if you collect a great amount of detail everywhere, and from everybody, and about everything they do, you can then always *roll it up* and summarize anywhere. This is a *just-in-case* approach in anticipation of any future remote questions. The term *accuracy requirements* is not in most accountants' vocabulary. As a result, their ABM models tend to become excessively large. Ultimately they may become unmaintainable and unsustainable. Eventually the ABM system does not appear to be worth the effort. I am not criticizing or attacking accountants. Years of training reinforce their high need for precision. However, ABM requires a bias toward practical use of the data.

One explanation for oversized ABM models is that at the outset of an ABM project it is nearly impossible to predetermine what levels of detail to go to. There are so many interdependencies in an ABM model that, as a result, it presents a problem. It is almost impossible to perform one of the earlier work steps of the traditional information technology (IT) function's systems development project plan, *data requirements definition*. ABM rapid prototyping, a technique that quickly resolves this problem, is discussed in the sidebar "Activity-Based Management Rapid Prototyping."

What is missing in most ABM implementations is a good understanding of what factors actually determine the accuracy of the ABM-calculated outputs. That is, what are the major determinants of higher accuracy of final cost objects? The following assertion will likely be counterintuitive not only to accountants but also to everyone who designs and builds ABM systems. ABM's substantially improved accuracy relative to traditional approaches actually resides more in the ABM cost assignment network itself than in the activity costs and in the activity driver quantities. That is, the reason that the products, service lines, channels, and customer costs are so reasonably accurate has less to do with their input data than with the architecture of the cost flow paths that make up the ABM cost assignment network.

Achieving success with ABM initially begins with overcoming the ABM leveling problem—right-sizing the model to a proper level of detail.

Activity-Based Management Rapid Prototyping: Getting Quick and Accurate Results

The ABM leveling problem can be partly solved using the increasingly popular technique of ABM *rapid prototyping*. This is a method of building the first ABM model in a few short days, relying on knowledgeable employees, followed by a few weeks of iterative remodeling to scale up the size of the model. But in addition to this highly managed trial-and-error approach, effective leveling of the ABM model can be achieved through better thinking. Figure 12A illustrates ABM iterative remodeling.

Enhance iteration enhances the use of the ABC/M system.

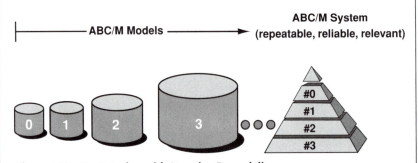

Figure 12A   Prototyping with Iterative Remodeling

In a closed absorption cost assignment system, there is a zero sum error, and error dampens out into cost objects. Figure 12B shows several curves that all have the same ultimate destination: perfectly accurate cost results, where the accuracy level is represented by the vertical axis. The horizontal axis represents the *level of administrative effort* to collect, calculate, and report the data. As explained previously, for each incremental level of effort to collect more and better data, there is proportionately less improvement in accuracy. The asymptotic curves represent the error-dampening effect of offsetting error.

Activity-Based Management Rapid Prototyping *(Continued)*

When the goal of the initial ABC system is profitability reporting, poorly designed and misleveled ABC systems will yield less accuracy despite greater effort!

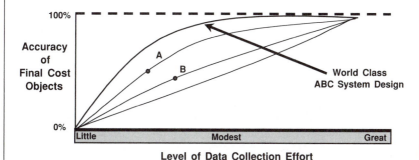

ABC Project Team A is achieving higher accuracy with much less effort relative to ABC Project Team B.

Figure 12B   Balancing Levels of Accuracy with Effort

The question "Is the climb worth the view?" is applicable to ABM. That is, by building a more detailed and slightly more accurate ABM model, will the answer to your question be better answered? Avoid the creeping-elegance syndrome. Larger models introduce maintenance issues. ABM rapid prototyping accelerates a team's acceptance of ABM by quickly giving them a vision of what their completed ABM system will look like—once scaled to its proper level of detail—and how they will use the new ABM information.

EVOLUTION OF THE COST ASSIGNMENT VIEW

To summarize Part Three up to this point, in the late 1980s activity-based costing was initially described as a two-step indirect cost allocation scheme to more accurately calculate how resources convert into product costs. However, activity-based costing cost assignment structures are now recognized to have *multistage* reassignments, not just two steps. There are activity-to-activity assignments for indirect and support costs, which cannot directly reflect variation from final cost objects, and there are also cost object–to–cost object assignments. An example of the latter assignment type is the cost to process a special order (versus a standard order), traced to a specific customer or a group of customers consuming a unique quantity and mix of products, services, or outputs.

The model in Figure 12.2 is analogous to Charles Darwin's model for the evolution of the species. The left graphic is like a single-celled paramecium or amoeba. The middle graphic is analogous to reptiles, amphibians, and snakes. The right graphic is like humans beginning to walk upright.

In Figure 12.2 the left graphic is primitive. It represents traditional accounting's *cost allocation* method, which simply and arbitrarily redistributes the source costs into destinations such as product costs, without regard to logical causality. Many financial controllers still allocate costs this way.[1] But without any causal relationship, there is an expected, undesirable error in calculating the costs of cost objects. The results are inaccurate costs. The financial controllers who continue to allocate costs this way are misleading their end-users with flawed data.

The middle graphic in Figure 12.2 represents the ABM two-stage cost allocation model, in which the expenditures for resources are assigned at the work activity level, not at a department level (i.e., using verb-adjective-noun grammar to define activities). But this method is too simplistic to be adequate.

The right-hand side of Figure 12.2 symbolizes the activity-based costing vertical cost assignment as a multistage cost assignment network with an expanded

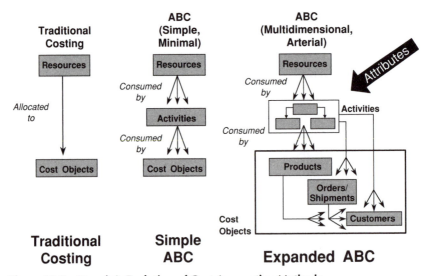

Figure 12.2   Darwin's Evolution of Cost Accounting Methods

Two Alternative Equations for Costing Activities and Cost Objects

There are two alternative approaches for computing activity costs and the costs of cost objects, such as products. The two approaches differ based on which data one prefers to collect or calculate, and on how an organization prefers to use feedback data to *control* its costs. The two approaches are as follows:

1. **Activity driver equations.** First, activity costs are derived (via surveys, timesheets, estimates, etc.). Then the quantity, frequency, or intensity of the activity driver is collected per each activity. A unit cost rate per each activity driver is computed and then applied to all of the cost objects, based on their unique quantity of the activity driver events (e.g., number of invoices processed). This is recalculated for each time period for each work activity.

2. **Cost object equations.** This approach begins with an in-depth time measurement study of work tasks and processes. In the study, the per-unit time elements for various (and optional) processing steps for each product (or product group) and each type of order are surveyed with deep time studies. Then each product and type of order is profiled with an equation specifying the sum of the number of transactions (e.g., events) for each product or type of order. Finally, the quantity of the products and order types is counted for the period and *back-flushed* against each product's or order's standard minutes-per-event to calculate an activity cost. This activity cost assumes the standard rate and is not the actual activity cost. The premise that this assumption is acceptable is that micromeasured activities do not vary much over time. What drives requirements for expenses is the varying mix and volume of products and type of orders.

Figure 12C displays where these two approaches are located with respect to the ABM cost assignment network and how they differ. The *activity driver equation approach* solves for cost of the cost objects by measuring or estimating activity costs and tracing them per events (i.e., activity driver quantities). In contrast, the *cost object equation approach* begins with product and order type profiles, collects volume and mix data, and then solves for the activity costs, assuming the standard times are correct and incurred. It starts with a low level of characteristics of the cost object. This approach appears to reverse-calculate to determine the activity costs.

(Continued)

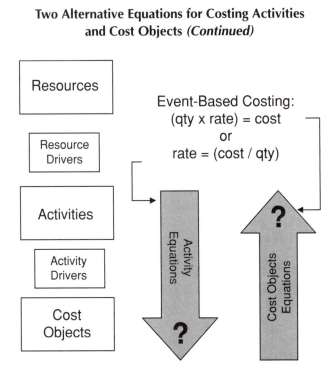

Two Alternative Equations for Costing Activities and Cost Objects *(Continued)*

Two knowns solve for the unknown dependent variable.

Figure 12C   Two Cost Equation Approaches

The *activity driver equation approach* solves for the activity driver rate by assuming that data for the other two factors can be collected or reasonably estimated. The *cost object equation approach* solves for the activity cost, at a standard cost, by presuming that processing times for each product's (i.e., output) characteristics have been measured, profiles for each product configured, and then the product mix volumes reported. The superior ABM software can compute costs in both directions.

Regardless of which equation-based approach is used, be cautious to first recognize the primary reasons you may be pursuing ABM data. Then, presuming there will be some interest in using the ABM for operational cost control and feedback, be clear what type of feedback costs you will be more interested in.

multistage structure that allows for intermediate activities and activity drivers, and cost objects being traced into other cost objects (i.e., the predator food chain). This graphic is labeled as the arterial ABM model to distinguish it from the obsolete two-stage ABM model. Thus, the three modules of the ABM model have now matured to become a multistage network of activities and objects. This cost assignment network has the flexibility to link resources to their cost objects—and the tracing relies on cause-and-effect relationships. Hence, the complete cost assignment network leads to much greater accuracy of cost object costs.

In summary, the evolution of the vertical activity-based costing cost reassignment network starts with the simplistic and arbitrary allocations of the traditional accounting system, and it ends with a multistage network of costs flowing through activity-based costing's three cost modules. This multistage arterial costing network is capable of detecting greater diversity and variation not only in product costs but also in all final cost objects, including different types of customers.

NOTE

1. "The State of Management Accounting: The Ernst & Young and IMA Survey (2003)," at www.imanet.org.

13

OPERATIONAL (LOCAL) ACTIVITY-BASED MANAGEMENT FOR CONTINUOUS IMPROVEMENT

A common misconception is that the scope of an activity-based management (ABM) system must be enterprise-wide. The misconception is that the expenses included in the system must account for *all* the employees in the organization and one-hundred percent of a time period's expenditures. (Or, alternatively, the expenses must include *all* the people in a substantial portion of the organization, such as a factory or service-delivery arm.) People with this misconception have usually been exposed only to ABM models or systems that are used for calculating the total costs of a product or service line used to determine their total profitability. Operational ABM is the focus of this discussion.

Operational ABM is applied to subsets of the organization for process improvement rather than revenue enhancement and profit margin increases. The objectives of operational ABM are process improvement, productivity increases, and asset utilization. Price and revenue information to determine profit margins is not included with operational ABM. This data is reserved for strategic ABM, which is discussed in the next chapter.

In this chapter I will first discuss how an organization's enterprise-wide ABM model can be divided into multiple *local* ABM models, representing departments or processes that can subsequently be consolidated into their *parent* enterprise ABM model. I will then describe the pursuit of operational ABM benefits via activity analysis, cost driver analysis, and scoring ABM with attributes, such as for nonvalue-added costs.

CONSOLIDATING ABM "CHILDREN" SUBMODELS INTO A PARENT MODEL

I like to view local ABM models using an analogy of a symphony orchestra con-ductor in rehearsal, first working the violins, then the trumpets, then all the stringed instruments, then all the brass instruments—and finally the entire or-chestra in a live concert. The combined orchestra represents a consolidated par-ent ABM model, with local ABM models rolled up into a parent model, performing as a repeatable and reliable system.

Commercial ABM software now enables consolidating of the local, chil-dren ABM models into the enterprise-wide, parent ABM model. Figure 13.1 illustrates how a railroad organization separated its operational ABM models from its strategic models. Note how the final cost object outputs of the chil-dren submodels become the inputs as final cost objects in the parent strategic ABM model.

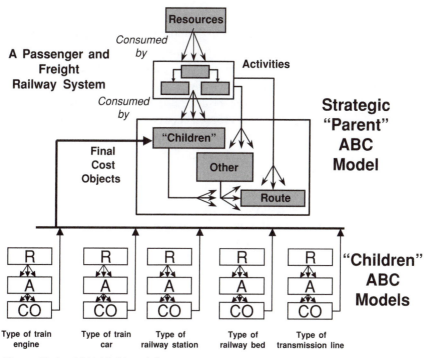

Figure 13.1   ABM Multimodels

Local ABM model data are used for tactical purposes, often to improve productivity. In contrast, the consolidated enterprise-wide ABM model is often used for strategic purposes because it helps focus on where to look for problems and opportunities. Also, enterprise-wide models are popular for calculating profit margin data at all levels, including channel-related and customer- and service-recipient-related profit contribution layers. I encourage readers who are interested in a more in-depth understanding of this topic to go to www.wiley.com/go /performance and read how a railway organization optimized its route profitability (i.e., strategic ABM) while concurrently driving productivity improvements and cost reductions with multiple operational ABM models that fed into the strategic ABM model.

OPERATIONAL ACTIVITY-BASED MANAGEMENT MODEL ANALYSIS: A HIGHWAY ROAD MAINTENANCE EXAMPLE

A government automobile road maintenance and repair department does not directly service individual types of cars or trucks or service individual types of drivers. The inherent diversity originates in the type of road. It is the characteristics of the road that cause the work crews to do more or less work. The road bed is the only practical way of connecting an output of the department's workload back to the used resources (e.g., types of trucks, garages, employees, etc.).

The ABM model design lesson is this: Final-final cost objects are at the end of the *predator food chain* that was earlier described. The *end-of-the-road* cost objects consume all of the cost assignments that occurred prior to piling up into them. Some cost assignments are direct to them, but in increasingly overhead-intensive organizations, most costs trace to final-final cost objects as indirect costs.

There can be dozens of characteristics that result in the four-lane urban expressway being so much more expensive relative to other types of roads after the effect of distance has been removed (i.e., per mile or kilometer). The level of activity costs used to serve the roadbed is inherently governed by the type of roadbed. The ABM assignment relies on cost object drivers; the activity drivers have already completed their mission to trace the workload costs into their cost object.

Figure 13.2 illustrates fictitious costs that compare the unit cost of the output of work for each type of road's cost per mile. This type of report is very popular with ABM users. It provides not just the total unit costs of the output—now validly computed—but it also subdivides that total unit cost among the various work activities that are being consumed.

This deeper visibility of activity costs within a unit of output provides a form of internal benchmarking, which lends itself to the identification and adoption of

Type of Roadbed Costs						
Roadbed Types						
Number of Lanes	Road Surface	Location	Total Cost	Number of Miles	Work Activity	Unit Cost per Mile
Four	Asphalt	Interstate	$270,137,078.40	125,342		$2,155.20
					Cut grass	$120.00
					Electronic signs	$334.25
					Fill potholes	$150.00
					Plow roads	$975.60
					Paint stripes	$450.50
					Replace signs	$124.85
Two	Bituminous	Rural	$29,783,384.10	43,578		$683.45
					Cut grass	$220.00
					Electronic signs	$0.00
					Fill potholes	$65.00
					Plow roads	$250.00
					Paint stripes	$112.20
					Replace signs	$36.25
Four	Asphalt	County	$95,567,207.84	65,672		$1,455.22
					Cut grass	etc.
					Electronic signs	etc.
					Fill potholes	etc.
					Plow roads	etc.
					Paint stripes	etc.
					Replace signs	etc.

Figure 13.2   Unit Costs of the Output of Work of a Total Unit Cost

best practices in other parts of an organization. It allows the employee teams and managers to ask much better and more focused questions of themselves. ABM becomes an excellent focusing tool highlighting where to look for potential changes for improvement. The employees can intelligently discuss what underlying factors are leading to the large relative costs compared to the other final cost objects. In this way the ABM cost assignment network's final cost object module provides insights to stimulate teams to think and to discuss how their limited resources are being used and may be better used.

ACTIVITY ANALYSIS TO IMPROVE THE COST STRUCTURE

The vast majority of ABM data are applied locally. The objective of local ABM models is not to calculate the profit margins of products, service lines, and customers; it is to compute the diverse costs of outputs to better understand how they create the organization's cost structure. In addition to analyzing the impact of diverse cost objects, there is also activity analysis and cost driver analysis. Figure 13.3 reveals the link between an activity driver and its work activity. In a

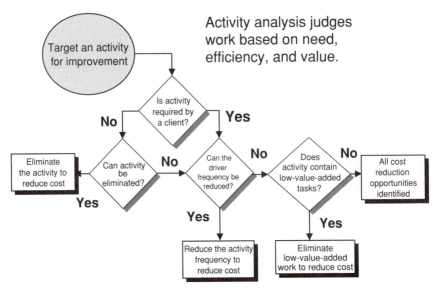

Figure 13.3   Activity Analysis

simple fashion it describes how each work activity can be judged based on its need by the product or customer, its efficiency, and its value content.

Some managers believe that the only way to truly reduce costs is to remove the work activity altogether. They believe there is little point in trying to do cheaply what should not be done at all. That is, a job not worth doing is not worth doing well. Regardless of how one attacks achieving improvements, the main message here is that work is central to ABM. What do we do? How much do we do it? Who do we do it for? How important is it? Are we very good at doing it?

USING THE ATTRIBUTES OF ACTIVITY-BASED COSTING

ABM systems provide for distinguishing work activities either by including them in a cost assignment structure (i.e., sustaining cost objects) or by tagging their costs as an overlay (i.e., as attributes). Attributes are considered by many involved with ABM implementations as more powerful than ABM's calculation of costs. Management consultants enjoy applying a variety of attributes to help their clients better *see* their cost structure and its behavior.

What are attributes? Traditional cost accounting methods do not provide any way for individual costs to be tagged or highlighted with a separate dimension of cost other than the monetary amount that was spent. An example of a range of tags that can be used to score activities is "very important" versus "required" versus "postponable." These are popular ways of measuring value-added costs and where they are located. The idea is to eliminate low-value-adding activities and improve higher-value-adding activities, thus enabling employees to focus on the worth of their organization's work. As another example, the quality management community uses attributes to calculate the cost-of-quality (COQ). Figure 13.4 illustrates the three popular COQ categories for grading work activities. Categories themselves can be broken down into subcategories for more refined reporting.

In contrast to ABM's objective cost reporting of the facts, attributes take the ABM data an additional step by making the data very suggestive of what actions to take. Two popular examples include the *level of importance* (i.e., value) and *level of organizational performance*. For the first example, the objective is to determine the relation of work or its output to meeting customer and shareholder requirements. The goal is to improve those activities that add value and minimize or eliminate those that do not. For the second example, the objective is to focus on efficiency and effectiveness.

Figure 13.5 illustrates the four quadrants that result from combining these two attributes for performance (vertical axis) and importance (horizontal axis). Organizations can see, for example, that they are spending a lot of money doing

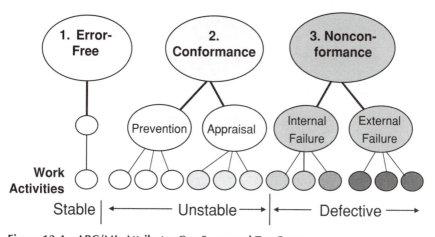

Figure 13.4   ABC/M's Attributes Can Score and Tag Costs

Scoring and tagging activities can assist employees to determine what directional actions to take with that work.

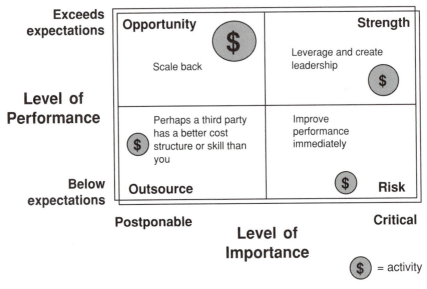

Figure 13.5   ABC/M's Attributes Can Suggest Action

things they are good at but that they have judged to be unimportant. The activity costs for such unimportant activities would be in the upper-left quadrant. In this example it is obvious the organization should scale back and spend less on that kind of work. Each quadrant involves a different suggestion. The lower-left quadrant suggests outsourcing the work since activities there are not well performed but are also not a required core competency.

In summary, the objective of operational ABM is continuous process improvement and general cost management. In contrast, the objective of strategic ABM is revenue enhancement and quality of profit improvement.

14

STRATEGIC ACTIVITY-BASED MANAGEMENT FOR CUSTOMER AND CHANNEL PROFITABILITY ANALYSIS

This chapter describes the insights gained from validly measuring customer profitability and how organizations apply performance management (PM) systems to actively manage changing strategies to increase profit, reduce cost, and improve performance throughout an organization. Initially, traditional accountants questioned why they should depart from collecting, summarizing, and reporting procedural transaction detail for strategic uses of cost accounting data. That resistance changed. The previous chapter focused on reducing costs. But cutting resources can only go so far—there is a limit. You can take out bodies, but you can't take out the work. This chapter focuses on revenue enhancement and quality of profits associated with the sales.

ARE ALL OF YOUR CUSTOMERS PROFITABLE TO YOU?

It is no longer sufficient for an organization to be lean, agile, and efficient. Its entire supply chain must also perform as it does. If some of its trading-partner suppliers and customers are excessively high-maintenance, those suppliers and customers erode profit margins. Who are the troublesome suppliers and customers, and how much do they drag down profit margins? More importantly, once these questions are answered, what corrective actions should managers and employees take?

Some customers purchase a mix of mainly low-margin products. After adding the *costs-to-serve* for those customers *apart from* the products and ser-vice lines they purchase, these customers may be unprofitable to a company and to that company's extended value chain. Other customers who purchase a mix of relatively high-margin products may demand so much in extra services that they also could potentially be unprofitable. How does one properly mea-sure customer and supplier profitability? How does one deselect or *fire* a cus-tomer or a supplier? After the less-profitable customers and suppliers are identified, they can be migrated toward higher profits using *margin manage-ment* techniques.

If two customers purchased from a company the exact same mix of products and services at the exact same prices during the exact same time period, would both customers be equally profitable? Of course not. Some customers behave like saints and others like sinners. Some customers place standard orders with no fuss, whereas others demand nonstandard everything, such as special delivery requirements. Some customers just buy your product or service line, and you hardly ever hear from them. Others you *always* hear from—and it is usually to change their delivery requirements, inquire about and expedite their order, or re-turn or exchange their goods. Some customers require more post-sale services than others do. In some cases, just the geographic territory the customer resides in makes a difference.

If you added up all the costs of your employees' time, effort, interruptions, and disruptions attributed to high-maintenance customers, *in addition* to the costs of the products and base service lines that they draw on, might you find that you do not make any profit on them? It's possible. But most organizations do not know whether this is case. These observations have been around a while as this quote from 1922 is evidence:

> "Very often, although a cost system may be nearly perfect and all possible factory economies may have been effected, a manufacturer may nevertheless show losses due to inadequate control over his selling and administrative expenses. In fact, unless the same (costing) principles are applied in controlling selling and administrative costs (as for production), the entire advantage gained through efficient low-cost production may be lost."[1]

Similar questions can be asked about the inbound costs from suppliers. Are some suppliers so much more difficult to work with that the cost ultimately drags down the organization's profits? If all these *extra* costs are passed on to cus-tomers by ultimately increasing prices to the end-consumer, what is the risk that your entire supply chain will finally push that consumer to switch to a substitute or a competitor's product or postpone the purchase altogether?

PURSUIT OF TRUTH ABOUT PROFITS

With better cost data a company can answer questions about its customers and suppliers, such as the following:

- Do we push for volume or for margin with a specific customer?
- Are there ways to improve profitability by altering the way we package, sell, deliver, or generally service a customer?
- Does the customer's sales volume justify the discounts, rebates, or promotion structure we provide to that customer?
- Can we realize the benefits from our changing strategies by influencing our customers to alter their behavior to buy differently (and more profitably) from us?
- Can we shift work to or from some of our suppliers, based on who is more capable or who already has a superior cost structure compared to ours?

To be competitive, a company must know its sources of profit and understand its cost structure. A competitive company must also ultimately translate its strategies into actions. For outright unprofitable customers, a company would want to explore passive options of substantially raising prices or surcharging them for the extra work. It can also be more assertive and terminate the relationship. For already profitable customers, a company may want to reduce customer-related causes of extra work for its employees, streamline its delivery process so it costs less to serve customers, or alter the customers' behavior so that those customers place fewer workload demands on the company.

What kinds of customers are loyal and profitable? Which customers are only marginally profitable or, worse yet, losing you money? Activity-based management (ABM) is the accepted methodology to economically and accurately trace the consumption of an organization's resource expenses to those types and kinds of channels and customer segments that place varying demands on the company.

Revisit Figure 12.1, the ABM cost assignment network. It shows the framework for how ABM traces, segments, and reassigns costs based on the cause-and-effect demands triggered by customers and their orders. As previously described, ABM refers to these triggers as *activity drivers*. When the cost of processing a customer's orders is subtracted from the sales amount for those orders, a company can really know whether it actually made or lost money over time. A company will also know prospectively whether an accepted price quote for a future customer order will be profitable.

Many employees in the sales function are evaluated on commissions that are based on sales volumes, so they don't place much importance on costs and profits. The emphasis for variable compensation will eventually need to include customer profits, so attention needs to be shifted to the bottom line. The issue here is not only determining the profit contribution of customers, including accurate costs for the products they buy, but also understanding the elements of customer-specific work that make up the entire costs to serve *each* customer.

It is no longer acceptable to *not* have a rational system of assigning so-called nontraceable costs to their sources of origin, whether those sources are suppliers, products, or customers. ABM is that rational system, and when it is bundled with planning and scorecards as an enterprise PM system, the collective system becomes a powerful tool suite for taking the right actions. Senior management constantly adjusts strategies. A PM system is continuous, providing actionable information to everyone.

BENEATH THE ICEBERG: UNREALIZED PROFITS

Traditional methods of costing products result in under- and overcosting from flawed, volume-based averaging methods of cost allocation. The profit margin math subtracts the true ABM product and service line costs from the sales and revenues. The profit margin is always a derivative—it is the money that is left over. With ABM, the costs shift from what everyone had believed them to be, while the price and volume do not shift but remain unchanged. As a result, the profit margins are also revealed to be substantially different than what the organization had believed. This result is also due to the fact that margins are usually very thin, so even slight changes in costs make a difference.

Figure 14.1 is a graph of how *unrealized profits* can be hidden due to inadequate costing methods. The accountants are not properly assigning the expenditures based on cause and effect. The graph is of each product's cost, net of sales, to reveal *each* product's and service line's profit.

The products are rank-sorted left-to-right from the largest to the smallest profit margin rate. The very last data point equals the firm's total net profit, as reported in its profit and loss (P&L) statement. Statisticians call this the Stobachoff curve. For this organization, total revenues were $20.0 million with total expenses of $18.2 million, to net a $1.8 million profit, but the graph reveals the distribution of the mix of that $1.8 million net profit. Although not empirically tested, experiences with these measures show that the total amount of the profits, excluding any losses, usually exceeds two-hundred percent of the resulting reported net profit; greater than one-thousand percent has even been measured.

The last data point in Figure 14.1 exactly equals the *total* reported profit, but

Profitability profiles are like electrocardiograms of a company's health. After sales are attached to the ABC costs, this graph reveals that $8 million was made on the most profitable 75% of products—and then $6 million was conceded back!

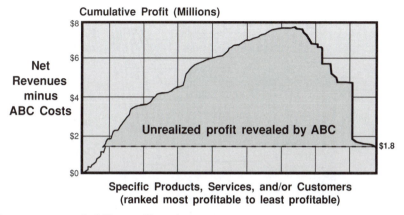

Figure 14.1   Profitability Profile Using ABC

that single point gives no visibility to the parts. As a result, the curve looks like a fishing pole catching a fish. Think of the last data point as being on a vertical metal track; it can only slide up or down (where the imaginary fish is on the hook). By looking at the graph this way, it reveals that products and service lines to the left of the peak, where an item's sales exactly offset its costs, are also fair game for increasing profits. Many people only focus on the losers to the right. (This graph has also been referred to as "profit cliffs" and as "whale curves," but a fishing pole analogy adds the concept of spring and motion to lift the end point—raise profits upward.)

Figure 14.2 clarifies the graph in Figure 14.1. It reveals the information that constitutes a single data point on the right down-sloping side of the "fishing pole" graph. The figure illustrates that for each product, service line, or customer, its final cost object's activity costs have piled up in it like sediment layers on the bottom of a river. The assignment comes from the ABM cost assignment network, where each activity driver and rate apportions the proper amount of activity costs consumed.

PM systems combine ABM with planning and performance measure and alignment tools; but what makes PM so appealing is that it is work-centric. The foundation for PM is built on what people and equipment do, how much they do it, and why.

Accountants rarely isolate and directly charge customer-related activity costs to the specific customer segments causing these costs. As a result, in financial

For this product or service offering, the pricing does <u>not</u> recover the costs-to-make and costs-to-serve.

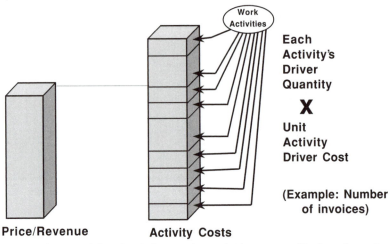

ABC not only provides insight to the relative magnitude of each activity cost element, useful for comparative purposes, but also for the product's or service's cost drivers and driver quantities.

Figure 14.2   Revenue–Bill of Activity Costs = Profit / Loss

accounting terms, the costs for selling, advertising, marketing, logistics, warehousing, and distribution are immediately charged to the *time period* in which they occur. Consequently, the accountants are not tasked to trace them to channels or customer segments. Today's selling, merchandising, and distribution costs are no longer trivial costs—they are sizable. There should be a focus on the customer contribution margin devoid of simplistic and arbitrary cost allocations. Companies with goals of sales growth at any cost need to temper their plans with a goal of *profitable* sales growth.

HOW DOES CUSTOMER SALES VOLUME RELATE TO PROFITS?

Figure 14.3 reveals the typical data points for the intersection of individual customer sales volume and profit that constitute the same data points shown in the fishing pole diagram (Figure 14.1).

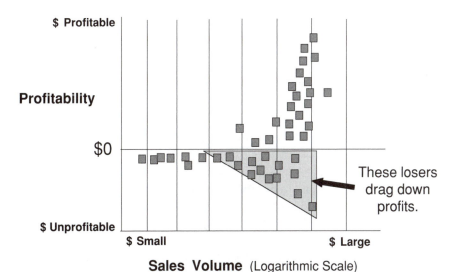

Customers tend to cluster. Medium-volume customers can be much more profitable than large-volume customers!

Figure 14.3   Customer Sales Volume versus Profits

Figure 14.3 indicates that there are clusters:

- Small-volume customers may be, to a high degree, unprofitable. (Note that this does not automatically suggest abandoning all of them, because some may be the seedlings that will grow into forests, becoming the large, profitable customers of the future.)
- For many of the larger customers, profits grow exponentially.
- For a sizable group of large customers, however, profits are minimal or, worse yet, nonexistent and negative.
- There can be medium-sized customers that, as a collective group, bring in a large share of the total profit.

The shape of any organization's customer base's profitability profile curve will be unique. Knowing the types of customers that cluster in the various profit/loss zones of Figure 14.3 can be valuable in determining what actions to take.

PM goes even further by bundling these profit margin and cost measurement tools with employee scorecard tools to assure that any decisions are aligned with the company's strategies. PM resides in a Web-enabled environment, so employees can much more quickly analyze, communicate, and take actions. The vision and strategies coming from the top down, and the feedback results coming from the bottom up, are important for actively managing an organization. PM serves as that bridge between strategies and operations.

ABM CUSTOMER PROFIT AND LOSS STATEMENT USING PROFIT CONTRIBUTION LAYERING

With activity-based costing, unlike the traditional P&L statement, profit contribution margins are reported more like the layers of an onion. An ABM P&L view shows that first, exclusively product-related margins can be viewed, and without the misleading distortions from product-related overhead cost misallocations. (Traditional overhead cost allocations apply volume-based factors without correlation, not *consumption-based activity drivers* that possess cause-and-effect, if-then relationships.) Then, as customers consume (i.e., purchase) their unique quantities of the mix of products and service lines, where some products may be stand-alone profitable and some not at the product level, the customer-related costs-to-serve are combined to calculate the next profit contribution margin layer. The onion is peeled back another layer.

A true ABM system operates as a reassignment system. The following material refers to Figure 12.1, the ABM Cost Assignment Network. This structure is the key to revealing the profit margin layers for each customer and to generating customer-specific P&L statements.

Figure 14.4 expands on the ABM Cost Assignment Network's final cost object module in Figure 12.1. It displays two layers of a *nested* consumption sequence of costs. The metaphor for this consumption sequence, as previously described, is the predator food chain. The final-final cost object, which in this figure is the customer, ultimately consumes all the other final cost object costs, except for the business sustaining costs.

Each of the major final cost object categories (e.g., supplier, product/service line, and customer), has its own *sustaining costs*, which are also assignable to its end-product or end-customer.

In the ABM Cost Assignment Network, each product previously incurred its own activity costs with a cause-and-effect relationship, not with an arbitrary indirect cost allocation. This method of costing thereby creates layers of costs. Figure 14.5 is an example of an individual customer profitability statement. Using ABM, there can now be a valid P&L statement for *each* customer as well as logical segments or groupings of customers.

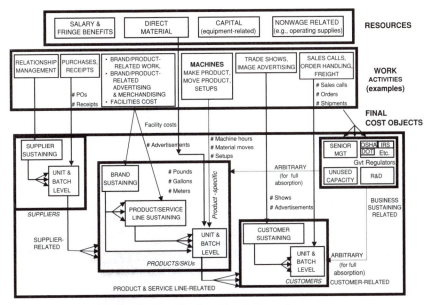

Figure 14.4   ABC/M Profit Contribution Margin Layering

CUSTOMER: XYZ CORPORATION (CUSTOMER #1270)

Sales	$$$	Margin $ (Sales − ΣCosts)	Margin % of Sales	
Product-Related				
Supplier-Related Costs (TCO)	$ xxx	$ xxx	98%	
				Product-Related Costs
Direct Material	xxx	xxx	50%	
Brand Sustaining	xxx	xxx	48%	
Product Sustaining	xxx	xxx	46%	
Unit, Batch*	xxx	xxx	30%	
Distribution-Related				
Outbound Freight Type*	xxx	xxx	28%	
Order Type*	xxx	xxx	26%	
Channel Type*	xxx	xxx	24%	Customer-Related Costs
Customer-Related				
Customer Sustaining	xxx	xxx	22%	
Unit, Batch*	xxx	xxx	10%	
Business Sustaining	xxx	xxx	8%	
			8% Operating Profit	
Capital Charge** (inventories, receivables) xxx		xxx	−2%	
			6% Economic Profit (for EVA)	

* Activity cost driver assignments use measurable quantity volume of activity output.   **Capital charges can also be directly charged
(Other activity assignments traced based on informed [subjective] %s.)   as imputed interest to products and customer.

Figure 14.5   ABC/M Customer Profit and Loss Statement

With an ABM P&L, the individual products and service lines purchased can be examined in greater detail; they comprise a mix of high and low margins based on their own unit costs and prices. In other words, in a customer-specific P&L summary, the product or service line is reported as a composite average, but details about the mix are viewable. In addition, within each product or service line the user can further drill down to examine the content and cost of the work activities and materials (the *bill of costs*) for each product and service line.

The crucial challenge is not to just use ABM to calculate valid customer profitability data but then to *use* the data, and use it wisely. The benefit comes from identifying the profit potential and then realizing it and fulfilling it via smart actions. A primary feature of PM is that it structures the analysis, places it in a strategic context, and encourages instant communications and actions.

MIGRATING CUSTOMERS TO HIGHER PROFITABILITY

What does all this information reveal? First, it quantifies what everyone may already have suspected: All customers are not the same. Some customers may be more or less profitable based strictly on how demanding their behavior is. Although customer satisfaction is important, a longer-term goal is to increase customer and corporate profitably. There must always be a balance between managing the level of customer service to earn customer satisfaction and the impact that doing that will have on shareholder wealth. The best solution is to increase customer satisfaction profitably. Because increasingly more customers will expect and demand customization rather than standard products, services, and orders, understanding this balance will be important. ABM data facilitate discussions about arriving at that balance. Many managers are unwilling to take any actions until presented with the facts.

In the company P&L in Figure 14.5 there are two major layers of contribution margin:

1. By mix of products and service-lines purchased.

2. By *costs-to-serve* apart from the unique mix of products and service lines.

Figure 14.6 combines these two layers. Any single customer (or cluster) can be located as an intersection. Figure 14.6 provides a two-axis view of customers with regard to the two layers just described, the *composite margin* of what each purchases (reflecting net prices to the customer) and its *costs-to-serve*. Each quadrant of the matrix represents a zone in which four different types of customers can exist.

Figure 14.7 shows various customers as points of an intersection on the

Customers with high sales volume are not necessarily highly profitable.
Customer profitability levels depend on whether the net revenues recover the
customer-specific costs-to-serve.

Types of Customers

Very Profitable

Product Mix * Margin

High (Creamy)

Passive/ "Champions"
· Product/service is crucial
· Good trading partner match

Savvy/ "Demanders"
· Pays top-shelf price
· Costly to serve

Cheap/ "Acquaintances"
· Price-sensitive
· Low service & quality requirements

Aggressive/ "Losers"
· Leverage their buying power
· Buying low margins

Low (Low Fat)

* Unique to each customer (their basket of purchases)

Nominally demanding

Very demanding

Very Unprofitable

Cost-to-Serve

Figure 14.6   ABC/M Customer Profitability Matrix

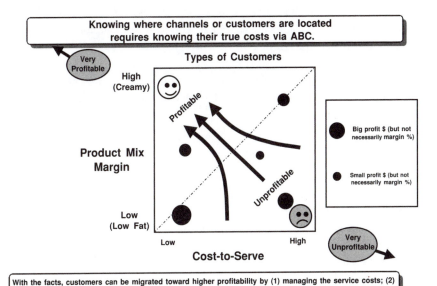

Knowing where channels or customers are located
requires knowing their true costs via ABC.

Types of Customers

Very Profitable

Product Mix Margin

High (Creamy)

Profitable

Unprofitable

Low (Low Fat)

Low   High

Cost-to-Serve

Big profit $ (but not necessarily margin %)

Small profit $ (but not necessarily margin %)

Very Unprofitable

With the facts, customers can be migrated toward higher profitability by (1) managing the service costs; (2)
reducing their services; (3) renegotiating prices and/or shifting their purchase mix to richer products.

Figure 14.7   Migrating Customers to Higher Profitability

matrix in Figure 14.6. The objective is to make all customers more profitable, represented by driving them to the upper-left corner. Note that migrating customers to the upper-left corner is equivalent to moving individual data points in the profit profile in Figure 14.1 from right to left. Knowing where customers are located on the matrix requires ABM data.

Segmenting customers with ABM requires some different filters, which we will discuss next.

SEGMENTING CUSTOMERS BASED ON THEIR DEMAND BEHAVIOR AND MAINTENANCE NEEDS

Many companies categorize their customers based on their geographic location, their demographics (e.g., elderly, youth, affluent, etc.), or their shopping behavior. These categories are useful for sales and marketing studies, but the delineation for understanding customer-related costs requires *value segmentation*. Figure 14.6 illustrated the four types of customers that could fall into multiple demographic categories.

Another way of labeling the four quadrants in the figure that is separate from each demographic or alternative customer segment is to refer to customers as four types of *valued* customers. This framework can facilitate formulating customer management strategies:

- **Champions.** These are the best type of customers. They are loyal, purchase a lot from you, and can be nearly effortless to service. You want to nurture and reward them.

- **Demanders.** These *savvy* customers may generate nice profits but they make heavy, uncompensated demands on your resources. You want to grow their revenues but manage how they cause you costs. One approach is to encourage them to use self-help processes, such as a bank's ATM.

- **Acquaintances.** These are the *cheap* customers. You would not want to build your business based on them, but you enjoy having them because they contribute marginal profits with relatively low maintenance. Growing revenues with them is okay—but do it economically. They are price-sensitive and may not put much importance on your levels of service or quality.

- **Losers.** These are the *aggressive* customers who drain your resources and time, yet provide little—and probably negative—financial return. Their size and volume may have exacted a negotiated pricing discount beyond what was perceived as profitable to you. Alternatively, they may be the type who hops around among you and your competitors. You may want them to permanently defect to competitors and avoid them in any win-back campaigns.

Another critical reason for knowing where each of your customers is located on the profit matrix is to protect your most profitable customers from competitors. Because so few customers account for a significant portion of the profits, the risk exposure is enormous. This highlights the importance of high customer retention rates, the value derived from customer loyalty, and the opportunity cost of losing profitable customers.

OPTIONS TO RAISE THE PROFIT CLIFF CURVE

What does a commercial organization do with the customer profit information? In other words, what actions can an organization take to increase its profits? This is all about the "M" in ABM, the *managing* of costs and profits. Some customers may be located so deep in the lower-right corner of the customer profitability matrix that the company will conclude that it is impractical to achieve profitability with them and they should be terminated. After all, the goal of a business is not to improve customer satisfaction at any cost but rather to attempt to manage customer relationships in order to improve long-term corporate profitability.

Although this is a partial list, increasing profitability can be accomplished by doing the following:

- Manage each customer's *costs-to-serve* to a lower level.
- Establish a surcharge for or reprice expensive cost-to-serve activities.
- Reduce services.
- Introduce new products and service lines.
- Raise prices.
- Abandon products, services, or customers.
- Improve the process.
- Offer the customer profit-positive service level options.
- Increase costs on activities that a customer shows a preference for.
- Shift the customer's purchase mix toward richer, higher-margin products and service lines.
- Discount to gain more volume with low cost-to-serve customers.

Before doing anything and acting hastily, it is important for anyone interpreting the profit distribution diagram to understand the following key issues about the diagram:

- This snapshot view of a time period's cost does not reflect the *life-cycle costs* of the products, service lines, or customers that have consumed the resource and activity costs for that particular time span.
- The information represented in the graph should not be prematurely or spontaneously acted on. Analysts must appreciate the large difference between what information is and what making an actionable decision is. They are not the same.

BEWARE THE LEARNING ORGANIZATION: COMPETITORS

As progressive organizations gain proficiency and mastery with the business intelligence provided by ABM, they can be formidable. What those companies are recognizing is that each individual customer affects the profitability of their brand products, base services, and market segments. The effect is due to the customer's purchasing habits, delivery location, discount/rebate structures, or other diverse ways in which it places demands on its suppliers. When equipped with ABM's superior data, competitors can cherry-pick the premium-profit customers of their competitors. They can also strategically price for new product entry.

NOTE

1. William B. Castenholz, "The Application of Selling and Administrative Expense to Product," *National Association of Cost Accountants (NACA) Yearbook*, 1922.

15

PREDICTIVE COSTING, PREDICTIVE ACCOUNTING, AND BUDGETING[1]

Information technology computing power has now made it possible for business analysts and planners to apply advanced methods for budgeting and to estimate the costs for alternative decisions. These methods provide more accurate answers than traditional cost estimating methods that often simply extrapolate historical cost amounts and rates. However, these advanced cost estimating methods come with a price: They require a greater administrative effort.

This chapter addresses the shortcomings of traditional budgeting as a fixed *contract* negotiated a year ahead based on assumptions of certain external market and competitive pressures, which are actually likely to change. One of the popular solutions advocated to fix traditional budgeting is activity-based budgeting (ABB). However, as you dig deeper into understanding budgeting and planning, you discover that you have entered into a much broader world of forecasting and marginal (incremental) cost analysis. Forecasting includes cost estimating, presumably linked with projections of demand. ABB and its companion, activity-based planning (ABP), which are now popularly combined as activity-based resource planning (ABRP), will be considered in this chapter.

WEARY ANNUAL BUDGET PARADE: USER DISCONTENT AND REBELLION

Why is there increasing interest in ABRP? In part the interest is due to increasing problems with the annual budget process, and not just because individuals are not getting the approval for funding they want. They are disturbed by the budgeting process altogether. Executives and employees are all recognizing that a fixed *contract* budget does not transmit the continuously changing and relentless market pressure, nor competitor actions. There is great cynicism about budgeting as a bureaucratic exercise disconnected from reality. The other reason for discontent is that everyone senses that a better way to budget exists, such as with business modeling and less invasive rolling financial forecasts. The suite of methodologies in performance management (PM) provides better ways to motivate people.

Traditional Budgeting: An Unreliable Compass

Activity-based planning and budgeting is a better approach to forecasting the location and level of resources and budgeted expenditures than traditional budgeting methods. It recognizes that the need for resources originates with a demand-pull triggered by customers or end-users of the organization's services and capabilities. In contrast, today's traditional basis for budgeting tends to extrapolate the level of resource spending from the past, but the past is not a reliable indicator of the future.

Figure 15A contains some sarcasm about traditional budgeting in the form of a check-the-box survey.

Our Budgeting Exercise . . .

☐ is a death march . . . with few benefits.

☐ takes 14 months from start to end.

☐ requires two or more executive tweaks at the end.

☐ is obsolete in two months due to reorganizations.

☐ starves the departments with truly valid needs.

☐ caves in to the loudest voice and political muscle.

☐ rewards veteran sandbaggers who are experts at padding.

☐ is overstated from the prior year's use-it-or-lose-it spending.

☐ incorporates last year's inefficiencies into this year's budget.

Figure 15A   Quiz: Check the Boxes

Traditional Budgeting: An Unreliable Compass *(Continued)*

Traditional budgeting motivates unintended and wrong behavior. It wastes lots of time, usually hides excessive and unneeded spending, involves gaming to protect self-interests, leads the sales force to attempts to pull a customer order earlier than needed, and ultimately can result in unethical cooking of the books.

Traditional budgeting is backward-oriented and simply takes last year's expenses plus a small amount for inflation. This method implies that the budget process starts with the current level of expenses; however, today many managers believe that the budget should flow from the levels of future outputs to determine the needed resources. It should reflect anticipated changes in the marketplace that hopefully the strategy is reacting to. Activity-based budgeting, in effect, flows in this more appropriate *opposite* direction. It logically assists in determining what levels of resources are truly required to meet the future market-driven demands placed on an organization.

Often when there is a substantial change in a management technique, it stems from a combination of dissatisfaction with the current methods and a vision of what a replacement method would look like. With strategy mapping, scorecards, and ABRP we have both conditions present.

Why are executives, managers, and employees cynical about the annual budgeting process?

- As *executives* discover how their strategy maps and scorecards can be the link to budgets, typically the financial department's disconnected exercise, they see the flaws in budgeting as a short-term, focused, "make next year's numbers" report rather than a guiding instrument to successfully execute their strategy by aligning behavior. The budget gives a false sense of security. Strategy maps with scorecards make the strategy operational, and linked budgets provide for how to do it.

- *Managers and employees* have different gripes. They find the process is too long, too detailed, and excessively burdensome. In addition, they view budgeting as a political game that still usually results in some departments being overfunded while others continue laboring as have-nots. This latter group of workers toils without relief. With organizational downsizing, senior management has often removed the bodies but they have not taken out the work. Across-the-board percentage cuts in manpower, some of the slash-and-burn variety, are likely to cut into the muscle in some places while still leaving excess capacity in others.

Fortunately there is a vision of what a better way of budgeting looks like. Rather than as a spending control, the broader purpose for a budget should be to predetermine the level of resources that will be required, such as people, material, supplies, and equipment, to achieve an expected or desired amount of demand for employee services—meaning demands for their work. ABB advocates are interested in the notion of *resource requirements* as being the result, not the starting point. They want to be able to first estimate oncoming customer and management demands, and then estimate the *supply* of resources, in terms of cost, that will be needed to match that supply with the work demands.

In short, ABRP advocates want to reverse the traditional budget equation and start with the expected outcomes, not with the existing situation. Effective budgeting should be a closed loop. It begins with strategic objectives (ideally from a strategy map), considers the projects and plans required to achieve those objectives, and finally determines the funding needed to make the plans actionable. The expected process steps and results of the plan provide metrics (ideally reported via a scorecard) to evaluate and monitor the objectives. Too often, planning starts with a budget and ends with it because the tools in the accounting department are limiting and not integrated.

The ABRP approach leads to less detailed yet meaningful continuous, or *rolling*, financial forecasts that can be periodically refreshed, rather than a year-long committed contract that restricts managers. Rolling financial forecasts allow for faster reactions to external events, revised strategic objectives, and changes in resource allocations.

ACTIVITY-BASED COSTING AS A FOUNDATION FOR ACTIVITY-BASED PLANNING AND BUDGETING

As activity-based costing (ABC) moved into the early 1990s, some companies began leveraging the activity cost data for more operational purposes, to change and manage the same ABC-calculated activity costs that were accumulating in their product and service line costs. They discovered that their personal computer-based ABC models were useful for modeling their cost behavior. They increasingly began using their activity costs and the ABC-calculated unit cost rates for intermediate work outputs and for products and services as a basis for estimating costs. Popular uses of the ABC data for cost estimating have been to calculate customer order quotations, to perform make-versus-buy analysis, and to budget.

The activity-based costing data were being recognized as a predictive planning tool. It is now apparent that the data have a tremendous amount of utility for both examining the *as-is*, current condition of the organization and achieving a desired *to-be* state. (A more robust version of ABM, called resource consumption accounting [RCA] is based on a German accounting practice for marginal cost analysis and flexible budgeting for operational control. RCA is a comprehensive approach that focuses on resources and capacity management logic with ABM principles.)[2]

Cost estimating is often referred to as what-if scenarios. Regardless of what one calls the process, the fact remains that decisions are being made about the future, and managers want to gauge the consequences of those decisions. In these situations, the future is basically coming at us, and in some way the quantity and mix of activity drivers will be placing demands on the work that we as an organization will need to do. The resources required to do the work are the expenses. Assumptions are made about the outputs that are expected. Assumptions should also be made about the intermediate outputs and the labyrinth of interorganizational relationships that will be called on to generate the expected final outcomes.

Major Clue: Capacity Only Exists as a Resource

As most organizations plan for their next month, quarter, or year, the level of resources supplied is routinely replanned to roughly match the firm customer orders and expected future order demands. In reality, the level of planned resources must always exceed customer demand to allow for some protective, surge, and sprint capacity. This also helps improve customer on-time shipping service performance levels.

The broad topic of unused and idle capacity will likely be a thorny issue for absorption costing. A key will be recognizing that capacity can only be associated with resources, not with work activities. Activities have no capacity—they draw on it from resource. As management accountants better understand operations, they will be constantly improving their ability to segment and isolate the unused capacity (and the nature of its cost) by individual resource. Managerial accountants will be increasingly able to measure unused capacity either empirically or by deductive logic based on projected standard cost rates. Furthermore, accountants will be able to segment and assign this unused capacity expense to various processes or owners, to the sales function, or to senior management. This will eliminate overcharging (and overstating) product costs resulting from including unused capacity costs that the product did not cause.

WHERE DOES ACTIVITY-BASED RESOURCE PLANNING AND BUDGETING FIT IN?

In forecasting, the demand volume and mix of the outputs are estimated, and one then solves for the unknown level of expenditures that will be required to produce and deliver the volume and mix. One is basically determining the capacity requirements of the resources. Estimating future levels of resource expense cash outflows becomes complex because resources come in discontinuous clumps. That is, resource expenses do not immediately vary with each incremental increase or decrease in end-unit volume. Traditional accountants address this with what they refer to as a "step-fixed" category of expenses.

The ABRP method involves extrapolations that use baseline physical and cost consumption rates from prior-period ABM calculations. Managerial accountants relate ABRP to a form of flexible budgeting (which is normally applied annually to a 12-month time span).

Figure 15.1 illustrates how capacity planning is the key to the solution. Planners and budgeters initially focus on the direct and recurring resource expenses, not the indirect and overhead support expenses. They almost always begin with estimates of future demand in terms of volumes and mix. Then, by relying on standards and averages (such as the product routings and bills-of-material used in manufacturing systems), planners and budgeters calculate the future required levels of manpower and resources. The ABRP method suggests that this same approach can be applied to the indirect and overhead areas as well or to processes where the organization often has a wrong impression that they have no tangible outputs.

Demand volume drives activity and resource requirements. ABRP is forward-focused, but it uses actual historical performance data to develop baseline consumption rates. ABP and ABB assess the quantities of workload demands that are ultimately placed on resources. Beginning with the "Start" box in Figure 15.1, ABRP first asks, "How much activity workload is required for *each* output of cost object?" These are the activity requirements. The next question is, "How much of each resource is needed to meet that activity workload?" In other words, a workload can be measured as the number of units of an activity required to produce a quantity of cost objects. The determination of expense does not occur until after the activity volume has been translated into resource capacity using the physical resource driver rates from the ABM model. These rates are regularly expressed in hours, full-time equivalents (FTEs), square feet, pounds, gallons, and so forth.

As a result of these calculations, there will be a difference between the existing resources available and the resources that will be required to satisfy the

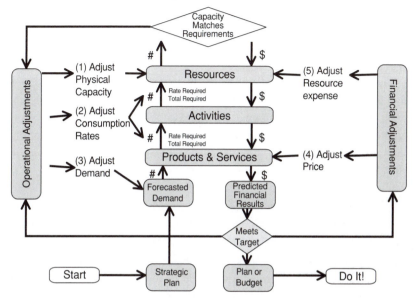

Figure 15.1   Activity-Based Budgeting and Activity-Based Planning Require Making Adjustments

Source: www.CAM-I.org

plan—the resource requirements. That is, at this stage organizations usually discover they have too much of what they do not need and not enough of what they do need to meet the customers' expected service levels (e.g., to deliver on time). The consequence of having too much implies a cost of unused capacity. The consequence of having too little is a limiting constraint that, if not addressed, implies an erosion in customer service levels.

Therefore capacity must be analyzed. One option is for the budgeters, planners, or management accountants to evaluate how much to adjust the shortage and excess of actual resources to respond to the future demand load. Senior management may or may not allow the changes. There is a maximum expense impact that near-term financial targets (and executive compensation plan bonuses) will tolerate. These capacity adjustments represent real resources with real changes in cash outlay expenses if they are to be enacted.

Assume that management agrees to the new level of resources without further analysis or debate. In the downward flow in Figure 15.1, the new level of resource expenditures can be determined and then translated into the costs of the work centers and eventually into the costs of the products, service lines, channels, and customers. This is classic activity-based management (ABM)—but for a future period. Some call this a *pro forma* ABM calculation. The quantities of the projected drivers are applied, and new budgeted or planned costs can be calculated for products, service lines, outputs, customers, and service recipients. At this point, however, the financial impact may not be acceptable. It may show too small a financial return.

When the financial result is unacceptable, management has several options other than to continue to keep readjusting resource capacity levels. These other options may not have much impact on expenses. Figure 15.1 reveals five numbered types of adjustments that planners and budgeters can consider to align their expected demand with resource expenditures to achieve desired financial results. Management can *physically* take the first three steps:

1. **Adjust capacity.** Additional manpower, supplies, overtime, equipment, and the like can be purchased for shortages. There can be scale-backs and removals of people and machines for excesses.

2. **Adjust consumption rates.** If possible, the speed and efficiency of the existing resources can be cranked up or down. If, for example, the increase in manpower makes a decision uneconomical, fewer people can be hired, with an assumed productivity rate increase.

3. **Adjust demand.** If resources remain constrained, demand can be governed or rationed.

The latter two options are operational but also affect the level of resource expenses required. After this cycle of adjustments balances capacity of supply with demand, if the financial results are still unsatisfactory, management can make two incremental financial changes:

4. **Adjust pricing.** In commercial for-profit enterprises or full cost recovery operations, pricing can be raised or lowered. This directly affects the *top-line* revenues. Of course, care is required because the price elasticity could cause changes in volume that more than offset the price changes.

5. **Adjust resource cost.** If possible, wage levels or purchase prices of materials can be renegotiated.

This approach has been called a *closed loop activity-based planning and budgeting* framework.

Absorption costing is descriptive; the only *essential* economic property costing you need to deal with is *traceability* of cost objects back to the resources they consume. However, the descriptive ABM data is used for predictive purposes—the data provide inferences. In contrast, ABRP is predictive. It strives to monitor the impact of decisions or plans in terms of the external cash funds flow of an organization.

In the predictive view, determining the level of resource expenses gets trickier because it requires consideration of an additional economic property: *variability.* The variability of resources is affected by two factors: (1) the step-fixed function, because resources come in discontinuous amounts; and (2) *reversibility* of resources, because the time delay to add or remove resource capacity can range from short to long.

Financial analysts simplistically classify costs as being either fixed or variable within the so-called *relevant range* of volume. In reality, the classification of expenses as fixed, semi-fixed, semi-variable, or variable depends on the decision being made. In the short term, many expenses will not and cannot be changed. In the long term, many of the expenses (i.e., capacity) can be adjusted.

Framework to Compare and Contrast Expense Estimating Methods

Figure 15B presents a framework that describes various methods of predictive cost estimating. The horizontal axis is the planning horizon, short-term to long-term, right to left. The vertical axis describes the types and magnitudes of change in demands of the future relative to the recent past.

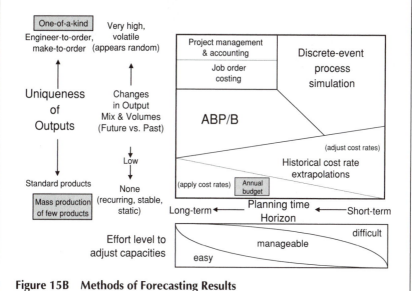

Figure 15B   Methods of Forecasting Results

(Continued)

Framework to Compare and Contrast
Expense Estimating Methods *(Continued)*

The lower part of the figure illustrates that the effort level to adjust capacity becomes easier farther out in time. It describes expenses as becoming more variable and less committed as the planning horizon lengthens. On the short-term horizon, an organization would not add or reduce employee manpower levels to match daily workload requirements, so there is a step-fixed cost function. It takes a while to convert in-case resources into as-needed ones. However, committed expenses (in-case) today can be more easily converted into contractual (as-needed) arrangements in a shorter time period than was possible 10 years ago. Fixed expenses can become variable expenses. The rapid growth in the temporary staffing industry is evidence. Organizations are replacing full-time employees, who are paid regardless of the demand level, with contractors who are staffed and paid at the demand level, which may be measured in hours. In short, historical cost rates can be more easily applied for longer-time-frame decisions; there are fewer step-fixed expense issues.

There are no definitions for the boundary lines between the various zones, and there is overlap as one estimating method gives way to another as being superior. But how much do the various conditions need to change before additional decision support is needed to validate the feasibility or completely evaluate a decision? That is a good question. I am investigating the question of just where the zones begin to overlap. So far, it appears that ABRP has substantial applicability across a wide set of conditions.

Figure 15B illustrates in the upper-right corner that as the time period to adjust capacity shortens and, simultaneously, the number of changes in conditions from the past substantially increase, it becomes risky to rely exclusively on extrapolation methods for cost forecasting. Discrete-event process simulation, which can evaluate and validate decisions in any zone, may especially provide superior and more reliable answers in this upper-right zone relative to the other methods.

A commercial organization ultimately manages itself by understanding where it makes and loses money, or whether the impact of a decision produces incremental revenues superior to incremental expenses. Organizations are increasingly achieving a much better understanding of their contribution profit margins using ABM data. By leveraging ABM with ABRP and discrete-event process simulation tools, an organization can plan better. It can be assured that its plan is more feasible, determine the level of resources and expenditures needed to execute that plan, then view and compare the projected results of that plan against its current performance to manage its various profit margins.

All this may seem like revisiting an Economics 101 textbook. In some ways it is, but here is the difference: In the textbooks, marginal cost analysis was something easily described but extremely difficult to compute due to all of the complexities. In the past, computing technology was the impediment. Now things have reversed. Technology is no longer the impediment—the thinking is. How one configures the ABRP model and what assumptions one makes become critical to calculating the appropriate required expenses and their pro forma calculated costs.

NOTES

1. The ideas in this chapter on activity-based resource planning (ABRP) are based on excellent research from a professional society, the Activity-Based Budgeting Project Team of the Consortium of Advanced Manufacturing International's (CAM-I) Cost Management Systems (CMS) group. More information is available at www.cam-i.org.

2. More can be learned about RCA at www.rcainfo.com.

16

ACTIVITY-BASED MANAGEMENT SUPPORTS PERFORMANCE MANAGEMENT

Part Two described how activity-based management's (ABM) fact-based information supports strategy mapping and scorecards. Figure 16.1 illustrates how activity-based costing data provides a solid base for strategic ABM (i.e., doing the right things—effectiveness), operational ABM (doing them well—efficiency), and strategy mapping. In the lower level of the pyramid, ABM transforms transactional data into meaningful information for discovery and insights about process costs and product/channel/customer costs for measuring profit margins. Moving up the pyramid, ABM then puts the activity-based costing information to use with analytic horsepower.

Equipped with ABM information for both planning and subsequent feedback, a company can monitor performance by means of scorecards for accomplishing the initiatives and managing the processes that support the strategic objectives. Strategy maps, scorecards, and ABM are foundational for performance management (PM).

ACTIVITY-BASED MANAGEMENT AND ITS FUTURE

Future competitive differentiation will be based on the rate of speed at which organizations learn, not just the amount they learn. An organization should not be too late to understand and master ABM as the route to understanding its operational cost behavior and its customer profitability. It should also not want its trading partners to be blind to where they themselves make or lose money. Understanding customer profitability will be a key to collaboration between trading partners to remove mutual waste and provide a basis for jointly beneficial discussion.

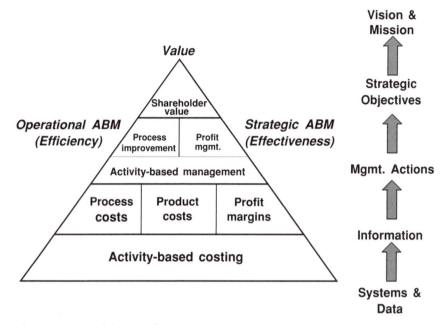

Figure 16.1   Activity-Based Management Supports Strategy Maps

An overarching issue in ABM is the perception of it as just another way to spin financial data rather than as mission-critical managerial information. The Information Age can be mind-boggling. In our future, as technology advances, so will the demand to access massive amounts of relevant information. The companies that survive will be those that can answer the following questions:

- How do we access all this information?
- What do we do with it?
- How do we shape the data and put it into forms with which we can work?
- What will happen when we apply technologies developed *during* the Information Age *for* the Information Age?

Clearly, as information technology (IT) evolves, organizations will increase their effectiveness. Further, as markets change, companies and organizations will encounter global competitors that increasingly look to information and IT for competitive advantage. ABM is involved in this broad arena of *outsmartmanship*.

ABM puts the *management* back into management reporting. For those who are involved with ABM projects, the key is to create and orchestrate change rather than merely react to it and attempt to make the best of a poor situation. It will be fun watching organizations move from their learning stages into mastery of building and using ABM systems.

ABM is the next-generation absorption costing system. Ten years from now we will look back and acknowledge ABM as mainstream, as today we view standard cost accounting systems. Having all these cost and margin data is only a beginning. People have to act on and make decisions with the data. But in the land of the blind, the one-eyed man is king.

In Part Four we will describe an organization's core business processes that involve suppliers, customers, and shareholders. All benefit from these foundational methodologies for PM.

PART FOUR

Integrating Performance Management with Core Solutions

"There are three classes of people: Those who see. Those who see when they are shown. Those who do not see."
Leonardo da Vinci (Florentine painter and inventor), *Note Books*, c. 1500

The usefulness and utility of strategy map, scorecard, and activity-based cost management (ABC/M) systems become real in the context of an organization that is making products or delivering services to satisfy customers, users, and stakeholders. The next five chapters touch on how performance management (PM) can integrate with other *core* solutions. Core solutions are methodologies that apply to all industries rather than specific ones, and entire books have been exclusively written about each of them.[1]

FIVE INTELLIGENCES OF PERFORMANCE MANAGEMENT

Figure P4.1 uses the same upside-down pyramid from Figure 1.1, but this time it highlights the solutions in the intelligence architecture that an organization directs at its customers, its suppliers, its employees, and its shareholders (or stakeholders for public sector and not-for-profit organizations). These solutions are

145

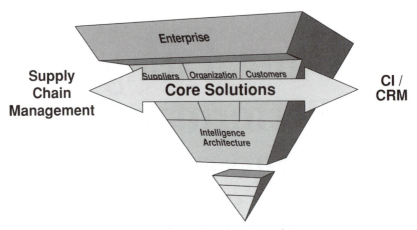

Figure P4.1   Core Solutions Apply to All Industries and Sectors

not so much inward-looking within an enterprise, as if it operates in isolation, but rather these solutions seek to manage the interorganizational impact from interacting with its upstream and downstream trading partners, and by so doing reward its workers and owners.

Each of these *core* solutions is referred to as an *intelligence* to keep with the theme of an intelligence architecture that sits on top of information technology's (IT) transaction-based operational application software in Figure 1.1. In the following chapters, five major elements of the intelligence architecture that have PM linkages are discussed:

- Customer Intelligence and Customer Relationship Management (Chapter 17)
- Supplier Intelligence: Managing Economic Profit across the Value Chain (Chapter 18)
- Process Intelligence with Six Sigma Quality and Lean Thinking (Chapter 19)
- Shareholder Intelligence: Return on Whose Investment? (Chapter 20)
- Employee Intelligence: Human Capital Management (Chapter 21)

Before we dive into each of these, I would like to briefly discuss the ambiguities of the term *value*. It concerns me that there can be trade-offs between adding value to customers that destroy value for shareholders. I am hopeful that within my lifetime advances in the quantitative side of PM will be able to model the linkages from customer satisfaction metrics to measures of shareholder wealth creation. In Chapter 21 I reveal what this model might look like.

CONFUSING PURSUIT OF VALUE ENTITLEMENT

One of the most ambiguous terms in these discussions about business and government is *value*. Everybody wants value in return for whatever they exchanged to get value. We can have endless philosophical debates about the definition of value. The ancient Greek philosophers have already put a lot of time into that. The much more interesting question for the 21st century is, "Whose value is more important?" In the supply chain there are three groups who believe they are entitled to value: customers, shareholders, and employees. Are they rivals? Is there an Adam Smith-like invisible hand controlling checks and balances to maintain an economic equilibrium so that each group gets its fair share? After the expected cost savings from a project are realized in part or whole, how will the financial savings be divided among these groups?

Figure P4.2 illustrates the interplay among the three groups. Customers conclude that they received value if the benefits or pleasure they received from a product or service exceeds what they paid for it. At the opposite end of the figure are the owners, shareholders, and lenders. They also have entitlement to value. As investors, if their investment return is less than the economic return that they could have received from equally or less risky investments, then they are disappointed; they would feel they got less value.

The weighing scale in Figure P4.2 indicates that there is a trade-off between

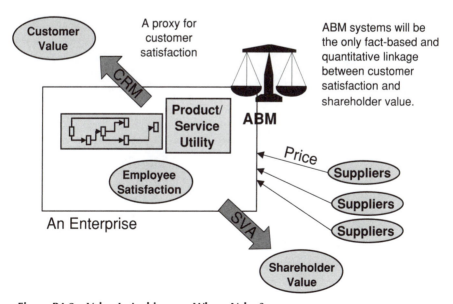

Figure P4.2   Value Is Ambiguous: Whose Value?

customers and shareholders. Under certain conditions, increasing customer satisfaction can result in reducing shareholder wealth. For example, if the enterprise drops its prices too much or adds many more product features and services without a commensurate price increase or gain in market share and sales volume, then the shareholders give up some of their value to their customers.

Figure P4.2 also involves supplier-employees, which includes the executive management team. Their perceived entitlement is their job value. For many this is their security and financial compensation. Heroes of the 20th-century labor union movement, such as Walter Reuther of what is today's AFL/CIO labor union in the United States, confronted Henry Ford for "a fair day's pay" for hourly workers. In today's more mobile knowledge worker labor pool, employees who are dissatisfied with their job value simply vote with their feet by switching to pursue a greater-value job with another employer. Or they become contractors and establish their own value with their own fees or billing rate.

Figure P4.3 decomposes Figure P4.2. The two ultimate core business processes, encompassing the specific ones, that are possessed by any organization on the planet are represented by the solid arrows. The two are (1) take an order or assignment, and (2) fulfill an order or assignment. When stripped to its

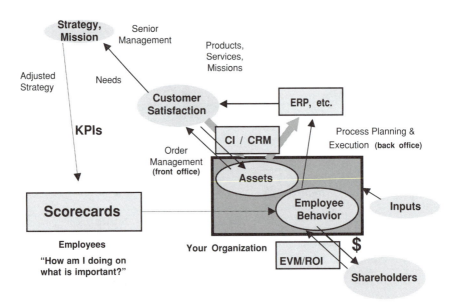

Figure P4.3 How Do They All Fit Together?

core, that is what *any* organization does. Can you name one that doesn't? Figure P4.2 reveals that the IT world has named the support systems for these two mega-processes as *front office* and *back office* systems. Other IT systems serve as components in managing the value chain.

The concept of value is imbedded in Figure P4.3. The three groups entitled to value are defined as follows:

1. **Shareholder value.** This is measured by economic value management (EVM) methodologies, which detect whether the profit margin generated from satisfying customers is also sufficient to reward shareholders and lenders beyond risk-adjusted investment returns that investors and lenders could achieve elsewhere, including financial returns from financial market instruments, such as U.S. Treasury bonds. Accounting profits are not economic profits (see Chapter 20).

2. **Customer value.** The *front office* customer intelligence (CI) and customer relationship management (CRM) systems are intended to maximize communications, interactions, and sensitivity to each customer's unique needs. (See Chapter 17.)

3. **Supplier-employee value.** The *back office* enterprise resource planning (ERP) and advanced planning systems (APS) ensure effective execution to *fulfill orders*. The PM strategy mapping and scorecard systems ensure that specific groups of people, equipment, and other assets are performing in high alignment with senior management's strategies.

ABC/M data permeate every single element of Figure P4.3. As earlier mentioned, ABC/M itself is not an improvement program or execution system like several of those systems in the figure. ABC/M data serve as an enabler for these systems to support better decision making. However, a strong case can be made that ABC/M links CI/CRM to shareholder value, which, as previously mentioned, is heralded as essential for economic value management. The tug-of-war between CI/CRM and EVM is the trade-off of adding more value for customers at the risk of reducing wealth to shareholders. ABC/M is the only financial calculation engine that can quantitatively translate changes in one value to measure the impact on the other. In my opinion, the key event that will catapult ABC/M to front-and-center as an essential PM methodology will be the recognition that ABC/M modeling can be the best link between what now appear to be disparate systems. We know they all connect, but we struggle with how they do it.

Part Four concludes by describing how information technologies—namely data warehousing; data mining, with its powerful extraction, transform, and load (ETL) features; and business analytics (e.g., statistics, forecasting, and optimization)—all produce data from diverse source platforms transparently. That is, these technologies convert raw data into intelligence—the power to know.

NOTE

1. See Paul Greenberg, *CRM at the Speed of Light* (McGraw-Hill, 2002); and Michigan State University, *21st Century Logistics: Making Supply Chain Integration a Reality* (Oak Brook, IL: Council of Logistics Management, 1999, www.clm1.org).

17

CUSTOMER INTELLIGENCE AND CUSTOMER RELATIONSHIP MANAGEMENT

This chapter discusses why mass marketing of products is being eclipsed by direct one-to-one marketing with customers and prospects; how customer information is used by powerful customer relationship management (CRM) tools (e.g., automated campaign management systems; customer call center response systems); and why measures of customer profitability (and its next-generation measure, customer lifetime value [CLV]) will eventually integrate with customer-facing tools.

WHAT IS THE ROI OF MARKETING?

The economic boom of the 1990s in North America was fueled by a steady supply of relatively cheap capital. The economy was investment-driven. However, going forward, the future economics will be demand-driven. Why? Customers, not capital, will generate the next wave of dynamic economic growth. In the past, companies focused on building products and selling them to every potential prospect. But many products are one-size-fits-all and have become commoditylike. To complicate matters, product development management (PDM) methods have matured and accelerate quick me-too copying of new products by competitors.

The consequence is this: As products become commodities, the importance of services rises. That is, as differentiation from product advantages is reduced or neutralized, the customer relationship grows in importance. There is an unarguable shift from product-driven differentiation to service-based differentiation.

151

Strategists all agree that differentiation is a key to competitive advantage. The implication is clear: Profit growth for suppliers and service-providers will come from building intimate relationships with customers, and from providing more products and services to one's *existing* customer base. Earning, not just buying, customer loyalty is now mandatory. But how much do you spend in marketing to retain customers, and which type of customers should you spend more on? Which marketing channel capacity or marketing activity should you spend more or less on? What tailored offer can you up-sell or cross-sell to a customer on an inbound call? How do you prioritize which customers should get which type of communication? Few organizations can answer these questions.

Estimating the return on investment (ROI) of purchasing equipment is near science. In contrast, determining the ROI of marketing is a wing and a prayer. There is a rumored quote from a company president stating, "I am certain that half the money I am spending in advertising is wasted. The trouble is, I do not know which half." Whether someone ever said that is unimportant. It sounds like a real concern—and it applies to the marketing budget too. Marketing spends the money, and the company hopes for a miracle. Was that last e-mail spam we sent a waste or did it hit gold?

Today the margin for error is slimmer, and mistakes are more costly. Without knowing what generates sustained growth in sales, market share, and profitability, the marketing function relies on imperfect metrics, anecdotes, and history that may have been a result of unusual occurrences unlikely to be repeated. Customer intelligence (CI) and CRM address this problem. CI and CRM will be defined shortly, but they evolved from the shift from the 1950s mass marketing to the use of customer database marketing systems. (Read the sidebar, "Transition from Mass Marketing to Customer Database Marketing Systems," for a historical perspective.) These systems are not synonymous with *direct* marketing. Direct marketing refers to circumventing retailers or distributors and directly contacting customers by mail, telephone, or e-mail. Database marketing, which can include direct marketing as a channel, differs in that it requires an understanding of unique customer needs and then tailoring products and marketing campaigns to reach them.

CI is sometimes referred to as *analytical CRM*, whereas CRM (as just described) is referred to as *operational CRM*. Regardless of the semantics, collectively, CI and CRM are customer database marketing methods that accomplish identifying, getting, keeping, and growing customers. There are two main uses: (1) to maintain a dialog with customers, and (2) to promote offers to targeted sales prospects. The goal of CI/CRM is to place the customer or target prospect experience at the center of the organization's priorities and to ensure that incentive systems, processes, and information resources leverage the relationship by enhancing the experience. CI and CRM help attract new customers by first profiling existing customers and testing their responses to promotions, and then identifying sales prospects with similar characteristics.

Segmenting customers into logical groupings is key to CI/CRM. How should segments be defined and what are their key differences? What characteristics of a segment are most predictive? How do customers move between segments over time, and how can their migration be proactively managed? Which are most profitable? Which are more difficult to retain longer term? Which segments respond to which communication channels and types of marketing messages? The understanding of customers resident in CI, typically done in the background, helps drive CRM and ideally proactively manage customers.

Rather than fret about competitors, the message from CI/CRM is that the best way to outperform competitors is to focus on customers. Furthermore, it is generally accepted that it is substantially more expensive to acquire a new customer than to retain an existing one—and satisfied existing customers are not only likely to buy more but also to spread the word to others like a referral service. A company's interactions with a customer or sales target are the all-important currency of CI/CRM—but what does each interaction truly cost and what is its payback? Questions related to the ROI from marketing can be answered by integrating the performance management (PM) tools described in Parts Two and Three with the core methodologies discussed here in Part Four.

CUSTOMERS: THE ULTIMATE SOURCE FOR ECONOMIC VALUE CREATION

One thing is sure: Customers are one constant in a world of uncertainty and change. In Chapter 20 I will discuss creating value not only for customers in the form of satisfaction but also for an organization's investors and owners in financial terms of economic value. However, the unchallenged belief that increasing sales volume is the only key can lead companies to depressed profitability just to sustain sales growth. Some customers are unprofitable to conduct business with. What matters is to shift mind-sets and thinking from sales volume at any cost to *profitable* sales volume.

Security investment analysts and stock brokers struggle with placing a market value share-price on stocks. Many of them fall back to focusing on short-term financial results as a substitute or proxy for long-term potential. One way to help shift the investor's focus to long-term value creation is to take a closer look at a company's customers. When an organization's customer base is expanding and its existing customers are being managed to higher levels of profit (see Part

Three on customer profitability computed with ABM), there is a foundation in place to manage even higher profit growth.

So customers really matter. A way for investors, shareholders, and a management team to think about measuring a company's promise for long-term *economic value* growth performance is to measure its customers. How many customers does it have? How much profit is it earning from each customer today and in the future? What types of customers are the best to up-sell? What kind of new customers are being added and what is the growth rate of additions?

(Later in this chapter I will discuss measuring *customer lifetime value* [CLV] as a predictive measure computed in financial terms. Since changes in customer behavior are usually not volatile, CLV may be useful to understand profit momentum. CLV measures are not interrupted by one-time charges and other short-term but substantial financial statement surprises.)[1]

Customers will always exist. However, customers have widely varying demands—and their demands are increasing. Ideally, the cost-to-serve component of each customer's profit contribution should therefore be measured to provide economic visibility. That is where ABM fits in. But let's not get ahead of our story.

Internet-enabled e-commerce is irreversibly shifting power from the seller to the buyer. This power shift results from the buyer's access to so much more information for product education and comparison shopping. The result is the consumer will become king or queen. Customers have an abundance of options; and now they can get information about products or services that interest them in a much shorter amount of time than what today appear as the antiquated ways of the past. The customer is in control more than ever before. Consequently, from a supplier's perspective, customer retention becomes even more critical, and treating customers as a lifetime stream of revenues becomes paramount. In a later section in this chapter, "Customer Value Measurement Using Customer Lifetime Value," I will describe ways to link customer revenues to organizational profits. They should never be assumed to always go in the same direction.

With e-commerce, each customer can express his or her unique desires and will increasingly search for customized goods and services. Technology is making this possible. As widely varying customization and tailoring for individuals becomes widespread, how will supply chain manufacturers and distributors distinguish their profitable customers from their unprofitable ones? The answer can be provided with ABM customer profitability calculations.

However, the level of profitability is only one variable or factor for formulating a personalized marketing strategy. CI and CRM involve as many variables as are relevant to keep buyers buying from you. Other examples of variables may be geodemographic or behavioral. Geodemographic variables include gender, age, income level, family status (single, married with young children, empty nesters, retired, etc.), recent purchase history, or where they live. Behavioral variables may include customers being loyal, cautious, early adopters, spendthrift, sophisticated, and so on. Analytic CRM examines combinations of these to maximize offer response rates.

Transition from Mass Marketing to Customer Database Marketing Systems

A historical perspective will aid in understanding the marketing revolution that is under way.

Customer intelligence/customer relationship management (CI/CRM) systems evolved as a result of advanced information technology and large databases used to refine marketing and sales efforts. The CI/CRM tools enable companies to target individual customers or micromarket segments with pinpoint accuracy and manage the dialogue and interactions. In the earlier applications of operational CRM (without much analytical CI) in the 1990s, the goal was simply to promote products and emphasize key services to specific types or groups of sales prospects or existing customers. Early operational CRM also focused on cost savings by automating business process work flows or lowering transaction costs, such as in call centers.

Much has changed now. The emphasis since then is on growing revenues, not simply lowering costs. And today mainframes have migrated to the desk top. The Internet takes relating to customers a step further by blending computing and communications into a platform-independent, globally accessible, and universally usable medium. Analytical CI, based on customer database marketing systems, has evolved as an important companion to operational CRM. For example, call center CRM tools may guide the telemarketer to make shorter calls to increase the number of calls, whereas analytical CI can increase the likelihood of acceptance of an offer during a call. A factor in deploying analytical CI is the marketing strategy that may be requiring a shift from increasing market share via more sales to increasing profit by better understanding customer profiles.

It used to be that lowering costs and quickly bringing products to market could ensure a company's success. Now e-commerce is creating a customer-focused approach to business. One of the earliest books on this topic was *The One to One Future: Building Relationships One Customer at a Time*, by Don Peppers and Martha Rogers.[a] Their premise was that it is no longer sufficient

(Continued)

Transition from Mass Marketing to
Customer Database Marketing Systems *(Continued)*

to offer products and use advertising to attract customers—now a business needs to understand *each* customer's unique requirements. That is, following World War II, mass marketing was appropriate; a company produced standard products and sold them to large common groups of customers, usually via mass media. "One size fits all" was accepted. But no longer. The CI/CRM way of thinking has shifted the concept of "share of market" to "share of wallet."

Most people in developed countries own the basic material things they require, like clothes, furniture, and appliances. What they are more interested in are the subtle differentiators that the world of fashion has focused on— quality items that people emotionally bond with, such as brand names. Having choice among product or service line diversity makes people feel like individuals or like part of a group they gladly relate to (e.g., Starbucks). Customer database marketing can monitor customers' unique preferences with one-to-one dialogues.

The economics of profit support CI/CRM. It is exponentially more expensive to acquire new customers than to retain existing ones. Hence, customer satisfaction, always suspected as important, is now officially sanctioned as essential and critical. In short, the message is that suppliers must now continuously seek ways to engage in more content-relevant communications and interactions with their customers. This includes proactively anticipating customer needs.

Increasingly companies are realizing that improving their profitability requires more and better customer contact and more intimate customer relationships. And indiscriminate mass marketing techniques are shifting to database marketing, sometimes called *relationship marketing.*

Although the marketing and sales functions clearly see the links between increasing customer satisfaction and generating higher revenues, the accountants have traditionally focused on encouraging cost reduction as a road to higher profits. The wise managers recognize that some of the best profit-generating opportunities come from improvements, such as attaining higher quality, that achieve both lower costs and higher revenues from increased customer satisfaction.

---

[a]Don Peppers and Martha Rogers, *The One to One Future: Building Relationships One Customer at a Time* (New York: Currency/Doubleday, 1997).

NEED FOR CUSTOMER INTELLIGENCE/ CUSTOMER RELATIONSHIP MANAGEMENT

A force leading to the need for analytical CI and operational CRM systems involves the growing distance and anonymity between those operating the business and their customers. My father and mother operated a mom-and-pop delicatessen in Chicago for 30 years, and my family knew all our customers on a first-name basis. Today it is nearly impossible for a company to manage the growing number of communication channels in which a customer can and will interact with a business. These can include by phone, Internet Web site, e-mail, letter mail, or in person. What is even more problematic is ensuring *consistent* customer-facing behavior among all of the employees in an enterprise. The customer's interactions with the business are typically handled by a variety of employees in different roles and situations responding to the different channels. The employees may be unaware of tailored strategies or desired service levels for handling particular customer groups. Inconsistent experiences are likely being created for customers, who are acutely aware of them and will behave accordingly.[2]

A lesson learned from the supply chain management discipline, at least from a materials management and new product development standpoint, is "I even need to better know my customer's customers." There are supply chain management software tools that allow such transparency across the supply chain.[3]

Ironically, the now accepted term *customer relationship management* may not be the ideal term because you do not truly manage customers. Rather, you enhance their relationship with your company through good experiences and interactions. In the end, an objective of CI/CRM is to offer and deliver the *right* product or service via the *right* channel to the *right* customer at the *right* time—and to do this in a pleasurable way from the customer's point of view.

An emerging trend in CI/CRM is the emphasis on maximizing the response from an *inbound* interaction, such as where the customer initiates calls to a customer service center, rather than scripting an *outbound* call intended to sell as much standard product as possible. Customers are getting saturated from a bombardment of outbound sales solicitations, and they have pain threshold limits. A more profitable impact may come from a tailored up-sell or cross-sell offer at the moment a customer calls in based on what you know about them. This is a nonintrusive solution where an increased response rate is more likely. The higher impact results from having current and relevant customer data combined with analytical intelligence about which type of customer may be receptive to which type of offer. CI provides understanding of customer preferences that can translate into purchases.

CI/CRM FIGURE-EIGHT CONTINUOUS CYCLE

Customer intelligence management has been referenced but not yet differentiated from customer relationship management. Because the two are not the same, they will now be discussed. Figure 17.1 helps illustrate the differences and will aid in our understanding of how business software tools facilitate customer-focused processes:

- **Customer intelligence (CI).** This is the internal, company-facing repository of data used to determine and analyze customer segments and then used to formulate strategies in order to satisfy and retain *each* customer segment. *Analysis* is the key word. CI is an internal process for truly understanding who your customers are and what they want from you. CI anticipates their needs. The results of CI are then put into action by CRM. CI leverages data warehousing and data mining tools for data extraction, reorganizing, and analysis.

- **Customer relationship management (CRM).** These are the operational methods and tools, such as *marketing campaigns*, to interact with customers and new sales prospects regardless of the communication channel. CRM and CI bi-directionally feed each other input data in a continuous figure-eight cycle, as illustrated in Figure 17.1. Operational CRM generates transactional data that feed input to CI (as well as do other systems). Analytical CI then converts this data into actionable business information that becomes the input to operational CRM for further customer interactions or communications.

An objective for operational CRM is to ensure that customers enjoy consistently good experiences to increase their loyalty and the likelihood that they will purchase again from you—and possibly refer your business to others. That is, the goal is to forge long-term relationships with customers by consistently delivering exceptional service and tailored products for repeat business and referrals. *Consistent* treatment of customers is a key descriptor because customers can become finicky and impatient with one poor experience (i.e., below their ever-rising expectations), causing them to explore alternative providers—competitors.

The "Start Here" symbol at the bottom of Figure 17.1 represents the initial

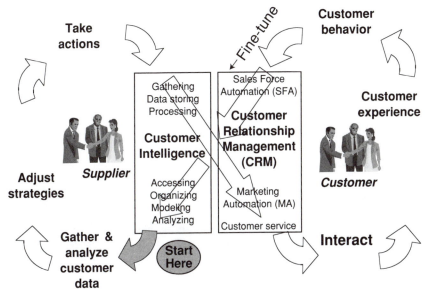

Figure 17.1   Analytical CI and Operational CRM

analysis of customers. This presumes that much customer data has already been collected and is easily data-mined. The arrows reveal the iterative process cycle, shown in the shape of a figure eight. Much of the customer data in the *back office* CI (analytical CRM) side is typically captured in the right-side operational CRM. This explains why the figure-eight loop operates as a continuous cycle.

The cycle starts with analyzing customer data to synthesize and distill patterns. After that, marketing analysts formulate strategies that are tailored to the various microsegments of customers and are obviously intended to motivate customers to continue purchasing the supplier's goods and services. The next steps involve mobilizing the organization to execute the strategies; this can range from new product development programs to new value-added services that support existing products and service lines.

The process cycle next crosses into the *front-office* CRM domain, where the customer is *touched* and feedback about their responses is collected. Powerful sales force automation, marketing automation, and customer service tools are applied here:

- **Sales force automation.** Think of this as a salesperson's traditional business card Rolodex, contact directory, and sales pipeline forecasts, but now completely automated with much more data. Sales force automation helps manage the life cycle of every sales opportunity to its success-ful conclusion. It allows for managing the sales pipeline and funnel to better forecast when actual sales events will occur, remove administra-tive work by automating routine tasks, and empower a sales team with call-tracking history and relevant intelligence about prospects and customers.

These tools also include contact management, proposal management, quote generators, and sales lead and order tracking. When combined with a CI (analytical CRM) tool, this provides a single gathering point to enable a unified view of each customer for all employees. Conversely, it also pro-vides each salesperson (e.g., a bank loan officer) an automated book of their accounts.

- **Marketing automation and optimization.** These tools aid in profiling customers based on dozens of characteristics (e.g., preferences, buying be-havior, purchasing frequency, recency of purchase, and demographics). The tools are not based on marketing theory but rather on actual customer behavior, as research has demonstrated that good indicators of a customer's future behavior is their past behavior and their profile. After the CI formu-lated data has been collected, *marketing automation* tools then push out each campaign, survey, or contest to customers and prospects, as well as re-ceive and analyze the responses. With advanced marketing automation tools, customer responses can be anticipated. Personalized messages, po-tentially with offers or incentives to purchase or act, can be immediately pushed back to the customer. *Marketing automation* tools go a step further by maximizing profit by balancing the customer's likeliness to purchase with the organization's ability to deliver, including its channel's capacity constraints or its operation's capacity or planned offer inventories. These tools are also foundational to customer loyalty programs, such as airline frequent flyer programs.

- **Customer interaction centers.** Call centers are today's factories for ser-vicing customers. Everyone has received unsolicited marketing phone calls or toggled through an automated answering system to receive online help service from a person. With the addition of a CI (analytical CRM) tool, call center employees are enabled to not only interact more effectively with a customer, but to also expand their service call into a sales call raising the top line. As mentioned earlier, leveraging and finessing a customer-initiated inbound interaction to push a campaign message has been recognized by marketers as being substantially more effective than traditional outbound marketing campaign solicitations.

These tools, when combined, provide for interactions through all communi-cation channels—e-mail, call centers, mailing brochures, advertisements, newsletters, and so on. These are all *touch points* with customers and prospects. Every channel can engage the customer with a dynamically personalized and compelling experience by leveraging marketing, sales, and customer support. Each interaction is an opportunity to gain knowledge about customer prefer-ences—and to strengthen the relationship. I touched earlier on the perils of cus-tomers and sales targets receiving inconsistent messages. The problem is that each of the communication channels may unknowingly use their own customer intelligence data to interact with a customer without realizing that a *different* message may be being delivered to the *same* customer via another communica-tion channel. A common CI system provides the foundation to integrate with and feed all of an organization's different communication channels. This then provides a *consistent* personalized message from the receiver's view—consis-tent across all channels.

CI/CR CODEPENDENCIES

With the analytical/operational CI/CRM tools working in harmony, customers' responses triggered from marketing campaigns can be individually tracked and compared against their anticipated reactions. With e-mail or call center cam-paigns, the analysis of customer responses can be timely and so sophisticated that the marketing campaign itself, with all customer response traffic monitored on the supplier's computer servers or Web site, can be modified within hours or days following the start of the campaign. This is noted with the "Fine-tune" ar-row in the figure where iterative learning over time increases the effectiveness and response levels of future interactions. In addition, preliminary trials with control groups can also be tested to refine the marketing campaign prior to its full rollout. There can be dozens of parallel campaigns, each tailored to its spe-cific customers' microsegment.

The level of sophistication of marketing campaigns can be mind-boggling. The appeal from *behavior-tracking technology* is tantalizing to marketers. By monitoring and analyzing customer behaviors, it becomes immediately appar-ent when any statistically sensitive deviations or changes from normal behavior take place. An example would be, customer inactivity which may signal attri-tion. When this *event trigger* technology is combined with intelligence derived from data mining, a company has powerful intelligence to use when interacting with a customer to re-alter their shopping behavior. The communication may be in *real time*, or it may be *right time* where a delay is more appropriate; and the customer interaction can be via any communication channel, possibly inbound or outbound. Additional event triggers may include lifetime events, such as marriages or school graduations, that may be anticipated or reported from other sources. In short, CI/CRM tools provide a single, unified view—a comprehensive, cohesive, and centralized view of a customer—that can dynamically adjust based on feedback.

Good CI and CRM helps organizations make smarter decisions faster. A work flow or business process without the ability to measure, analyze, and improve its effectiveness simply perpetuates a problem. In sum, CI and CRM allow end-to-end functionality from sales lead management to order tracking—potentially seamlessly. CI includes data warehouses that are used by analytical applications that dissect the data and present it in a form that is useful; and CRM executes CI's plans.

Returning to Figure 17.1, the process cycle then flows continuously as a figure eight. The feedback about customer behavior—whether in response to a marketing campaign or as monitored consumer preferences—crosses back into the analytical CI domain, where that data is again gathered and analyzed for the next reformulation of strategies. Dozens of campaigns and strategies of different magnitudes can continuously and concurrently cycle with this CI/CRM process. Each campaign may target a unique promotion to a particular niche market.

To summarize, the main codependencies between CI and CRM are these:

- CI systems are analytical and need to extract from the front-office operational CRM systems data useful for analysis (e.g., customer, transactional, and third party data). Ideally, CI drives CRM.

- CRM systems need to surface the intelligence generated from the analytical CI systems to be more effective and actually make use of the derived intelligence.

Data Mining Analytical Tools Discern the Relevant Information

Customer relationship management (CRM) systems are intended to aid an organization in optimizing value and satisfaction for its customers through the methods that the organization uses to communicate with them, sell to them, and service them. Through integration, customer intelligence and customer relationship management (CI/CRM) allow marketing, sales, and service employees to coordinate as they plan, gather data, track events, and organize

Data Mining Analytical Tools Discern
the Relevant Information *(Continued)*

themselves from presales to postsales for both prospects and existing customers. Unfortunately, typical operational CRM software tools lack the necessary analytical rigor, defaulting to an emphasis on collecting data and displaying standard sales reports (e.g., sales pipeline) or popular marketing parameters (e.g., customer's last purchase date, sales amount, and purchasing frequency).

Progressive CI/CRM tools with powerful data mining functions provide much more business intelligence. The analytical CI system facilitates the integration of the front-office, customer-facing CRM systems to ensure coordination and sharing of a consistent message. That is, data from multiple communication channels can be consolidated to create CI for each customer or microsegment, and then the analytical CI system can formulate and push the appropriate intelligence into the front-office CRM channels.

For example, imagine that a company enjoys a surge in sales. What really made the difference? A price reduction? A new display? The timing being a holiday weekend? A new advertisement? A competitor's price increase? With excessively clustered segmentation and broad-brushed averages, marketers can be deceived by inferring causal relations with coincidences. But with today's data mining software and transactional detail, marketers can discern cross-effects. Simple statistical regression analysis models examining price/volume change elasticity relationships can be analytically upgraded with mixed modeling techniques that explore dozens of variables. These can generate predictions about the impact of a specific marketing event on specific products or services at a particular store or branch.

By analyzing more granular microsegments and subpopulations that reveal relatively greater differentiation, not only can more predictable outcomes be forecasted, but the relevant variables may not be necessarily demographic (e.g., age, income level, gender) but rather nontraditional (e.g., the source of the initial purchase, time of day when purchased).

Averaging can introduce problems. For a new product rollout, a retailer's national advertising and promotion budget should not be distributed evenly to accounts across the nation. Obviously, you shouldn't try to sell diapers if your store is located across the street from a Toys 'R Us retail store. One answer does not work everywhere. With data mining tools, you can minimize missing opportunities to stock products or launch promotions at a subset of stores or to a subset of customers (not just demographically segmented). Conversely, you can prevent overstocking where there is less likelihood of demand.

INTEGRATING CUSTOMER PROFITABILITY WITH CI/CRM

Acquiring and retaining customers must eventually be recognized as an organization's most important *core* process. A key to releasing the value of CI/CRM lies in differentiating your products and services in relation to the existing or future levels of profitability of each customer segment. A key assumption must be that all customers are not created equal. If a company does not know the current or potential profitability of its customers, then it is likely misallocating its scarce and valuable resources. Very profitable customers may be underserved while less profitable ones are receiving too much effort and attention.

Managing customers with a gut-feel based on intuition can lead toward assuming that increasing sales volume equates to success. Having a way to value different types of customers is a powerful tool to develop customer-centric strategies and subsequently determine with what level of priority and effort to engage each customer segment.

Based on customer analysis, CI/CRM transforms customer expectations into personalized experiences to acquire, retain, and service customers—and on a large scale. Real-time automated customer response analysis, regardless of the touch points, means quick yet tailored adjustments to marketing campaigns. But CI/CRM is not free. Where are the ROI cutoffs? Furthermore, given that an organization has scarce finite resources, then the benefits of effort should ideally exceed the costs of interactions. Therefore, an organization would do better to focus its energies on building economic value for its shareholders by serving the needs of the more profitable and potentially profitable customers. In a sense, these customers are the partners selected to grow the supplier's business and wealth creation.

What ABM adds for CI/CRM are key elements of information usually neglected or excluded from CI/CRM systems:

- What level of absolute and relative profit contribution does the customer provide today and potentially in the future?
- What actionable steps can economically increase each customer's profit contribution margin layer for high payback?
- How are we doing on what is important? Is the direct marketing and customer planning for a specific customer worth it?

Conversely, operational CRM systems can aid ABM since they already capture customer transactional interactions, so they can be extended to integrate with ABM. But unfortunately, operational CRM, like many evolving methodologies, is a constant target of criticism. Cynicism in the form of humor is usually a precursor to the improvements that fix shortcomings. Some of the sarcastic alternative definitions of the CRM acronym are "costs reams of money," "causes real migraines," and "can't really matter." Traditional CI/CRM's weak treatment of incorporating financial profitability into its analysis is an example of CI/CRM's shortcomings.

A CRM system may give its users misleading information. Without the facts, system users may conclude that their best customers are the biggest spenders. With ABM and profitability data, companies are routinely surprised to learn that key accounts can erode product or service line margins with excessive customer support, customization requests, and other hidden costs. This means a supplier's customers with large sales may be unprofitable! And customers potentially like them may be attracted by a sales force that lacks an appreciation of the large hidden costs that they can trigger.

Good customer profitability information leads to clearer thinking about where to allocate one's limited resources. For example, with CI/CRM systems, companies will experiment with customer communication programs designed for certain effects. However, if, for example, a company's revised direct mail campaign attracts teenagers or pension-dependent senior citizens instead of the targeted affluent market, then the campaign's follow-up costs may never be recovered from revenues. An ABM customer profitability system detects problems like these. A company's total revenues might be increasing, but are they the right kind of revenues? Perhaps not, if the incremental costs exceed the incremental revenues.

Regardless of whether the focus is on the top line (sales) or middle line (costs), profitability measured by each customer (or customer segment) is becoming critical. It is inevitable that customer profitability reporting will become standard reporting. Customer profitability reporting, enabled by ABM, brings marketing, sales, operations, and accounting together to analyze and improve customer profitability. By using customer profitability data, the demarcation lines for ROI cutoffs can be drawn, and the CI/CRM systems can stop wasting employee time and the company's scarce resources on types of customers that are not worth the effort it takes to pursue them. This doesn't mean making foolish decisions about customers. Analytical CI systems should be designed to send into the operational CRM systems customer intelligence *derived from the profitability data*. So, for example, a bank teller should not say to a customer, "You've got a low profit score, so therefore I cannot waive your service charge," but rather, "I'm sorry. I can't waive your service charge."

Without measures of customer profitability in CI/CRM systems, proclamations about CRM and customer value management strategies are, at best, statements of good intentions. One should not construct one-to-one customer propositions, a CRM tactic, unless one understands the profits and profit potentials of individual customers and their expected behavior from the proposition. Beware of unintended consequences. CRM systems are a promising start but not the final bell. Without the measure of customer profitability, CRM systems have not fulfilled their potential.

Without customer profitability data, the team using a CI/CRM system may potentially be investing greater effort and resources which, even if successful, may also be permanently unprofitable. For example, the sales function can possibly be selling more, earning higher commissions, yet producing lower overall profits. How? As we learned in Part Three, this can result if the mix the sales force is selling shifts from profitable to less profitable (or unprofitable) products and services. At a minimum, ABM provides data to prioritize where sales efforts should be invested.

Companies who already have ABM cost measurements can advance their application of CRM to determine if a customer is spending, or will spend, enough on the right items to warrant a higher marketing effort. Alternatively, an ABM-enabled supplier can adjust its marketing effort, including its level of marketing expenses, to optimize the expected profit from a customer segment—not more or less than is needed to maximize the return.

So why should ABM be combined with CI\CRM? CRM systems are extremely customer-centric, whereas ABM is work-centric. CRM cares about customer feelings and preferences. ABM pays attention to how product and customer diversity both require and consume greater resources. In isolation, operational CRM provides a partial picture. When combined with ABM, CI/CRM gives a fuller picture. This allows a change in mind-set for the marketers to rebuild customer behaviors on a foundation of fact.

Together, ABM and customer profitability analysis provide a basis for managerial decision making and actions. The information available from these methods is essential to attain corporate goals and strategies and to increase profitability. The company can diagnose, understand, and alter its programs' costs. As a bonus from analyzing customer profitability, the costs of poorly designed internal processes can be highlighted with the likelihood of removing profit-harming effects otherwise undetected. Customer relationship management systems without ABM are limited.

The success of ABM and customer profitability reporting systems can be measured as much by the employee awareness these systems raise as by the decisions and actions they directly affect. The analysis, discussion, and understanding of the drivers of customer-related costs can motivate managers to improve their own performance.

CUSTOMER VALUE MEASUREMENT
USING CUSTOMER LIFETIME VALUE

A superior method than measuring last period's ABM-calculated customer profitability is to think of each customer as an investment with its own ROI. This math gets trickier than measuring customer profitability levels because, just like with an investment portfolio, you need to consider factors other than what did happen. These factors include the following:

- The cost of acquiring different types of customers.
- The projections of *each* future period's revenues less assignable costs (i.e., net profit) for *each* customer (i.e., profit contribution growth rates).
- The cost of capital (this implies that a discounted cash flow [DCF] equation is used).
- Estimates of customer *churn*—customers who abandon a company for a competitors; substitutions; complete terminations; or customers who rejoin a company (i.e., customer retention time).

With these factors, by using DCF math, you can equate the future stream of net cash flow (profits) into a single cash amount (i.e., the *expected value*) of profit stated in today's money. This amount is called *net present value* (NPV), and it is derived from the span of a customer relationship beginning today to a future point in time (e.g., ten years forward). This single NPV amount is called the *customer lifetime value* (CLV). CLV is the sum of the profits to be received from a customer (or customer segment), discounted for the future of that cash in the future, measured over the life of the relationship with that customer. CLV is appealing in theory and principle. It is a predictive exercise based on modeling.

CLV's forward-looking view can reduce risks from focusing on the existing rate of profits from various customer segments. For example, a retailer may have two customers with the same current profit level. However, if one is a young dentist growing a successful practice and the other is approaching retirement, then their future potential profitability will obviously be diverging.

CLV's usefulness comes from varying its parameters to see the outcomes in financial terms of wealth. Additional usefulness of CLV is that it can shift an organization's focus from the short-term stock price management toward long-term payback efforts to manage the variables for *each* customer segment: the acquisition investment, profit contribution level and growth rate, as well as retention time. This way each customer can be considered as an investment, with potential to manage its ROI.

Calculating Customer Lifetime Value: A Primer

To better understand customer lifetime value (CLV), let's look at a hypothetical CLV equation. The top equation in Figure 17A shows CLV for an *existing* individual buying unit[a] (e.g., consumers, household, a customer company), say for a five-year planning horizon.

Individual Buying Unit
(e.g., consumer, household, customer company)

CLV = Net Present Value (for each *existing* customer) =

  (direct profit from base service) x (probability still a customer)

  + (incremental profit from additional services) x (probability customer chooses)

  + (variable profit from items/services purchased) x (est. volume & mix purchased)

  + (probability of default on bill) x (est. account balance defaulted)

  + sum of [(cost for free services) x (est. # of free services used)]

Enterprise CLV

CLV =

  the acquisition cost of *new* customers

  + sum of [CLV of all existing customers]

  + sum of [CLV of all new customers]

Figure 17A   Customer Lifetime Value Equations

In this one equation, the significant components of a customer relationship—revenues, expenses, and customer demand behavior—are comprised in a single measure. Further, the equation includes pricing, costs of products and services, credit risk, customer retention rates, and up-selling.

The appeal of CLV includes these facets:

- It focuses on the customer as the influencer of a company's profitability rather than the products and service lines (although they are included in the CLV equation).

- It does not include the prior *sunk cost* incurred when originally acquiring the customer, nor the past profit contribution levels of the specific customer. It strictly looks forward in time.

Calculating Customer Lifetime Value: A Primer *(Continued)*

- It includes probabilities. These will obviously introduce some errors, but unless there is a bias, error in individual customer segments will average out and offset in the enterprise-wide total CLV.
- The planning horizon can be limited to two to six years. With discounted cash flow's (DCF) *net present value,* the impact of time on the *expected value* quickly diminishes beyond the fifth or sixth year out. Regardless, most marketing programs should be examined for these shorter terms.

The top equation in the figure was for existing customers. In the lower equation for prospective new customers, the cost of acquiring the prospect has been added to the equation. (The same principles of ABM tracing shared expenses would apply.) Also, the sum of all existing and new customers is combined to compute an enterprise-wide CLV value. This number can be analyzed on a stand-alone basis as well as trend-analyzed over time.

---

[a]CLV can be calculated for an individual buying unit or a grouping or segment of similar customers. However, the greater the segmentation, the more visible will be differences and impact from different programs, mixes, and customer drivers. Hence, there is more information to slice and dice.

For an in-depth discussion on measuring and applying customer lifetime value measures, go to www.wiley.com/go/performance.

PREDICTIVE CUSTOMER LIFETIME VALUE VERSUS ACTUAL (HISTORICAL) CUSTOMER PROFITABILITY

ABM adaptors have proven they can repeatedly and reliably report and score customer profitability information. The benefits with actual customer profitability reporting come from the insights managers and analysts gain by comparing profiles of customers with varying degrees of profitability. This information alone may be sufficient to formulate new marketing strategies and to budget future marketing spending for higher payback.

However, the current sources of customer profitability do not necessarily make an entirely reliable predictor of future customer profitability. The predictive thinking involved with adjusting the parameters in the predictive CLV model (combined with ABM and ABP customer profitability model) is where the true value of CLV resides.

NEXT-GENERATION CUSTOMER RELATIONSHIP MANAGEMENT: A COMPETITIVE EDGE

In the past, competition has been based primarily on products, whether they are tangible ones, from manufacturers, or intangible ones, like an auto loan, from service providers. But now there is a higher form of competition coming in the future, beyond just selling products. For suppliers to retain customers for life, it will be essential that they collaborate in some form that is mutually beneficial to their customers, their employees, and their shareholders.

Many believe that with today's integrated information tools, suppliers have realized that superior service, speed, and convenience are the key to retaining customers and increasing market share. However, acceleration in new product development and innovation are powering every company's competitors' ability to achieve service, speed, and convenience. So it is a race.

The real challenge for suppliers is to find different and additional ways to create customer value. Lots of people talk about this, but few have discovered what it takes. Some competitors will add value by focusing on the *customer's experience*. This will apply somewhat less when commodities are purchased, but even those purchases can be spiced with an experience. Adding value to a customer's purchasing experience requires a deep understanding of what a customer values. Very few companies or consultants have moved into this territory. Strategy consultants rarely touch this area and prefer to stick to giving traditional marketing advice. Consumer product companies may not know the ultimate consumer's psyche.

In the end, services will be added to products, and unique services will be tailored to individuals. To relate back to PM, strategy maps and scorecards will guide the marketing functions. Obvious KPIs will be retention rates, acquisition rates, customer satisfaction levels, transaction volume, credit risk occurrence, fraud occurrence, current customer profitability, and customer lifetime value. ABM data will be essential to validate and prioritize the financial merits of *which* services to add and for *which* customers. ABM data will also be essential for a supplier's host system, with rule-based costing and profit margin acceptance testing capabilities, to influence customer demand in a way that is in harmony with the supplier's existing cost structure.

CRM systems are intended to ensure that customer satisfaction is addressed so that true customer value is provided. Enterprise resource planning (ERP) and advanced planning systems (APS) are intended to ensure that good execution and organizational effectiveness are present. PM strategy maps and scorecards are intended to ensure that the work of employees aligns with senior management's strategies. But it takes ABM data to ultimately compute key leading performance indicator measures that ensure that shareholder value and wealth are being created.

ABM data are foundational. They measure whether customers are consuming more resources than they are paying for, and ABM points employees to opportunities for improvements and corrective actions.

CI/CRM, SHAREHOLDER WEALTH CREATION, AND ABM

ABM is a complement to CRM systems, with compelling benefits. It enables a company to draw a more complete picture of its customers. This is key to understanding what to do with a customer and how much to do it.

Possibly even more important, ABM links CRM to shareholder value, which is heralded as essential for economic value management. This will be discussed in Chapter 20. The true tug-of-war is now becoming clear. It is the trade-off between adding more value for customers but at the risk of reducing wealth to shareholders. Not enough people realize how important this link is that connects customer value with shareholder value. ABM will serve as the weighing scale, in the form of a calculator, to help companies measure the trade-offs. ABM and its customer profitability (and its advanced CLV view) link each customer to the shareholders as if each customer is an investment. CI/CRM systems are designed to then grow those investments. These issues are the topics of the next chapter.

NOTES

1. Steve Skinner, *CRM*, January/February 2003, 47.

2. Paul Greenberg, *CRM at the Speed of Light* (Berkeley, CA: McGraw-Hill/Osborne, 2002), 8.

3. For example, see SAS Value Chain Analyzer at www.sas.com.

18

SUPPLIER INTELLIGENCE
Managing Economic Profit across the Value Chain

"Today the cost department of the average business is looked on as a right arm of first importance in management. Without the cost department today 90 percent of our businesses would be out of existence. . . . The cost department of the future is going to have more effect on the business and on the general management of business than any other single department. . . . And, gentlemen, in my opinion the major portion of the work of the cost department of the future is going to be applying recognized principles of cost analysis to sales expenses, for there is the greatest evil in present-day industry, the high cost, the extravagant, outrageous cost, of distribution."[1]

—James H. Rand, President,
Remington Rand Company, 1921

For the past 20 years, many managers have viewed the functions comprising their value chain as a mysterious black hole that moved and shuffled boxes and was best avoided. Any other area of management was more exciting. Executives have found greater appeal in programs such as total quality management starring six sigma, lean operations with just-in-time (JIT) practices, and, of course, enterprise resource planning systems (ERP), the latest wave of promise. The value chain had not been a hot topic up until now. With hindsight, the value chain now reveals itself to be a patchwork of centuries-old business practices fraught with redundancies and inefficiencies. Now that excess manufacturing costs are viewed as having been nearly squeezed to the last few drops, and service delivery times are increasing in importance, management's attention has been shifting to value chain management.

This chapter will focus on measuring interfirm cost behavior between the many pairs of buyer/seller trading partner relationships that collectively add up to the cost behavior across the extended value chain. But before diving into issues involved with measuring costs and collaborative relationships, let's first discuss broader value chain initiatives.

VALUE CHAIN INTELLIGENCE

Optimizing an organization's value chain begins with understanding customer demand. Consider this observation: In the value chain there is only one independent decision being made, and all of the other thousands of decisions are dependent ones. What is that single independent decision? It is the ultimate end-consumer choosing to exchange his money with a purchase. Subsequent to that, all stick replenishment and service decisions, loaded with production and logistics decisions, are governed. This is so profound that it makes me wonder why the term *supply chain management* was not initially coined as *demand chain management*.

The performance management (PM) tools are enablers for the value chain intelligence suite of solutions. This solutions suite includes demand planning, inventory replenishment planning, price optimization, and *spend* management:

- **Demand planning.** Reliable forecasting is the key. Statistically sound large-scale demand forecasts serve as a foundation for all levels of business planning. Effective forecasting tools dynamically adjust to irregular demand series and also take into account the impact of sales promotions. This must be done for every item at every level of detail because one shortage can prevent an assembled product. Hence the need for a large-scale forecasting system. A strong competency in demand planning provides the foundation for demand creation—generating higher profits with customer-influencing techniques.

- **Inventory replenishment.** Using reliable forecasts, economic-aware replenishment strategies are the key. That is, desired levels of service are blended with alternative rules or policies for different types of items, such as between repeatedly ordered, fast-moving items or their opposite types. Replenishments ideally should be planned by categories, often down to the item-by-item plans; and multiscenario analysis should allow exploration and comparison of different options. Here detail is needed because sometimes you have to get close down to the bottom where the dirt crops up. That is not to say that summaries by item categories won't provide useful insights. They will, but detail is useful. The goal is to optimally meet expected demand at lowest cost with maximum service levels. I like to humorously think of this replenishment as "It isn't distribution if items aren't moving."

- **Price optimization.** Just look to the airline industry for how they dynamically adjust prices up to the last hour before a scheduled flight takes off. Of course, an empty seat on an airplane is an opportunity for profit lost forever because their unused capacity becomes immediately perishable at lift-off. But product-making and service-providing companies must still consider the effects of unused and available capacity as well as the restricting impact of physically constrained resources, whether they be workers or equipment. Understanding customer preferences and price elasticity is the key. Effective customer management systems can leverage intelligence from historical patterns and adjust the patterns from newly collected data.

- **Spend management.** All companies spend money, but few are really good at it. Poor spend visibility, poor sourcing, and poor contract compliance are symptoms. Having a complete and auditable view of all spending with each supplier is key to driving volume discounts on price and other negotiated concessions. However, organizations with multiple diverse purchasing systems, often a result of a binge of acquisitions, can rarely have a single aggregated view of the spend volume, at the item level, with each of their suppliers.

  Maverick spending and poor data integrity complicates matters, including cases where there are multiple part numbers for the *identical* physical part. Short-term approaches to gather "low hanging fruit" savings are nice starts, but not enough to maximize buying leverage. Effective spend management systems scrub, cleanse, filter, classify, and unify large-scale purchasing data, including forecasts of purchases, to optimize their supply base management. Supplier contracts with volume discounts from suppliers can be negotiated once you have the facts.

PM tools in the value chain suite of solutions shifts a company's objectives to longer horizons, and they broaden its perspective from minimizing silo-based costs to maximizing customer value. There are interdependencies among the value chain suite of solutions described above. For example, forecasting is an input to replenishment decisions. Software vendors now offer the tight integration of this suite of solutions. The challenge is for companies to gain proficiency in applying them.

VALUE CHAIN ANALYTICS LEVERAGING ABM PRINCIPLES

A recently published Consumer Goods Technology/AMR Research Tech Trends Report reveals the two most pressing issues for companies are the pressures to reduce overall supply chain costs and to collaborate more effectively with trading partners. With so many steps across the supply chain, it is challenging enough to quantify the costs and profitability of one's own supply chain, let alone measure the effects caused by one's trading partners. But it is becoming necessary. What is needed is *financial transparency*—to see beyond the price a vendor charges and understand its cost behavior, as well as to understand how high-maintenance customers erode profits due to their work-demanding requirements. Because supply chains are now so tightly integrated, understanding both costs and the behavioral issues of resistance to collaboration is now critical. This chapter discusses both topics.

The term *collaboration* has been heralded as a key pillar to successful supply and value chain management. Many believe, however, that due to centuries of mistrust, collaboration between sellers and buyers is more shallow talk than action. In pre-Biblical times, if a buyer felt he had been ripped off when buying a camel or a goat, he never trusted a seller again. Those same feelings of buyers have been passed down through the generations. But now everyone is realizing it is no longer sufficient for your own company alone to be agile, lean, and efficient—you are dependent on your suppliers and customers both up and down your value chain to also be like you. Otherwise, they drag down service and reduce the entire value chain's profit with their extra costs. Therefore, regardless of this mistrust with historical adversarial relationships, collaboration is now becoming an important consideration because trading partners in value chains have substantial codependencies as well as mutual excess costs they can jointly remove—if and when they can identify them.

A key question, however, involves whether collaboration is more lip service than action. How do you get trading partners to genuinely collaborate when they mistrust each other? When is the appropriate time to collaborate? These are the questions discussed here, as well as how a company can attain financial transparency of the costs of its trading partners—its suppliers and customers.

Wherever a supplier is located in its supply and value chain, one can view *each* trading partner participating in the value chain as having a vested interest in a reasonably high level of productivity and effective performance exhibited by *all* the other participants in the chain. By working together in a collaborative manner, trading partners can collectively behave as an extended enterprise. They should ideally perform together as if they were one company. We are no longer in a what-is-good-for-me-is-bad-for-you era of business. Instead, in the future the emphasis will be "One team, one mission."

Genuine collaboration between buying and selling trading partners can be stimulated when suppliers and customers share open-book profit and cost data. Much better and more collaboration than we experience today can result when suppliers use data management and analytical tools, like activity-based management (ABM), specially designed to support analysis of value chain economics. However, there will be a sequence of events that will lead to earnest collaboration. Value chain analytical data initially provides companies with insights to their own cost behavior as well as *financial transparency* of their trading partners. Companies will eventually collaborate when they are ready—after they understand the cost dynamics occurring at their buyer/seller interfaces. Value chain analysis provides companies with that needed financial transparency to see where the adjacent costs lie *across* the value chain, and it provides them a competitive edge when they can use that knowledge to their advantage. But eventually they will leverage their value chain analysis (VCA) with their trading partners. That is, ultimately collaboration will occur when two or more trading partners jointly use *shared* data to seek programs, initiatives, or changes with mutual benefits.

Good costing methods, not flawed arbitrary cost allocations, can provide companies with boardroom-level information about how profitable each customer is to the supplier, and vice-versa. Applying a progressive approach to cost measurement of the value chain also delivers financial intelligence for companies to better understand the costs of their customers, suppliers, products, and processes as they move through complex distribution systems.

VCA can be used for internal studies as well as to provide two or more trading partners with a common costing methodology to objectively and *jointly* examine their mutual costs attributed to moving products across their shared value chain. This analysis in turn facilitates removing wasteful activities by applying trade-off analysis and what-if scenario analysis. In short, financial intelligence from transactional data transformed into managerial information is intended for focusing, initiating dialog, and ultimately generating higher financial returns. VCA can be applied internally across a company's complex postproduction distribution network as well as jointly with one's own external customers.

The pipeline across all the suppliers in the chain will continue to be filled and flow with inventory. Like a frictionless plane, a more synchronized, continuous flow of materials is more economical. It wastes less energy, which equates to less cost. Speed of material throughput, service, and information is becoming the rule of business. But today, a myriad of suppliers, customers, products, services, and transactions make managing the supply chain more complex than ever; and now managing also includes the information related to the inventory.

While technical advancements have created *more* of everything, including the opportunity to increase revenues, new challenges have also arisen. For example, organizations have extensive inventories to track and move, a greater number of new products to design and existing ones to make, quality issues to worry about, numerous suppliers to conduct business with, and finally, an ever-increasing need to acquire, retain, and satisfy customers in order to remain profitable.

To manage their value chains better, companies are using operational and transactional systems to collect data about each link in the chain. These systems are effective at producing data, but not at providing the knowledge needed to formulate decisions that maximize profits and make firms more competitive. Companies are deluged with data, but are no closer to the truth or relevancy.

INSIGHTS TO PROFITS AND COSTS ACROSS THE VALUE CHAIN

It is a fact of life that trading partners routinely create costs for each other. These costs are usually not intentional but are assumed to be just part of doing business. These unneeded costs are like that friction that slows the rate of profits. Figure 18.1 illustrates how the value chain includes multiple trading partners both upstream and downstream. Organizations must consider their linkages across the chain and their interdependencies.

Figure 18.1 demonstrates that the complexity of a supply chain requires considerable thought about selecting performance metrics and measuring costs. The supply chain is presented as a root-tree-branch scheme where the roots are the suppliers and the branches are the customers. Managers will increasingly require an understanding of what each potential supply chain means from an economic standpoint, including both profits and costs.

As the business-to-business (B2B) buyer and seller better understand their relationships at their interfacing touch points, then improved work flows—sometimes called *stickiness*—enabled with joint technologies will generate benefits. They will also tighten relationships and improve overall customer retention.

As an example, a customer requests that one of its suppliers deliver goods five days per week. What would occur if the customer could get by with deliveries on only three days per week? The effect would be that the customer's change in its ordering habits would save the supplier considerable time and effort. In another example, consider a purchasing agent who is required to physically examine and process a supplier's paperwork. What if that administrative paperwork could be

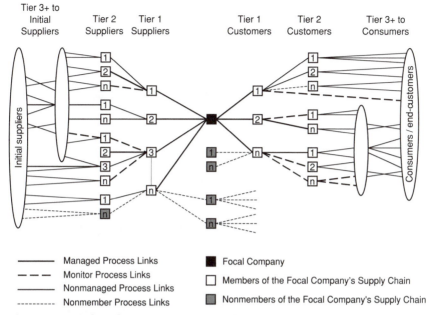

Figure 18.1   Value Chain Management Involves Linkages

Source: Adapted from Douglas M. Lambert, Martha C. Cooper, James D. Pugh, "Supply Chain Management: Implementation Issues and Research Opportunities," *International Journal of Logistics Management,* Vol. 9, No. 2, 1998, p. 2.

handled electronically (or be reduced, or not even required)? The effect would be that *both* parties might save time and effort—and ultimately save costs.

COLLABORATION CAN SOLVE A LOT OF SINS

How can redundancies and excesses be eliminated? One way to encourage collaboration between trading partners is for each partner to better understand how it affects the other's cost structure. Better yet, consider the benefits if *all* trading partners could credibly measure the cost impact that they create among themselves. Reliable measures can foster better communications, analysis, and understanding about how trading partners might *collectively* reduce costs.

There is a challenge, however. Altering trading partner behavior requires supplier/customer trust. Businesses have been wary of releasing information to trading partners even when that information will aid in mutual understanding—and one place where disclosure is needed is regarding an organization's cost structure. Since VCA and ABM systems are more user-friendly and useful than traditional accounting, trading partners are more motivated to collaborate in using the data as a form of open-book management to stimulate discovery of opportunities.

As trading partners remove the walls blocking sight of the others' costs and create financial transparency, they can better measure and understand how they create costs for each other. They can begin thinking about how to help each other reduce their collective costs. Trust in others must be well placed. Good collaboration leads to high-fidelity relationships. This chapter delves deeper into measuring interfirm profits and costs across the value chain, taking out unnecessary expenses, and freeing up capacity to serve better purposes.

THE INTERNET IS CHANGING EVERYTHING

Let's back up to understand the forces that are creating pressure on profits. First and foremost is the Internet. The Internet is shifting power from sellers to buyers—irreversibly. Search engines and greater and faster data access are prevalent among purchasing agents. The ability for the buyer to access knowledge and information about products is unbounded. Ironically, suppliers are assisting in the shift of power to buyers. How? Suppliers are providing increasingly more information about their products and services via their Web sites. As a result, the pressure on a supplier's pricing is immense. These pressures are not restricted to be between companies but they also exist among internal divisions *within* a company. Competition among businesses can get so blurry that business units in the same company can be customers, partners, and competitors. The inherent competition increasingly lies between different value chains selling different products. *Share of wallet* is displacing *market share* as a measure of business growth success. In short, it is the entire value chain that now requires scrutiny.

To complicate matters, as products increasingly become viewed as commodities, the importance of services rises. That is, as differentiation from product advantages is reduced or neutralized, the customer relationship grows in importance. There is an unarguable shift from product-driven differentiation to service-based differentiation. Services include the manner in which goods are moved and delivered. Strategists all agree that differentiation is a key to competitive advantage. In short, the increasing desire by different types of customer segments for unique requirements is forcing suppliers to respond with increasing flexibility. Of course, all of this extra effort and service comes with additional costs that can adversely impact profits.

Another problem involves pricing. How can a supplier or retailer know on which products to raise prices that will stick? And even more importantly, when you are operating at razor-thin profit margins, as with distributors and retailers, how many selling prices are unknowingly set at less than the product's market-landed cost—therefore at a loss rather than a profit?

In short, as widely varying customization and tailoring for different customer segments becomes widespread, how will value chain manufacturers, distributors, and retailers distinguish profitable customers or customer segments from unprofitable ones? And once known, what actions should they take to improve profitability based on this new knowledge?

Consumers and purchasing agents are becoming excellent at comparison shopping. For example, they typically perform exhaustive searches to identify the exact model of an appliance they want. After identifying which model they want, next they will search the Internet to locate the lowest price sources for their purchase. The Internet has shortened these shopping and buying experiences from days to minutes. Despite all of the dot-com dot-bomb hoopla, competition will continue to award consumers long-run savings generated from new technologies in the form of lower prices. That's economics at work. However, with the Internet leveling the playing field, suppliers, regardless of their size, will no longer be capable of protecting a niche market or enjoying as large or as long-lasting profit margins as they had in the past.

PRESSURE ON PRICES: HOW WILL SUPPLIERS COUNTER?

How can suppliers counter this power shift to their customers and the resulting pressure on their profits? Aside from the traditional continuous improvement programs (e.g., six sigma) to reduce their internal costs, suppliers have three ways to practice *collaborative management* to relieve pressure by involving their trading partners:

1. Mutually measure with their partners to identify change opportunities and remove unnecessary or redundant costs that buyers and sellers create with each other.

2. Alter or induce their customers' behaviors to minimize the power shift with unbundled menu-pricing and service level options that result in increased profits.

3. Understand their levels of profitability with different types of customers to rationalize how to deal with *each* customer or segment—and possibly share that data with specific customers.

Let's better understand the concepts of interfirm costs—those costs outside a company's four walls that are between and among trading partners. This is the financial transparency organizations crave. Today a company can only see its suppliers' invoice prices—not its suppliers' costs and profit margins behind the prices.

There is confusion with the term *collaborative management*. Some consultants and software vendors claim to offer products and services for value chain management, but with critical inspection these are usually limited tools—incomplete solutions to difficult questions like "How can we price our products to maximize category volumes and profits?" Traditional supply chain software tools focus on optimizing transaction management without a clear understanding of the key drivers of profit. These tools may not even qualify as suboptimizers. They leave organizations with little insight into what drives value chain performance and how it can be profitably improved.

Let's differentiate between a supply chain and a value chain:

- A *supply chain* is a network of autonomous or semi-autonomous business entities, collectively responsible for procurement, manufacturing, and distribution activities associated with one or more families of related products. It is simply the result of adding work (and costs) across the chain to fulfill end-consumers' desires.

- A *value chain* describes how businesses receive raw materials as input, add value to the raw materials through various processes, and sell finished products to customers. Various companies making profits along the chain accomplish this effort. It is an economic value creation chain.

Today, each participant in the value chain, including each step it performs, is increasingly scrutinized for the value it adds to the process. Weak performance will likely lead to removal from the chain. Everyone in a value chain ideally must be a high performer. Rather than having a brick wall separating the supplier and buyer knowledge of each other, there should be continuously looping decision support information with *financial intelligence* between (and among) trading partners. VCA supported with ABC data provides that communication medium.

Many supply chain software products, when their solutions are stripped to their core, are merely fancy schedulers or inventory optimizers rather than whole solutions. They are *operations only* systems that manage information about product flow from suppliers to users, but they do not necessarily improve profits or reduce expense. The goal is to eliminate expenses, not to shift them elsewhere—which may mean off-loading them to your unsuspecting trading partner. One company's cost reduction should not be another's cost increase. The net effect should ideally be validated as profit-positive for everyone involved.

If a supply chain software tool cannot measure *value* across the chain—bridging two or more trading partners—in sufficient detail to estimate realizable cost savings from projects and to support financial decisions, then it is hardly a complete *value chain* solution. Effective *collaborative management* tools should calculate and report the consequence and impact of decisions and changes, ranging from what-if scenarios to gap analysis between *as-is* and *to-be* business process reengineering proposals, and to other alternative opportunities relative to the status quo. VCA delivers the return on investment (ROI) that other vendor systems promise but cannot fulfill alone.

I just used the phrase "bridging two or more trading partners." As shown in Figure 18.2, the profit opportunities with substantial potential typically reside at this interface between suppliers and buyers rather than simply isolated within a company. VCA and ABM are ideal applications to shed light on this interface.

Let's further examine Figure 18.2. The value chain leverages information technology to perform as a *chain*. With improved communications and less uncertainty, buffer stock inventory is reduced everywhere. Buffer stock was traditionally used to protect companies from their unreliable suppliers and from unpredictable surges in demand from customers. But *demand-pull* methods, like *kanban*, as well as better forecasting methods, have changed the techniques for

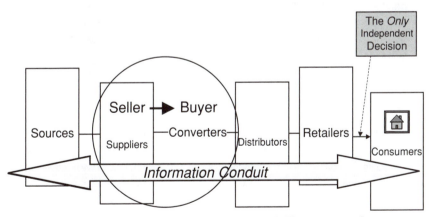

Untapped profit opportunities can be exposed. The process of measuring profits across the value chain can begin at any *seller/buyer interface* along the chain.

Figure 18.2   Profit Opportunities across the Value Chain

how producers make goods. Advanced planning and scheduling systems with powerful simulation logic are increasing the speed of material throughput and work flow with less waste. Risk and uncertainty are sliding to the side, taking inefficiency with them and allowing higher customer service levels. However, as cycle times are shortened, the importance and value of information rises. The importance of better forecasting also rises. And finally, relevant profit and cost information for value chain management is an increasingly important component of that information value set. The financial information validates the impact realized by the improvements.

In short, companies need a set of solutions that will analyze every aspect of the extended value chain and turn the available enterprise data into insight that can be acted on to guide intelligent decisions.

How Do Value Chain Analysis and Activity-Based Management (ABM) Complement Each Other?

Value chain analysis (VCA) and activity-based management (ABM) are both costing methodologies that can, if similarly modeled, calculate an *identical* cost for a market-landed stock keeping unit (SKU) and any steps along that journey. However, each costing method has its own sweet spot and focuses on solving a different type of problem. Consequently, each method typically measures different costs. For example, VCA includes the more directly attributable expenses to an SKU, excluding indirect overhead costs, which will not change in the short term. This allows VCA costing to focus on calculating the cost trade-offs between alternative what-if scenarios. In contrast, ABM measures and reports fully burdened costs (i.e., hidden indirect costs) of products, channels, and customers as an attention-directing viewer to determine where to focus.

Here is a broader description of these two methods:

- **VCA** is an industry specific solution, with predefined activities (e.g., receiving, put-away, replenish, loading) and material physical handling units (such as pallets, roll containers, cases, trays), which solves with *what-if* incremental costing the impact of alternative scenarios, typically measured against the *as-is* status quo. For example, if you change several products' container types, use a different route, and ship on different size trucks, where will the costs change—and by what amount? VCA is SKU-centric and can be thought of as direct-costing the increments of consumed cost

How Do Value Chain Analysis and Activity-Based Management (ABM) Complement Each Other? *(Continued)*

for every event uniquely *triggered* by each SKU and its associated material handling configuration (e.g., pallet, case, tray, unit). Examples of a *trigger* would be a move or a put-away.

- **ABM** software also measures and traces expenses consumed into calculated costs, but it focuses on the indirect preproduction product-making costs (often referred to as *overhead*) as well as the customer-caused (rather than SKU-triggered) *costs-to-serve* that are involved with front-office customer handling and service rather than SKU handling. ABM typically gives a broad snapshot of costs to determine what to focus on and where. (VCA typically is already focused, so it is used to test the costs and benefits of changes.) Popular applications of ABM are (1) to compute profit-and-loss statements for each customer (or customer segment) for profit margin analysis, and (2) to compare benchmarked work activity costs and their relative value-added and cost driver sources.

Figure 18A illustrates how VCA and ABM complement each other.

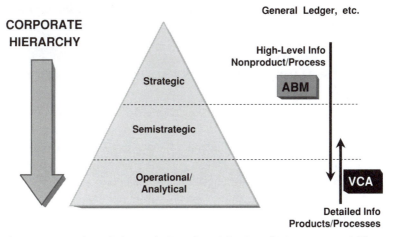

Figure 18A   Value Chain Analysis and Activity-Based Management Address Different Problems

(Continued)

How Do Value Chain Analysis and Activity-Based Management (ABM) Complement Each Other? *(Continued)*

In short, VCA focuses on products as they pass through processes that cut across multiple departments and potentially business partners. VCA enables rapid what-if return on investment (ROI) analysis used to evaluate alternatives. ABM is an increasingly accepted costing methodology used to calculate costs of diverse outputs, including products and customers, and what is causing those costs. ABM serves as an attention-directing mechanism to locate where to focus to inspire provoking questions about profit margin levels and unit-cost comparisons, all of which involve understanding what is causing the costs.

Business intelligence has been the missing ingredient in the supply chain market, and VCA fills that void. With a VCA system, suppliers and retailers can measure the effectiveness of their assortments, new product introductions, promotions, and various replenishment programs (e.g., collaborative planning, forecasting, and replenishment or factory gate pricing). A supplier can then preferably share this analysis and impact data with its trading partners for profit synergy, or it can alone discern the cost impact its proposed changes will have on itself and its trading partners.

JOINT SHARING OF VALUE CHAIN INFORMATION

Although the value chain starts with the gathering and conversion of raw materials and components, most of the focus in obtaining financial transparency is currently on the area from postproduction of the product manufacturer to the checkout counter of the retailer—meaning all the stages of material transfers in between. Suppliers today are challenged in their attempts to measure the costs of activities, processes, and product movements—from milling and manufacturing to storage, freight distribution, and delivery.

With removal of the information wall between a supplier and buyer resulting from the addition of proper information-based tools, each trading partner can finally answer questions like, "How can I accurately measure costs by channel, process, product, and customer at brand, category, or SKU levels, so I can identify potential savings?" When value chain financial intelligence and economics are jointly shared with a trading partner, the "I" in that question just asked becomes "we." The transparency of costs results in long-desired visibility. With VCA and ABM, operational costs provide that visibility in a language that matches an operational manager's and employee team's own understanding of their business. For example, the more handling of a product, the more costly will be the product's market-landed cost. A unified costing system would bond a pair of separate legal reporting entities as if they were a single entity.

VCA delivers financial intelligence so suppliers and buyers can reliably know their fully loaded market-landed cost to their customers and ultimately to their customers' end-consumers. VCA allows a company to look outside its operation in order to achieve maximum benefits from improvement initiatives. All value chain participants are realizing their chain is becoming intensely integrated with their trading partners' chains. Although VCA is typically initially used by suppliers for internal analysis to simulate the impact of changes on one's partners, VCA can do more. VCA can also provide two or more trading partners with a common costing framework to objectively and jointly examine their *mutual* costs attributed to moving products across their distribution system. The resulting financial transparency facilitates removing wasteful activities through trade-off analysis and what-if scenario analysis.

VALUE CHAIN ANALYSIS IS AN SKU-CENTRIC POSTPRODUCTION COST ACCUMULATOR

A VCA tool calculates costs across the value chain from a process-oriented view. Think of VCA as attaching yourself to an individual product and watching all the specific and proportionately shared costs accumulate into it as it traverses its path to its final delivery and in-store, point-of-sale purchase. In short, VCA is an SKU item-centric *direct cost* accumulator. VCA is less concerned with tracing indirect expenses to the SKU. With this direct cost data, more efficient and cost-effective logistics can be achieved by examining alternative route-to-market scenarios to scrutinize each step and the costs added or removed. For example, a supplier can finally see the impact on profit margins of serving a customer from a different warehouse. If this information is boldly shared with the customer, say in the situation where an extra day is required but margin improves two percent, then one possibility is that the customer will accept the day's delivery delay in exchange for half the cost savings. That is true, fact-based *collaborative management*.

VCA models are designed *horizontally* across time to monitor the flow of individual products and their costs as they move across time through the value chain. The VCA methodology, which is more applicable to the consumer packaged goods and retail industries, has preconfigured inputs, cost drivers, and outputs, which enables rapid analysis of products and their costs, as well as offering a mutually acceptable basis for financial transparency. By utilizing company-specific or standard consumption rates (e.g., time it takes to put a pallet into the storage location), combined with volumetric product data, processing times, and resource needs, costs can be derived. Hence, VCA is typically referred to as *bottom-up*, meaning to start with rates of the *pieces* to build up, accumulate, or summarize into the *whole*—including costs.

A VCA solution uses industry-standard language to foster communications across internal departments and external trading partners. It has an immense library of predefined work activities (e.g., receive, store, pick, move), product handling types (e.g., pallets, roll-cages, cases, units), and objects of attention (e.g., products, vehicles, routes-to-market, in-store fixtures, etc.). VCA combines standard industry terminology and metrics to enable rapid what-if modeling.

Traditional costing is typically flawed and misleading because the accountants use broad averages to compute cost rates. Effective costing involves modeling costs at lower levels of granularity. In this way, progressive costing models are very sensitive to the diversity and variation of how brands, categories, products, SKUs, service lines, and types of elements within channels uniquely place demands on activity costs. These demands on work, in turn, consume the resources, such as people and equipment. Figure 18.3 illustrates a branch of a cost assignment decomposition tree. This costing approach ultimately traces many-to-one cost relationships to pile up all of the financial general ledger expenses into customer costs via all of the SKU-triggered events.

The power of VCA is displaying visibility of costs *across* entities, such as from the manufacturer to wholesaler to distribution warehouse to the retail store outlet. It can run this breadth because VCA analysis is rarely about a holistic, enterprise-wide endeavor. With VCA, *what-if* scenarios are restricted to *incremental* costs of only the relevant things impacted—more of a *same as*, *except for* cost impact analysis. The impact being analyzed may be within a company's internal chain or involve analysis. But the impact usually involves two entities from two different companies. VCA enables organizations to do the following:

- Rapidly identify financial improvement opportunities.
- Enhance revenues and reduce costs by making better fact-based decisions.
- Facilitate the costing of products, customers, suppliers, and processes quickly and accurately within and across the extended value chain.
- Eliminate wasteful and redundant activities, processes, and policies, leading to a win-win and higher partners for both trading partners.
- Explore *what-if* scenarios for changes before implementation.

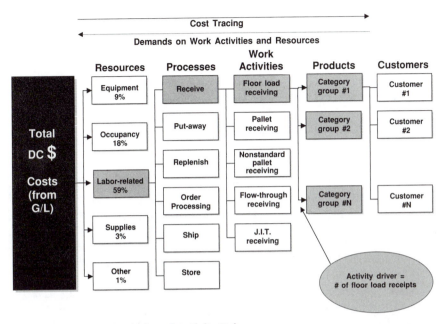

Figure 18.3   Cost Analysis and Activity Drivers

VCA is appealing for rapidly getting results because not only is commonly accepted standard terminology used, but agreed-on work-rate and conversion metrics can be used too. The lack of agreed-on measurement systems and improperly maintained data are key reasons that a tool like VCA is desirable.

In situations where two or more trading partners may both have an ABM system monitoring each other's unique cost demands, VCA combines them into a

History of Supply Chain Cost Measuring

In the 1970s, distributors and retailers began worrying about the individual profits and costs of each product and SKU. They applied a compact, ABM-like method called *direct product profitability* (DPP) to measuring the manpower effort of handling products relative to SKU pricing in order to measure profit contribution margins. But DPP only included direct costs, not indirect and overhead costs. DPP ignored any customer-related activity costs, such as taking orders or fielding inquiries, which are not caused by an SKU. (DPP was, in effect, an ancestor of value chain analysis.)

(Continued)

History of Supply Chain Cost Measuring *(Continued)*

In the 1980s, the purchasing function began examining the total cost of ownership (TCO), which acknowledges that the item purchase price on a vendor's invoice represents only a portion of the total cost of acquiring that item. Vendor performance also affects the costs of ordering, expediting, receiving, and inspecting. Vendors can cause extra costs with poor quality and failure to deliver on time. Burying these vendor-caused costs in overhead or general expenses obscures the costs. ABM data calculates the TCO measure by revealing these hidden costs and allowing them to be assigned to each vendor. Then ABM reassigns those costs into the purchased items, combining them with the purchase price—hence the TCO. Total cost of ownership addresses overhead costs that have been previously excluded from the DPP costing calculations.

By applying TCO to its vendors, an organization can assess how *interfirm* relationships affect its own costs. With TCO, companies can negotiate with or select upstream channel members based on *total* acquisition costs. Total cost of ownership measures can also enlighten buyers about how their own behavior affects their vendors' costs. It is a two-way street for cooperating trading partners in the supply chain.

Ultimately, the total landed marketplace costs of the supply chain are what matters to the consumer who is making the purchase choice at the end of the value chain. If the value chain's postproduction costs are high, then the prices to consumers will be also. As a consequence, the entire supply chain matters. Direct product profitability and TCO only capture an organization's *intrafirm* costs related to procuring, merchandising, and stocking product. A more complete supply chain costing system must also capture the downstream costs triggered by customers and their product and service orders. These are *costs-to-serve*. Figure 18B illustrates where TCO and DPP costs are captured in the ABM cost assignment network.

TCO and DPP costing methods are combined in an ABM system. Why is this relevant? By not capturing costs needed to see and understand the cost structure both upstream and downstream, a company within the supply chain will miss the opportunities for making interfirm cost trade-offs. In addition, passing the excess costs all the way through to the end-consumer inevitably reduces overall product demand for the entire chain.

The elegance of ABM is that it combines all the costs—upstream costs, the production costs, and the downstream costs.

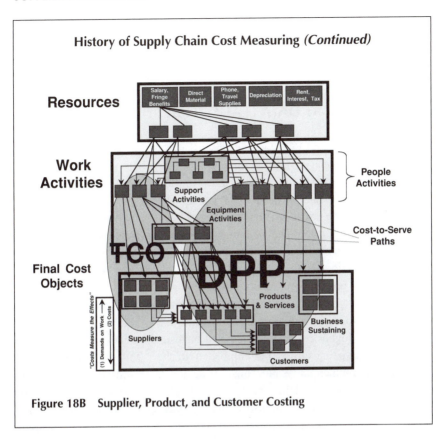

Figure 18B   Supplier, Product, and Customer Costing

single shared view while distinguishing who *owns* which costs. In these instances, VCA serves as a neutral and bilateral communication instrument for joint what-if analysis, including the monitoring of trade-offs. VCA provides a common costing platform for trading partners who participate so they can collectively understand the actual impact that different initiatives will have on all parties. Trading negotiations no longer need to haggle with questionable and partial data, but can use fact-based financial intelligence including previously hidden costs occurring below the gross profit margin line.

An appealing feature of VCA is it can quickly produce visibility to things never seen before (or guessed at) that can lead to improved results. VCA works with a company's *existing* data systems, extracting utility from information that has already been captured and stored. It measures costs in the chain to find a mutually acceptable base cost, which allows negotiation of shared rewards from implemented changes. Without an agreed base cost, quantifying change becomes debate that declines into argument. The pursuit of trust collapses again.

BETTER COST DATA LEADS TO BETTER DECISIONS

Together ABM data and VCA facilitate discussions and the making of fact-based decisions. Many managers are unwilling to take any actions until presented with the facts. Open-book sharing of cost and profit data, based on financial transparency, may be the catalyst needed to foster genuine seller-buyer collaboration. Many companies do not adequately understand how much of their cost structure is a consequence of the collective demands on work triggered by their suppliers and customers. Costs measure effects. Influencing a customer or supplier to behave differently to lessen the organization's employee workload is too often overlooked as a possibility to reduce costs.

Trading partners in a value chain are now realizing that as each optimizes its own internal processes and policies, some of the impact ripples externally, causing potentially higher costs to partners and thus suboptimizing the *entire* value chain. Costs are being shifted, not eliminated. In short, with the increased codependency of commercial relationships, achieving improved service levels and efficiency needs to be switched from inward-focused, *inside-the-four-walls* cost-reduction programs to *collaborative management* with supplier-facing and customer-facing initiatives. With VCA, a company can integrate both the supply and demand sides of its value chain, enabling cost analysis encompassing both inbound and outbound effects. Unfortunately, many businesses mistrust their *own* cost data. Most companies operate with a resigned acceptance that their cost accounting data is "a bunch of fictitious lies—but we all agree to it." Understanding true and actual costs is not the whole solution, but it is a big part of the solution to increase interfirm trust along the value chain and better manage the entire chain's costs and profit margins.

How can suppliers recover any of the power they are losing to buyers due to the Internet? I just described three ways of *collaborative management*. The common theme is that information technology is the ace in the hole for suppliers. VCA and ABM will inevitably be part of the suppliers' solution to regain power. Supply and value chain intelligence hits at the heart of the core competencies of solutions provided by software vendors offering business intelligence (BI) functionality: data access and management; transforming data; monitoring, reporting and diagnostics; award-winning analytics; and costing capabilities across the extended value chain—all on a flexible, scalable platform.

Information technology enables trading partners along the value chain to better coordinate and collaborate for mutual benefit. It is now evident that trading partners will require managerial accounting systems, powered with VCA and ABM, that are superior to the conventional accounting systems that all companies struggle with today.

NOTE

1. James H. Rand, "The Profit Element," *National Association of Cost Accountants (NACA) Bulletin*, vol. 9, no.2, September 15, 1921.

19

PROCESS INTELLIGENCE WITH SIX SIGMA QUALITY AND LEAN THINKING

"Nine times out of ten, in the arts as in life, there is actually nothing to be discovered; there is only error to be exposed."
—H. L. Mencken American editor,
in *Prejudices* (1922, third series)

Business process reengineering (BPR) was the rage of the improvement programs during the 1990s. BPR means different things to different people. In its earlier days BPR was all about radical change with the cheer "Don't automate—eliminate." That is, "Don't fix it—break it" and start anew. Early BPR advocated an intense focus on customers while concurrently attacking broad, cross-functional business processes with the use of IT as an enabler for new ways of doing work. With hindsight we now realize that what early BPR recognized was that information technology had progressed so far that traditional manual business processes, like the sales order entry process, could be totally redesigned by the inclusion of high-speed computing power.

In contrast to the punctuated change from BPR, and running alongside BPR during the 1990s, were the relentless *continuous improvement* programs aimed at gradually improving operations. These programs produce no major improvements but rather small incremental steps of productivity gains. However, later BPR began to include these programs too—any attempt to change how work is done. (The eternal *continuous improvement* programs, which evolved from the industrial revolution near the end of the 19th century, include quality management, systems analysis, and improved operations planning and scheduling systems.)

To some, BPR became a code word for employee layoffs. To others, they suspected BPR as a fad due to missed project implementation deadlines. One problem was that initial BPR was more consultant-driven without involving the people who actually did the work. Because of these negative connotations and overblown rhetoric from consultants and gurus *selling* BPR, late adopters of BPR principles stopped using the term. But, at some fundamental level, organizations will always apply commonsense principles for making improvements. When used in moderation, most of the concepts in reengineering have substantial merit.

There is now also a resurgence of reengineering around three areas not much touched in the first version:

1. Business-to-business processes related to supply chain management. This is because stronger and more automated linkages between suppliers and customers improve service and reduce expenses.

2. New product design and development. This is due to the need for compressed time for speed-to-market.

3. Marketing automation. The Web plus powerful combinations of databases and statistical forecasting tools allow laserlike pinpointing

At the same time that BPR was hitting its stride, and as was described in the section about the Internet in Chapter 18, the Internet, with its powerful search engines for comparison-shopping, is irreversibly shifting power from suppliers to customers and consumers. So the combination of BPR principles and the Internet truly accelerated changes in business processes.

However, before the explosion of these IT-based technologies occurred, the rate of change in productivity increases and process improvements moved at a slower pace. These slower-paced but relentless improvement programs, like quality management and refined scheduling systems, are the topic of this section. My point is that when a new idea, such as BPR, comes along, we must not forget about the old ideas—they still work. BPR should augment rather than replace other management ideas. I am less concerned with classifying change as being fine-tuned tweaking versus breakthrough transformation. What matters is whether it makes sense, and whether the calculated risks of the outcomes can be estimated.

The historical evolution that illustrates the convergence of these managerial improvement programs appears in Figure 19.1. The figure presents a time line that reveals how many of the older improvement programs from the last half of the 20th century are converging.

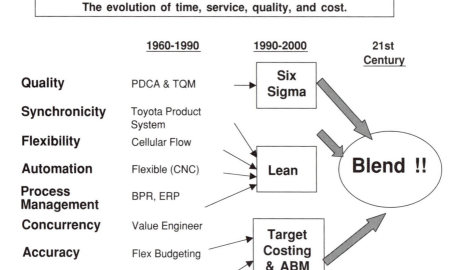

Figure 19.1   Time Line of Improvement Programs

The figure reveals that three broad concepts are the generational heirs to prior improvement methodologies:

1. Quality: Six sigma.
2. Operations: Lean management.
3. Managerial accounting: Activity-based cost management and target costing.

These three methodologies, despite having a somewhat different focus, have synergy. The message from each methodology is short and sweet. Six sigma addresses quality improvement and says, "Get perfect—analyze processes for zero-defects." Lean management says, "Get agile and strong—eliminate waste of all kinds and accelerate throughput with shorter cycle times." And activity-based management (ABM) says, "Get smarter—make better decisions."

Just as physicists are making advances at explaining the unification of the fundamental forces of nature (e.g., electromagnetism, gravity, and the subatomic forces), business managers are also seeing more interdependencies that became apparent only a few years ago. Figure 19.1 proposes that the three heir methodologies have strong interdependencies. Michael George claims that by combining lean management with six sigma, you get lean six sigma; and the synergy of the two together "has helped companies reduce manufacturing overhead 20% and inventory by 50% in less than two years."[1]

Part Three of this book described managerial accounting in great depth with an emphasis on ABM and activity-based resource planning. Additional information about managerial accounting and target costing that supports the new product development process is footnoted here.[2] This chapter describes the other two concepts of total quality management and lean operations thinking. Many companies are simultaneously implementing both methods and combining them as a unified methodology.

TOTAL QUALITY MANAGEMENT— WHAT IS QUALITY?

To some people *quality* might mean durability or richness in a product or a pleasurable experience. This is a *fitness-for-use* definition that relates to a customer's needs. In the 1980s this predominant supplier-oriented view defined quality as being a high conformance to the buyer's requirements or specifications, usually measured at the time of final product test. One of the risks of limiting the definition of quality to a supplier "doing things right" is that it can miss the customers' *real* needs and preferences.

More recently, quality has been considered from a customer satisfaction orientation to meet or exceed customer requirements and expectations. Sadly, prior to this change in attitude, phrases and terms like *high quality* and *customer satisfaction* were not noticeably present in the vocabulary of business and government; and in many cases where they have been spoken, the actions did not follow the words.

The recognition of the importance of the customer shifts the view from the sell side to the buy side. This shift is also consistent with the forces discussed that are driving the customer intelligence (analytical CI) and customer relationship management (operational CRM) movement. There has been substantial research about customer preferences, both stated and subconscious, with elaborate survey questionnaires, diagnostics, and conjoint statistical analyses. For example, "food" may be a customer's stated need, but "nourishment" or "a pleasant taste" are the real primary needs. A customer's ultimate perception of quality involves many factors. In short, the universally accepted goals of total quality management (TQM) are lower costs, higher revenues, delighted customers, and empowered employees.

WAS THE TOTAL QUALITY MANAGEMENT MOVEMENT A FAD?

In the 1980s, global competition began to cross borders. Quality levels started to become an issue for North American companies. North American consumers were increasingly purchasing foreign products with reputations of high quality. The threatened North American companies reacted. Some of their earlier improvement programs began with quality circles of employees but soon evolved into robust TQM programs that embraced much more in scope as a vast collection of philosophies, concepts, methods, and tools. TQM received substantial business media attention and was intellectually appealing. At an operational level, TQM was effective at identifying waste and accelerating problem solving for tactical issues. However, at a more strategic level, it was felt by many that TQM was not the magic pill that senior executives always seem to be searching for.

For a more in-depth description of the historical evolution of traditional TQM, up until the 1990s when it evolved into six sigma, go to www.wiley.com/go/performance.

RISE OF SIX SIGMA

In the early 1990s, skepticism about TQM began to take the bloom off the TQM rose. A disappointing pattern from past TQM projects had emerged. Just like most business improvement programs that senior management often hopes may be a solution to unleash productivity gains, the TQM movement was failing to demonstrate the large breakthroughs that it was promoted to accomplish. Part of the problem was that some of the TQM enthusiasts took a faith-based position and strongly suggested that managers and employee teams simply fully commit to improving quality. These TQM enthusiasts assumed that by pursuing TQM, then all of the other performance factors, such as levels of cost and service, would automatically self-correct and take care of themselves. The consequence was that results from TQM were below possibly inflated expectations.

Regardless of the historical explanation for skepticism about TQM, after initial improvements were experienced from TQM, executives began to question if there were enough results. In October 1991 *Business Week* ran a "Return on Quality" cover article questioning the payback from TQM. This exposed TQM to the scrutiny of the financial analysts, where expense and investment justification is tested by requiring a defensible minimum return on investment (ROI). In short, there was an ominous disconnection between quality initiatives and the bottom line. Increasingly more companies adopted quality programs, yet few could validate much favorable impact on profitability. At about this same time, other change initiatives, such as just-in-time production management and BPR, began capturing management's attention. TQM settled in as a necessary-but-not-sufficient backseat program.

As time passed, organizations worldwide began recognizing that TQM need not operate in isolation from other change initiative programs—it could be integrated. Management teams admitted to themselves that there had been drawbacks that had harmed TQM's reputation, such as nonverifiable measures, claimed but unrealized cost savings, and small projects that were too local and tactical. However, these same executives realized that with corrections, TQM could be repositioned as a more impactive business improvement program.

As a further impulse to renew interest in TQM, all manufacturers along the supply chains began to realize that they depended on each other and that poor quality from one trading partner mushroomed to affect others. Manufacturers began to expect, even require, minimal problems from their suppliers, such as off-spec products, because such flaws would quickly produce component shortages and lead to unplanned and profit-draining downtime. Unplanned events also made reacting to changes in schedules a difficult challenge. Manufacturers began demanding that their suppliers become formally certified with globally administered programs such as ISO 9000:2000.[3] These certifications serve as a form of insurance to a customer that a potential supplier's quality levels will be sufficiently reliable to minimize the likelihood of work disruptions caused by supplier shortages to the manufacturer's processes. (Some industries, such as automotive, have recognized that ISO 9000 does not go into enough depth to meet their specific needs and have written supplemental standards that do not replace but enlarge on ISO 9000.)

Eventually TQM began to qualify as one of the essentials in the new suite of management tools and methodologies, which we now view as performance management (PM) and its core solutions. Corporate role models of applying TQM emerged. Six sigma programs with "black belt" quality training at respected multinational corporations, like General Electric and Motorola, were heralded as keys to their successful performance. Six sigma became the next-generation TQM program.

One aspect of six sigma involves educating employees about how to measure the adverse impacts of variation and defects. The goal is to get employee teams to think in terms of perfection and zero defects. But another aspect of six sigma, one that is deeper and hopefully should sustain six sigma as an accepted methodology, focuses on identifying high-impact opportunities as project candidates.

Projects that are identified are prioritized by the likelihood they will produce bottom-line financial results. This is somewhat in contrast to some of the TQM projects from the 1990s that, for example, might involve providing mini-refrigerators for supervisors—a nice quality-of-life touch but questionable in how this produces higher profits. In order to assure that six sigma concentrates on high-impact-opportunity project candidates, six sigma introduces financial accountability as part of the approval process to initiate an improvement program. Any six sigma proposed project is expected to be justified on true cost savings (or future cost avoidance), where the benefits exceed the time and expense associated with the project.[4]

Six sigma is viewed as a paradigm shift in the quality arena. Veterans of quality management believe that quality just for quality's sake—meaning conformance to standard—is not sufficient. This sounds paradoxical. Quality is obviously needed to capture and retain customers, but quality must also be applied to the business itself. That is, when we examine the basic input-process-output model, the quality emphasis has traditionally been on the inputs and outputs, such as the purchased raw materials and components or the finished products. Six sigma assures there is emphasis on the *conversion* and paperwork-related *transaction* processes too. But six sigma goes much further and also suggests consideration of the business's financial health.

To validate an organization's claim to total quality, quality assessment mechanisms have been developed. For example, the Malcolm Baldrige Award, established in 1987, has become coveted as a sign of excellence in the United States. Europe honors its winners of the European Quality Award (EQA), and Japan has honored winners of the Deming Application Prize.[5]

TQM'S NEED FOR A FINANCIAL VIEW

Despite the quest for improved quality, global and local competitive pressures are making executives feel boxed-in, particularly given that pricing is market-driven. Executives are realizing that profit margin management will require visibility and relentless management of costs. TQM will be essential for managing costs. To complicate matters, some companies that have been *reengineered* may have become leaner and smaller from downsizing, but not necessarily fitter. The reengineering may have helped them to survive, but they may still not have a distinct competitive or quality advantage. In many cases, you cannot simply remove bodies if you do not also reduce the work; otherwise service levels deteriorate.

One of the obstacles affecting TQM initiatives, and other initiatives as well, has been the shortcomings of financial accounting methods. Part of the problem is the traditional emphasis of accounting on external reporting. Another part of the problem is the accountants themselves and deficiencies with their financial accounting system. As described in Part Three, the accountants' traditional general ledger is a wonderful instrument for what it is designed to do: to post and accumulate (i.e., categorize) financial transactions into their specific ledger account balances. But the cost data in this format (e.g., salaries, supplies, and depreciation) are structurally deficient for decision support, including measuring cost-of-quality (COQ). The accounting community has been slow to understand and accept this problem, but advances in technology and modeling capabilities are reversing that.

Resistance by quality managers has also delayed the acceptance of measuring COQ as an approach to improve processes. Some quality managers have become skeptical about measuring their COQ. They have seen increasing regulations and standards, such as the ISO 9000 series, where installing any form of COQ measurement was perceived as more of a compliance exercise to satisfy documentation requirements to become *registered*, rather than as a benefit to improve performance. A disadvantage of ISO 9000 is that it represents only a minimum standard, perhaps insufficient to induce competitive-advantage behavior. Also, due to its being written in general terms, with a manufacturing origin, ISO 9000 is open to interpretation with ambiguities for service sector organizations. Some complain that ISO 9000 serves as a documentation tool with little extension to apply as a managerial tool.

Resistance to COQ also stems from misconceptions. Some quality managers perceive quality and cost as competing investment choices, implying that there is a trade-off to make between the two. This thinking assumes that achieving better quality somehow requires more effort and therefore costs more. This is not necessarily true. But what matters most is the ROI from quality programs—and that includes top-line revenues as well. If quality programs are properly installed, productivity can be improved while also raising customer satisfaction. The combination of these two improvements eventually leads to increased sales, market penetration, and higher profits and returns.

SIX SIGMA: REPLACE BLIND FAITH WITH SHAREHOLDER ENTITLEMENT

Now six sigma is vying to exhibit staying power as a TQM program. Will it succeed, or is there an inherent flaw? A strong case can be made that it will succeed. Here is why. Low defects, timely delivery, and minimal cost will always remain key elements of business, but quality in business can and should be viewed from a profitability perspective. Hence, six sigma advocates that the classical scope of quality be expanded beyond customer satisfaction to also encompass satisfaction of the investor and shareholder. Six sigma proposes that unless expectations from both sides of the transaction are met—referred to as a *mutual valuation*— then true quality has not been achieved.

A popular definition of *quality* preferred by six sigma advocates is a state in which *value* entitlement is realized for the customer and the supplier (i.e., employees and shareholders) in every aspect of the relationship. It is predictable that there will be debates about trade-offs among shareholders, customers, employees, taxpayers, and the environment. The methods of COQ measurement will be useful to convert these debates into agreements.[6]

This new perspective acknowledges that investing additional capital intended to reduce defect rates will not be sustained unless shareholders and lenders feel assured of high-quality financial returns to them. In six sigma, financial data to support manager proposals for projects are absolutely required. So, just like customers who demand utility value, owners, investors, and lenders have a rightful expectation of profit value and wealth creation.

This broader notion of quality is well beyond classic TQM. For producers and service providers, it is no longer enough to just make and deliver quality goods and services. A quality business must exist as well. The intent of six sigma is to refocus on business economics as the driver of quality improvements.

A key to realizing the benefits from six sigma is to identify the vital few projects that will have the impact to keep organizations on their path to six sigma. The projects are like the stocks in an investment portfolio: They must produce returns. Specific cost savings or profit improvements are assigned by senior management, and "black belt" projects are defined to achieve the goals. Qualified employees are intensively trained as black-belt project managers. These individuals are next assigned several black-belt projects. The organization then relies on the black-belt managers and programs to achieve the results.

CATEGORIZING QUALITY COSTS: KEY TO MEASURING PROGRESS

Almost every organization now realizes that not having the highest quality is not even an option. High quality is simply an entry ticket for the opportunity to compete. Attaining high quality is now a must. Anything less than high quality will lead to an organization's terminal collapse. In short, high quality is now a prerequisite for an organization to continue to exist. The stakes are higher than ever.

To some people, quality costs are very visible and obvious. To others, the amount of an organization's quality costs is understated, and they believe that many of the quality-related costs are hidden and go unreported. How does one distinguish between *obvious* and *hidden* quality costs?

- Examples of *obvious* quality-related costs are rework costs, excess scrap material costs, warranty costs, and field repair expenses. These typically result from errors. Error-related costs are easily measured directly from the financial system. Spending amounts for these types of expenses are recorded in the accountant's general ledger system using the chart-of-accounts. Sometimes the quality-related costs include the expenses of an entire department, such as an inspection department that arguably exists solely as being quality-related. However, as organizations flatten and delayer and employees multitask more, it is rare that an entire department will focus exclusively on quality.

- The *hidden* poor-quality costs are less obvious and are more difficult to measure. For example, a hidden cost would be those hours of a few employees' time spent sorting through paperwork resulting from a billing error. Although these employees do not work in a quality department that is dedicated to quality-related activities, such as inspection or rework, that portion of their workday wasted due to an error was definitely quality-related. These costs are not reflected in the chart-of-accounts of the accounting system. That is why they are referred to as *hidden* costs.

The lack of widespread tracking of COQ in practice is surprising because the tools, methods, and technologies exist to accomplish reporting COQ. A research study[7] investigating the maturity of COQ revealed that the major reason for not tracking COQ was lack of management interest and support, as well as management's belief that quality costing is *paperwork* that does not have enough value to justify its performance. In short, for them it's not worth doing. Other major reasons for not tracking COQ were a lack of knowledge of *how* to track costs and benefits of COQ as well as a lack of adequate accounting and computer systems. Given the advances in today's data collection, data warehousing, data mining, and ABM system implementations, these reasons begin to appear as lame excuses—the technology is no longer the impediment for reporting COQ that it once was in the past.

Providing employee teams with visibility of both obvious and hidden quality-related costs can be valuable for performance improvement. Using COQ data, employees can gain insights into causes of problems. The hidden and traditional costs can be broadly categorized as follows:

- **Error-free costs** are unrelated to the planning, controlling, correcting, or improving of quality. These are the did-it-right-the-first-time (nicknamed "dirtfoot") costs.
- **COQ** costs are those that could disappear if all processes were error-free and if all products and services were defect-free. COQ can be subcategorized in the following way:

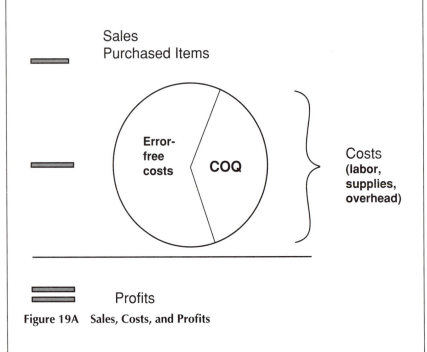

Measuring Cost-of-Quality: A Primer

Figure 19A uses a pie chart to portray, in financial terms, how an organization's sales, profits, purchased materials, and cost-of-quality (COQ) expenses might exist in an organization. In principle, as the COQ expenses are reduced, the result will be higher bottom-line profits.

Sales
Purchased Items

Error-free costs   COQ

Costs
(labor,
supplies,
overhead)

Profits

Figure 19A   Sales, Costs, and Profits

Measuring Cost-of-Quality: A Primer *(Continued)*

Figure 19B illustrates before-and-after COQ measures where quality programs have been initiated. Quality-related costs can be managed best when they are shifted from nonconformance to conformance costs.

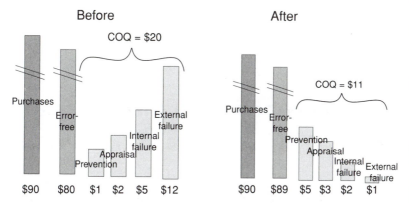

Figure 19B COQ Histograms: Getting Efficient with Conformance-Related COQ

Ideally, all four COQ cost categories should be reduced, but one may initially need to prudently increase the cost of prevention to dramatically decrease the costs of and penalties paid for nonconformance. This makes COQ more than just an accounting scheme; it becomes a financial investment justification tool.

The benefit from using an ABM system at the activity level is that it reduces debate. With traditional COQ measures, people can endlessly debate whether a borderline activity is a true COQ, such as scrap produced during product development that may arguably be expected. By starting with the one-hundred percent expenditure pool, *every* cost will fall into *some* category and always be visible. Each type of cost can always be reclassified later on, as people better understand how to use the data.

- *Costs of conformance*—the costs related to prevention and predictive appraisal to meet requirements.

- *Costs of noncomformance*—the costs (including detective appraisal work) related to internal or external failure to meet requirements. The distinction between internal and external is that internal failure costs are detected prior to the shipment or receipt of service by the customer. In contrast, external failure costs usually result from discovery by a customer.

An oversimplified definition of COQ is the costs associated with avoiding, finding, making, and repairing defects and errors (assuming that all defects and errors are detected). Cost-of-quality represents the difference between the actual costs and what the reduced cost would be if there were no substandard service levels, failures, or defects.

To get a much more in-depth understanding about COQ, go to www.wiley .com/go/performance.

DECOMPOSING COST-OF-QUALITY CATEGORIES

In effect, the technique to calculate a reasonably accurate COQ is to apply ABM and ABM's attribute capability. Figure 19.2 shows categories for work activities that are one additional level below the four major categories of COQ. This figure reveals how each of these subcategories can be tagged against the ABM activity costs. This kind of definition provides far greater and more reliable visibility of COQ without the great effort required by traditional cost accounting methods.

The quality movement has been a loud advocate for measuring things rather

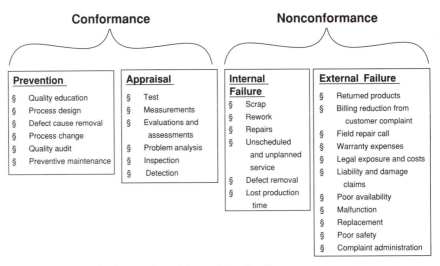

Figure 19.2 Typical Examples of Cost of Quality Components

than relying on opinions. It would make sense that measuring the financial implications of quality will become an increasingly larger part of the quality management domain.

SIX SIGMA AND ACTIVITY-BASED MANAGEMENT

There is a strong case that COQ measurements using attributes from the ABM methodology should be included among the six sigma tools. The disconnection between traditional quality programs and an organization's financial measurements and performance, however, serves as a wake-up call. The disconnection is an indication that there is a need for an improved understanding of quality. Methods like activity-based cost management are enabling quality managers and six sigma program managers to leverage the managerial accounting system to support their proposals, build stronger business cases, and measure accomplishments versus their expectations.

Some companies have been successful in using COQ and some have not. The difference is that successful companies use COQ as a management tool for identifying and prioritizing projects (which Juran defined as "problems selected for solution"), while unsuccessful companies have used it mainly as a scoreboard. To more effectively use COQ as a management tool, one should also track costs by specific problems and causes, as well as by departments and by the COQ cost categories.

The experience from quality management practitioners is that initially you can get a substantial amount of the value by working with existing data and making reasonable estimates—enough to get management's attention. In the past, companies risked getting bogged down in setting up what appeared then to be a sophisticated data system. However, with today's performance management (PM) systems, as described in this book, it is feasible and practical to get better and more complete data.

The reputation of the quality management movement has experienced a few waves of ups and downs. It became almost a religion for some years, and later was ridiculed. Hopefully, the addition of valid costing data will give the quality movement more legitimacy. A recent publication from one of the key sanctioning quality societies, the American Society for Quality (ASQ), contained a key definition. *ANSI/ISO/ASQ Q9004-2000* suggests financial measurement as an appropriate way to assess "the organization's performance in order to determine whether planned objectives have been achieved."[8] Hopefully there will be increased coordination among the quality, managerial accounting, and operations systems.

THE LEAN MANAGEMENT MOVEMENT

At the same time that the six sigma movement was evolving, operations management personnel began a series of improvement programs that evolved into what has today achieved programmatic status and is called *lean management*. How did "lean," its shortened nickname, come about?

Immediately following World War II, capital shortages forced the Japanese to adopt low-inventory methods of production. These just-in-time (JIT) production methods were opposite the batch-and-queue production methods practiced on all the other continents. During the 1990s, the production planning and scheduling community of all the other nations were learning how to refine the Japanese JIT methods. One of the attractions of synchronized demand pull-based material flow systems is that they require much less paperwork and manual recording of transactions. The resulting reduction in paperwork and other workloads caused by complexity (and resolved with JIT) led to the creation of the practices encompassed by this broader term, *lean management*.

Adopting lean management practices does not mean managers lose weight from a diet; it means the organization operates with a bare minimum of non-value-adding work. *Lean* can be defined as the opposite of its antonym, *fat*. For example, as customer demands become more volatile and unpredictable in the short term, a fat producer will not be able to keep up with its leaner and more agile competitors. Its very weight bogs it down.

The timing to adopt lean management thinking is now good because advances in information computing technology enable the performance of some new tricks, such as computer modeling and simulation.

LEAN MANAGEMENT BALANCES THE FLOW, NOT THE CAPACITY

A process and value stream view is fundamental to lean thinking. That is, lean management techniques create more of a process flow environment. The emphasis shifts toward flow management of the value stream. Control is easier with lean methods. Actual customer demand, rather than just an error-prone forecast of demand, is the trigger for factory-floor activities. Available-to-promise production-planning logic is replaced with more of a make-to-order (MTO) logic. One of JIT's goals is to configure the workers, products, and equipment in a way that reduces variability in the flow. Suppliers are often unreliable in their delivery and customers are often unpredictable. Traditional remedies are to carry extra raw material and finished goods inventory. In contrast, lean thinking strives for stability, with time buffers replacing inventory buffers as the insurance against uncertainty and fluctuations.

As mentioned, lean practices are the opposite of fat ones. Fat practices appear as too many people trained to do only a few narrow and repetitive tasks, often with long changeover times needed to produce the next batch. Fat practices produce obsolete inventory while having past due orders partially completed in the queue. The most basic practice of lean management is scheduling in relatively small finished-goods lot sizes as close to the customer order's quantity and due date as possible. Component buffer stocks should be maintained far back in the process (i.e., replenished as consumed).

Lean scheduling is contrarian to fat scheduling, which prefers running machines at fast rates and keeping them fully utilized. Lean scheduling adjusts the rate of output based on the input rate of customer demand. Having speed everywhere is less important. Flexibility is what matters. The critical principal with lean thinking is to balance the load of the flow rather than have extra just-in-case labor and equipment capacity everywhere. Any quality problems are quickly identified before much defective work can pile up.

The key lever for lean scheduling is to cross-train employees and thereby increase the flexibility of workers to move to where the demand is, rather than have them stationary, waiting for the demand to arise for them to use their special skill. Thus, by broadening the skill capability of the laborers, as in-process product inventory might build up, workers are able to shift downstream to relieve the load and accelerate throughput. In addition, lean management prides itself on eliminating complicated reporting and scheduling methods and replacing them with simple, often visual signage systems.

Reorganizing the physical layout of operations increases the payback of lean practices. Changes are made to the floor layout of work centers, such as creating U-shaped or circular cells of work stations, enabling workers to sit or stand back-to-back and to turn around to perform different tasks, in contrast to the fat practice of long assembly lines and side-by-side workers performing repetitive tasks. The closer proximity of the equipment in lean cells all but eliminates material handlers to move skids of products from place to place. In short, cellular layouts enable flexing the cell's output rate according to the demand rate, and flexing mainly focuses on the amount of labor assigned to the cell. Fat layouts typically are grouped by functions, whereas lean's cellular layouts organize work centers more around product families.

Modifications to work practices also improve the payback for going to lean. For example, with a lean work center cell there are no internal queues of in-process work product between operations. In contrast to fat purchasing, with its emphasis on bulk volume purchases for price discounts, lean purchasing favors a total-value-received view, including suppliers' delivery reliability, lead times, and administration simplification. Lean storage also favors a total-value view. Here the aim is to have the required materials kitted in advance or delivered directly to the line by the suppliers, eliminating double handling and unneeded storage space. And, of course, with lean management, there is no place for the traditional role of inspectors. Workers perform in-line self-inspection with the rule that defective production may not be passed on to a next operation. Defects or errors are resolved immediately without costly buildups.

LEAN ACCOUNTING VERSUS LEANER ACCOUNTING

Some of the advocates of lean management have extended their thinking beyond the material flow management space and into the cost accounting area too. They are proposing that the administrative effort to collect and manage all of the cost accounting records and transactions exceeds the benefits. They strongly suggest that, similar to the radical steps needed to accept JIT techniques, radical rethinking and changes are also needed for cost accounting and performance measurement methods.

The lean management community would prefer to see the accountants serve much more as change agents than as accounting police. These lean thinkers envision a cost accounting system with much less detailed reporting and transaction data collection. They would prefer measurement of only the vital few events that matter. Transactions are to lean accounting what inventory is to lean production. Transactions are viewed as waste and should be systematically eliminated. They see the accountants trapped in a role as bookkeepers with minimal time left over from the nonvalue-added drudgery of detailed data collection and reporting to assist in analyzing for improvements and innovation.

Some of the actions and changes that the lean management community would like from the accountants include the following:

- Eliminate variance reporting.
- Reduce the number of cost centers.
- Eliminate detailed labor reporting.
- Reduce the number of transactions for payables and receivables (by e-commerce with trading partners).
- Cross-train within the accounting department.

Some companies, however, confuse *lean accounting* with *leaner accounting*. Applying lean practices to many of the transaction-based work tasks that accountants perform makes great sense. However, reforms to how accountants compute managerial information to support decision making is another aspect. There is new risk if the proposed solutions overshoot their target. The cure should not be worse than the disease. For example, there are *lean* ways to compute costs of products and service lines, but they can follow costing principles—such as cause-and-effect rules—that already have improved managerial accounting in the last 20 years from its old, stodgy, flawed ways. Obviously, I am referring to ABM as a solution.

There is also little debate that performance measures for operations require a shift in emphasis away from local efficiency and utilization measures that can lead to suboptimizing behavior of the total enterprise. However, there is less solid footing for proposed changes based on lean thinking that are related to absorption costing and ABM. If reforms to managerial accounting that are based on lean thinking are too radical, organizations may find themselves reducing some expenses as if they are nonvalue-added spending rather than an investment with a healthy return.

One of the more radical proposals from the lean management community is to eliminate labor data collection and reporting systems altogether. A variation on this theme is to not bother to allocate any of the indirect and overhead expenses into product costs. In other words, leave those types of expenses unassigned. This latter method is referred to as *materials-only costing* because it only recognizes the direct material costs as being unique to the product costs. All of the rest are considered as costs belonging to the operations that are not distinguishable by any product. That is, all nondirect-material expenses are presumed to be a cost of doing business—not a product cost. The problem is this: If taken to the extreme of materials-only costing and a single factorywide direct and overhead expense rate, then any heterogeneity in equipment or in products is likely to result in over- or undercosted product costs relative to the product's true consumption of resource expenses.

Regardless of whether you think that materials-only costing makes sense, the source of the conflict is that the lean management people expect the accounting system to reflect the simplification and waste reduction efforts required in a lean environment.

A major tenet of lean accounting is that if the processes and value streams become more simplified, then there is less need for financial accounting, control, and measurement systems. But if this notion is taken too narrowly, it can be misinterpreted as if there is less need for applying financial analysis in teams for decision making. In fact, it should be the reverse. The margin for error is getting slimmer, and employee teams need greater, not less, proficiency in using financial data.

What may be an even worse unintended consequence of oversimplifying the lean costing system is the loss of visibility to view hidden waste. Today's traditional costing systems already hide waste by not identifying low-value-added activity costs that are baked into the standard costs. In short, all support costs are lumped into overhead. ABM resolves this by making support activity costs visible.

Ultimately we fall back to the "Is the climb worth the view?" test. The cost assignment model's network design and architecture need to be leveled up to a point where the diminishing returns of extra accuracy for extra level of effort of work is just not worth the benefit.

Lean accounting is simply absorption costing, using the same principles of activity-based management (ABM). Lean accounting simply applies some common sense by understanding that costing is modeling, and all cost models are stylized based on the decision support purpose they are intended to serve.

TIME, COST, AND QUALITY

In the past, organizations believed there were trade-offs among these three aspects of performance. The old line went, "Which two do you want to improve at the expense of the third?" Today organizations are realizing that all three can be improved simultaneously.

NOTES

1. Michael L. George, *Lean Six Sigma: Combining Six Sigma with Lean Speed* (New York: McGraw-Hill, 2002) 4, 36.

2. Gary Cokins, "Integrating Target Costing and ABC," *Journal of Cost Management*, Vol. 16 No. 4 (July/August 2002), 13; http://riahome.com.

3. ISO 9000, in its earliest versions, only required that there be a quality system, but did not demand that it be at a level that met customer expectations.

4. A related tool, Hoshin (sometimes called Policy Deployment) also provides a vehicle for focusing projects from the top down on strategic top management goals. Unfortunately, Hoshin was not widely used, especially where there was a great zeal to get on board with TQM and to get teams of

low-level workers going and give them a warm feeling of success—often without the support of middle managers.

5. While the Baldrige Award is indeed a terrific model, it has somewhat fallen short of its adoption level as the Deming Award in Japan. This is in part because it is viewed as a contest, so top management does not see the value of pursuing the process for the process's sake. The mentality related to the Baldrige Award is somewhat like "If you don't win, you lose."

6. Mickel J. Harry, "A New Definition Aims to Connect Quality with Financial Performance," *Quality Progress*, January 2000, 65.

7. Victor E. Sower and Ross Quarles, "Cost of Quality Usage and Its Relationship to Quality Systems Maturity" *Working Paper* series (Houston: Center for Business and Economic Development at Sam Houston State University, November 2002), 10–12.

8. American Society for Quality, *ANSI/ISO/ASQ Q9004-2000* (Milwaukee, WI: ASQ Quality Press, 2000).

20

SHAREHOLDER INTELLIGENCE
Return on Whose Investment?[1]

"The three most important things you need to measure in a business are customer satisfaction, employee morale, and cash flow. If you are growing customer satisfaction, your global market share is sure to grow. Employee satisfaction gets you productivity, quality, pride and creativity. Cash flow is the pulse—the vital sign of life in a company."
—Jack Welch, CEO (retired),
General Electric Inc.

We live in a world of contradictions. Executives are expected to deliver long-term value and growth but are pressured to produce consistently growing short-term profits. Are short-term profit results a valid predictor of long-term potential? How does the financial market assign a value to an organization's performance? These are questions that even professional consultants who espouse "maximize free cash flow" do not appear to have answers for. How can so-called economic value information be translated into a form that managers and teams can act upon?

The most prevalent method of valuing a publicly-owned and stock-traded company is by its market-quoted stock share price. This valuation method stems from the popular efficient-markets theory, which asserts that at any given moment the stock price is not only the best measure we have of the future value of a company, but it is usually an accurate one. The price of a stock, the theory goes, quickly incorporates everything publicly known about a company. Advocates defend the theory by stating that stock prices may appear too high or too low at times but this is only illusion. In short, the market presumably always knows.

In theory, the level of the stock share price at any point in time is influenced by several factors, such as cash requirements, profits, and cash flow velocity. Most security analysts adjust for limitations of audited financial statements and revert to cash flow–based measures. Security analysts subscribe to the belief that "Earnings are an opinion, but cash is a fact." The popularly followed investor Warren Buffet describes this as, "You just want to estimate a company's cash flows over time, discount them back, and buy them for less than that."

Changes in the quality of a company's income statement and balance sheet, both of which influence cash flows, include the impact of its decisions and selection of projects. All of these changes are predictable with calculable risks of moderately different amounts. Hence, if the determinants of value are measurable with understood risk, by knowing them and their relationships then the determinants' levers can be pushed or pulled to increase shareholder value.

This chapter explores value creation and how each function or department within an organization can understand how what they do impacts their organization's value.

WISE CASH OUTLAYS GOVERN ECONOMIC VALUE

Share price, like any price, is not that mysterious. It represents the currency value that two parties place on what is being bought or sold. For stock, it is the price at which shareholders are willing to buy *and* sell a share of stock. As with all commerce, this value depends on the particular requirements of the buyers and sellers. For example, what are their particular financial circumstances? And what are their forward-looking views of the benefits of a sale or purchase?[2]

Certainly, before the e-commerce bubble burst, the 1990s witnessed the impacts of baby boomers who believed the stock market was *the* investment vehicle, and of retirees who came to believe it was a safe, long-term investment.[3]

Today, company stock prices are increasingly volatile, seeming to jump around as knee-jerk reactions to press releases and news. One can debate whether a publicly traded company's stock share price, and hence its market value capitalization, is a *default* method for determining the value of a company in the absence of any better alternative valuation methodology, and whether stock share prices dynamically reflect the *correct* intrinsic value of companies. Stock price may be one method, but even the largest pension fund in the world does not use it alone in analyzing companies.[4] The California Public Employees' Retirement System (CalPERs) uses three pillars: stock price, corporate governance, and *economic value*. When using economic value, CalPERs looks at two aspects: (1) how much economic value the company is creating, and (2) whether the company has implemented processes to use economic value in the management of its business.

Perhaps, in part, this is because what increasingly accounts for a company's intrinsic value is how and where it deploys its spending and investments. While the corporation's strategy is an important signpost, its *execution* (i.e., wise investments) is what gets it to the destination. Any cash outlay is best thought of as an investment where its payback must exceed the cash outlay plus the *cost of capital*[5] of that cash outlay.[6]

SHARE PRICE MANAGEMENT OR VALUE MANAGEMENT?

A company's financial statements do not effectively report the consequences of previously deployed capital or the value of future capital expenditures and spending. Accounting profits do not equal economic profits. As Peter Drucker has noted, "Until a business returns a profit that is greater than its cost of capital, it operates at an economic loss," and unless accounting profits exceeds an enterprise's cost of capital, then it does not create wealth—it destroys it.

There is a principle in physics stating that nature abhors a vacuum and drives to fill it. Similarly with economic theory, capital eventually flows to the investment opportunities with the best returns because investors want to maximize their personal profits. This then transfers the responsibility to the company's management team to identify the best investment and spending opportunities for realizing and securing the capital's growth. Prioritizing projects and programs becomes a critical task for management.

A company may not compete directly with giants like the Ford Motor Company or General Electric, but all companies compete against each other in the financial markets—even privately owned companies. The companies yielding an acceptable financial return to investors and lenders survive and grow. Those that do not generate acceptable returns will be starved for renewal capital or will be charged a premium for raising future capital and financing. This places them at a relative disadvantage.

In short, generating modest accounting profits is not enough. Profits must be large enough to reward investors and lenders who have voluntarily risked their personal cash when they had risk-free alternative choices to invest their cash elsewhere, such as in money market funds. In other words, lenders charge interest on loans, while providers of equity capital have an opportunity cost of what they could have earned elsewhere. The accountants do deduct interest expenses on debt, but there is no comparable deduction for shareholders' opportunity costs in financial statements.

EPS (earnings per share) includes the lenders' charge and therefore is perceived by many to measure a company's ultimate accounting profit. It is calculated based on rules from generally accepted accounting principles (GAAP). But economists, including Professor Frank Knight of the University of Chicago in the 1920s,[7] have recognized that accounting profit and economic profit are not the same measure. In a sense, this implies that generated and retained earnings

---

Sarbanes-Oxley Act: Reform or Another Audit?

From the standpoint of public policy on modern capital markets, simply measuring earnings per share (EPS) lets the accountants off rather easily. Legislated reforms to address the financial scandals in the United States, such as the Sarbanes-Oxley Act, focus on the audits of financial statements. The real issue lies less with the accuracy of an audit but rather with its adequacy. The emphasis should be not on better traditional audits but rather on other forms of financial disclosure.[a]

The purpose of capital markets is to direct scarce capital to its highest uses. The highest uses depend on economic profits—rates of return—not on accounting profits. Yet the Sarbanes-Oxley Act explicitly references EPS and generally accepted accounting principles (GAAP) and thus may serve as a retardant to the application of economic profit data as the basis for good financial decisions. In the view of G. Bennett Stewart III, a pioneer in alternative forms of financial measures, earnings, and EPS as measured by GAAP are unreliable measures of corporate performance and stock market value.[b] I guess we'll all see if CEOs and CFOs are clever enough to use economic information for their internal decision making.

Although audited GAAP financial statements contain a statement of cash flows, it is not detailed enough to enable nonprofessionals to make their own cash-flow projections. Regardless, all financial statements are the result of management's opinion about a broad range of future situations and events that may or may not happen. For years now, security analysts have been cognizant of this as well as of the differences between accounting and economic profit. They use number-crunching software to reverse a CFO's accrual accounting, or *adjustments to reserves* to restate a company's financial performance in terms of cash flows. The appeal of cash flow measures will be discussed later in this chapter.

---

[a]Peter J. Wallison, "Give Us Disclosure, Not Audits," *Wall Street Journal*, June 2, 2003, A16.
[b]G. Bennett Stewart, "Why Smart Managers Do Dumb Things," *Wall Street Journal*, June 2, 2003, A16.

are free, so EPS encourages executive management to over-retain and waste shareholder capital by not redeploying it at desirable rates of return.

ECONOMIC VALUE MANAGEMENT: BEYOND ACCOUNTING PROFITS

Share price management, with its accounting manipulations that are fueled by pressure from financial analysts, will predictably lead to suboptimal short-term decisions. Share price management will hopefully give way to *economic value management* (EVM). But what is economic value management?

To address concerns with the limitations of financial accounting, corporate leaders are being attracted to management improvement programs that emphasize *value*. But as executives and managers investigate what economic value improvement programs are all about, they quickly realize there is much ambiguity involved: Whose value? What value? Value defined by whom? Value for customers or for shareholders? If for shareholders, is the market rational or schizophrenic in its valuation of publicly traded companies? If for customers, what risk exists that customers are given extra services with extra work effort and costs but without incremental price increases to recover the extra costs? In short, when spending decisions are made, will the shareholders ironically wind up paying with the destruction, not creation, of the company's wealth—and *their* wealth?

The objective to increase shareholder value and wealth is routinely verbalized in corporation annual reports and press releases. In the end, defining and executing strategies that satisfy customers in an economic way is widely accepted as the primary means of increasing shareholder wealth. However, this is accomplished by continuously investing in and redeploying the correct resources, both people and assets, in a way that motivates employees, guides better decisions, and produces more profitable results. How do you do this? That is what we will discuss here. But first let's understand some additional shortcomings of traditional financial reporting.

Financial statements do not report the intrinsic value of an enterprise or point to the location where economic value within an enterprise was created and will be created in the future. They partly reflect what has happened, but not what will happen; and even the historical reporting of accounting profits is somewhat misleading. The calculation of goodwill—basically the accountants' forced plug amount from a prior acquisition or merger event—has many interpretations. As an example of how unreliable goodwill can be, however, the goodwill amount in AOL Time Warner's equity capital valuation was adjusted down in January 2003 by billions of dollars in just a few months following AOL's acquisition of Time Warner when the goodwill accounting entry was posted for the combination of the two companies.[8] The original goodwill amount was obviously overstated. So much for the assumptions in that valuation! A better alignment of company performance and valuation measures is needed.

A company's balance sheet can particularly mislead the understanding of a company's *total* intrinsic value. As referenced in Part One about intangible assets, most companies find their share price–based market value is increasingly diverging from the balance sheet book value, a traditional Industrial Age measure. Recent Wall Street scandals have exposed companies whose accounting practices inflate the reported earnings and lack economic substance.[9]

BUSINESS VALUATION METHODS

The discipline of business valuation can be complicated. When a company intends to purchase another company, the alternatives for determining price valuation include the following:

- **Share price.** (Discussed earlier.)
- **Paying market price.** However, there is not much of a trading market for privately owned or thinly traded stock public companies.

Where Did the Accountants Go Wrong?

The limitations of financial statements are due in part to their origins. The history of an income statement reveals that it was created to report to investors, owners, and lenders how much profit was made from a single venture at the completion of that venture. An example would be investors in a tall ship's single 18th century trip across the Atlantic Ocean and back to export and import cargo. Because the venture was liquidated upon the trip's completion, the income statement and the balance sheet accurately reflected the profits and increase in wealth derived from the venture to pay back the investors and return to them a measured profit.

In today's modern age, however, we rarely see such full life cycle, beginning-to-completion investments, except perhaps for investors in a Broadway theatrical production. Modern enterprises do not liquidate themselves every year in order to provide accurate measures of income and wealth. Companies are not cargo schooners. They are a going concern. Although the balance sheet appears to capture the continuous build-up of wealth for a company as *retained earnings*, the balance sheet is weak in predicting liquidation value.

- **Comparison-based appraisals.** However, unlike comparative analysis for residential real estate, with active supply-and-demand relationships, there are insufficient transactions to glean a fair price.

- **Value the assets and liabilities.** I have already described why balance sheet *book balance* measures of goodwill and retained earnings, as well as omissions of intangible assets, render this approach unreliable.

- **Net cash flow.** The discounted cash flow (DCF) method acknowledges the time value of money in conjunction with the expected future returns of spending and investments generated across future time periods to equate to a *single* amount.[10] This amount is a perfect valuation—but its accuracy is subject to how reasonable the estimates are![11]

While valuation methodologies continue to be debated, one can only hope that more firms will recognize the cutting-edge benefits of *economic value management*, defined in Eleanor Bloxham's groundbreaking book of the same title. Before we discuss the distinctions in the cutting-edge application, however, let's look at the DCF and at historical economic profit and economic value methodologies. (We'll use the terms *economic profit* and *economic value* interchangeably, as that is the standard with most professional practitioners.)

ORIGINS OF DISCOUNTED CASH FLOW AND ECONOMIC PROFIT

More than 30 years ago economists, investors, and security analysts began to look beyond traditional financial accounting statements to simplify the reasoning behind their valuation of a corporation's stock price. The analysts began considering how they might determine a value for an enterprise as simply as they would value a child's lemonade stand. They disregarded all accrual accounting and judged whether the amount of money in the lemonade stand's cash-box register was increasing or decreasing. They focused on *cash flow*, not accrual accounting and the CFO's manipulations of *reserve balances*.

In 1961, Nobel Prize-winning economists Merton Miller and Franco Modigliani published an article that has been basic reading in business schools ever since.[12] They suggested that all the accrual accounting and adjustments the accountants use for external financial reporting are basically a smoke screen. They introduced and advanced the concept that shareholder value was a function of two net cash flow streams—the first from existing assets, reflected in the financial statements, and the second from future investments (e.g., microprojects), not yet reflected in the financial statements.

During the 1970s and 1980s, business schools graduated increasing numbers of MBAs and CPAs who understood the logic of DCF, further leading to its broader acceptance.

It is fine for earnings statements not to include the costs for all the resources used if there is only one investment, as in the case of cargo ships in the 18th century. But modern corporations invest on an ongoing basis. The paradox of "accounting profits up but shareholders' wealth down" is caused, in part, by the fact that the opportunity cost of equity capital cost is not included on the income statement. Thus, financial statements do not reflect how efficiently or poorly a company is using its capital, the cost of money, to generate its profits.

This is not a trivial matter. The measure for an investor's cost of equity capital can range widely, depending on whether they view their alternatives as low-risk U.S. Treasury bills or higher-risk high-tech growth firms. Only by earning more than its cost of equity can a company create wealth. The cost of equity is a critical cutoff rate, an invisible but profound dividing line between superior and inferior performance.

To resolve the problem of the omission of the cost of equity capital, early economic profit approaches add back after-tax interest expenses to net income and subtract the cost of both debt and equity capital as a *capital charge*. This type of performance measure would put shareholders and corporate managers into the driver's seat and bankers into the back seat. It would do so by shifting the attention of financial statements from a lender to a shareholder and investor orientation, and relegate lender information to footnotes.

In more sophisticated models, they also make other adjustments, which adjust net income due to issues in GAAP accounting.[13] Using economic profit provides a valuation of the company based on each period's projected economic profit (EP) with DCF math:

Valuation of a Company = Economic Value
$$= \text{Sum of PV of } [EP_{(p)} + EP_{(p+1)} + \ldots + EP_{(p+n)}]$$

where   PV = present value
   p = the period
   EP = economic profit (i.e., adjusted net income* reduced by a capital charge), calculated as follows:

Economic profit (EP) = [Adjusted net income
   $- \text{(average invested capital} \times \text{WACC)}]$

Or alternatively and equivalently,

$$\text{Economic profit (EP)} = [(\text{Adjusted net income/average invested capital })\\ - \text{WACC}] \times \text{average invested capital}$$

where WACC = the lenders' and equity owners' weighted average cost of capital

The magnitude of a period's economic profit doesn't matter as much (unless it is an alarming negative profit) compared to increases, and hopefully sizable increases, in the stream of economic profits in the future time periods. *Economic value* equates that stream of all future *economic profits* as a single amount. Hence, as the formula demonstrates, the key to value creation is to understand the elements that make economic profit rise. For many firms, value creation may relate to a combination of the following elements:

- Sales growth rate
- Operating profit margin
- Asset turns
- Incremental fixed capital investments
- Incremental working capital investments
- Tax rates
- Debt versus equity and leverage
- Weighted cost of capital
- Cash flow

In order for a company to plan for maximizing its economic value creation, firms will need know to how these elements interact and, more importantly, how these combined elements connect to operational decisions. It is important to move from theory to practice. And the key question is: "How do the efforts of employees and the current spending and future investments in resources generate perpetually increasing shareholder value?"[14]

VALUE CREATION FROM CAPITAL EFFICIENCY AND CASH TURNOVER VELOCITY

Many believe that the three major influences on economic profit or economic value, and wealth creation, are year-to-year revenue growth, healthy profit margins (relative to the industry), and good *capital efficiency*.[15] (An example of capital efficiency is an airline carrier getting the most from its fleet.) While most everyone understands the first two influences, the last one is less well understood.

Here is an alternative variation of the economic profit formula that does not change the calculated answer from the prior equations, but it forces you to think more deeply about the equation's elements:

$$\text{Economic Profit (EP)} = [(\text{Profit*/average invested capital}) - \text{WACC}]$$
$$\times \text{average invested capital}$$
$$= [\text{ROAIC} - \text{WACC}] \times \text{average invested capital}$$

where WACC = the lenders' and equity owners' weighted average cost of
                     capital

    ROAIC = return on average investment in capital, calculated as follows:

$$\text{ROAIC} = \text{Profit Margin [Profit */Revenue]}$$
$$\times \text{Velocity [Revenue/average invested capital]}$$
$$= \text{Profit*/average invested capital}$$

A review of the equations forces a company to evaluate its ability to generate more revenues from its invested capital (velocity) in conjunction with its profit margins, to assess its broader ROAIC percentage's annual performance—which in turn can affect its economic value or economic profit.

ECONOMIC PROFIT, CAPITAL EFFICIENCY, AND DECOMPOSITION TREES

A substitute for measuring economic profit is a measure called *cash conversion cycle efficiency* (CCC). CCC measures how efficiently cash is being converted from purchasing resources to selling the outputs and receiving the cash. CCC has also been called a company's "cash gap" and is computed with this equation:

$$\text{CCC} = \text{Cash Gap} = \#\text{ days inventory} + \#\text{ days accounts receivable}$$
$$- \#\text{ days accounts payable}$$

---

*Reported as earnings adjusted in the economic profit calculation.

Figure 20.1 illustrates a cash gap where cash is tied up for 120 days in this company's operating cycle that converts purchased resources into profits.

What good is a measure, however, if we do not know how to influence or directly impact its outcome? An effective way of understanding what levers to push or pull to improve economic profit is with a decomposition tree, similar to the classic DuPont equations. Figure 20.2 illustrates a decomposition tree used to compute a company's return on average invested capital (ROAIC).

Economic profit at each period end for a company can then be computed as shown in the shaded box of the right half of the figure. As noted earlier, the formula subtracts the lenders' and equity owners' weighted average cost of capital (WACC) from the period's ROAIC and multiplies the remainder times the average invested capital (AIC):

Economic Profit = (ROAIC − WACC) × average invested capital employed

With the decomposition tree, we can perform revealing analysis to aid in converting this obviously financial information into operational information needed to improve the financial results.[16]

Figure 20.3 visually displays some of the relationships of improvement pro-

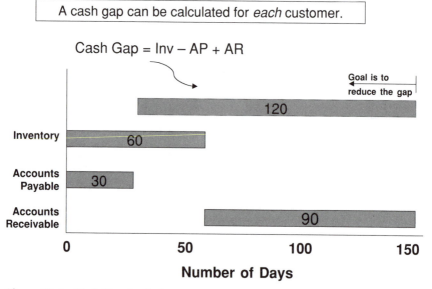

Figure 20.1   Cash Gap Analysis

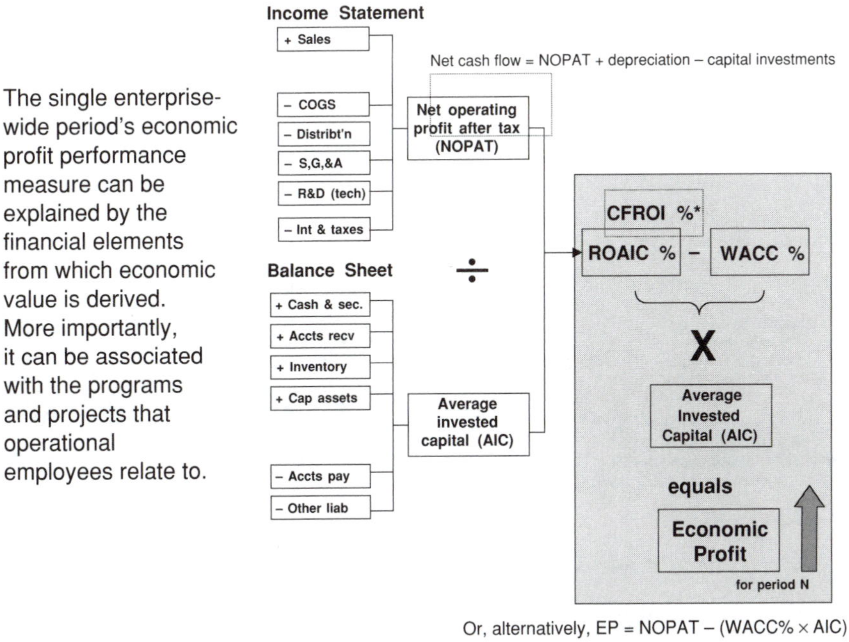

The single enterprise-wide period's economic profit performance measure can be explained by the financial elements from which economic value is derived. More importantly, it can be associated with the programs and projects that operational employees relate to.

Income Statement

+ Sales

Net cash flow = NOPAT + depreciation – capital investments

– COGS

– Distribt'n

– S,G,&A

– R&D (tech)

– Int & taxes

Net operating profit after tax (NOPAT)

Balance Sheet

$\div$

+ Cash & sec.

+ Accts recv

+ Inventory

+ Cap assets

Average invested capital (AIC)

– Accts pay

– Other liab

CFROI %*

ROAIC % – WACC %

X

Average Invested Capital (AIC)

equals

Economic Profit

for period N

Or, alternatively, EP = NOPAT – (WACC% × AIC)

Figure 20.2   EVM Decomposition Tree

grams and projects as they relate to the financial statements—and ultimately to period economic profits and their composite measure, economic value. This type of financial modeling connects projects, the lower levels of work that employees relate to, with the economic profit measures that executives are driving.

For more in-depth reading on the topics of cash conversion cycles and EVM decomposition trees, go to www.wiley.com/go/performance. There is also a description of an advanced technique to evaluate the average rate of return on capital (AROC) for planned spending decisions.

PERILS OF RELYING ON A SINGLE ECONOMIC VALUE MANAGEMENT NUMBER

An EVM metric, when reported as a single number, cannot be readily used for decision-making purposes. How does an organization communicate such measurement data downward to affect the behavior of the employees and managers?

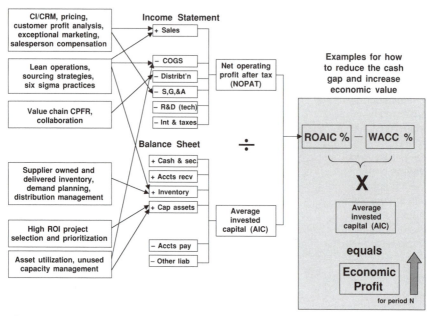

Figure 20.3   EVM Decompsotion Tree: Projects

How do the employees and managers know *which* actions that they influence or control most contribute to improving economic value and to maximizing shareholder value? Investments in one area, such as manufacturing, may detract from another area, such as distribution, that may hold an opportunity for relatively larger returns. As long as capital can be employed in other areas, it is not free—it has an opportunity cost since next-best alternatives exist. Linkages are needed between economic value measures and the functions *within* a business unit. In effect, senior management has been left with an ambiguity that lies between their economic profit measure and the performance measurement information that employees at the lower levels of a company's operations rely on daily as their operating signals.

It is my opinion that this proverbial *single* economic value measure reported for the company's president or the pay incentive compensation system (e.g., bonuses) must eventually be decomposed into its tree of subelements comprising the parts that contribute to it. This is data that employees can use to take actions. I favor tools that not only suggest what to improve, like profit margins, but also which specific costs of customers, products, and processes need to be changed to make those improvements.

Organization Performs an Endless Series of Projects

How does a company continuously increase its economic value? To begin with, a company cannot rest on its laurels of brand-name products and loyal customers. A company cannot coast without eventually slowing down. As Eleanor Bloxham illustrates in her book, a company's activities begin with capital investment.[a] A company continuously injects spending into an endless stream of projects. Product promotions and sales campaigns are examples. Some projects are large, while many are *microprojects*. Even receiving, processing, and fulfilling a customer sales order, the components of the cash-to-cash cycle that seems so repetitive, can be thought of as a microproject—no two sales orders are ever identical.

Think of a business model where a company works only on projects (e.g., an engineer-to-order company), but take your thinking to the extreme in terms of how this company uses resources. Imagine if this company terminates all of its employees each evening and rehires them the next day. Consider the overall impact of microprojects that have a range of very high and very low financial returns. Unfortunately for some employees, an unacceptable payback for their project-related effort might not justify hiring them back for the next day's work.

This approach, where all employees are thought of as daily subcontactors, would assure financial returns above the cost of capital. While companies typically retain their employees and consider their learning curves, companies rarely ever know, with any confidence, which projects are creating or destroying shareholder wealth. Only the net effect of all projects combined is reported as the company's net profit. The employees' work is rarely thought of as a recurring series of microprojects. If, as time passes, a company's composite collection of projects becomes less innovative, loses its impact on customers, or becomes less efficient, then the company's overall economic profit performance will inevitably suffer.

Financial statements do not shed much light on individual project economies and their individual returns. Significant changes from all of a company's concurrent projects are, as time passes, eventually reflected in the financial statements. This then reports whether the company is improving or falling behind. The message here is that the cost of capital matters in three places:

1. Selecting the correct projects with financial returns likely to exceed the cost of capital.

(Continued)

Organization Performs an Endless Series of Projects *(Continued)*

2. Monitoring the financial rate of return of existing projects to possibly adjust them midstream to minimize economic losses.

3. Reporting the financial rate of return of completed projects to learn what contributed to favorable or unfavorable returns.

In summary, the cost of capital is very relevant when making decisions about resources, and the decisions ultimately affect shareholders and owners.[b]

---

[a]Bloxham, *Economic Value Management*, 296–298.
[b]Details on adjustments to the value and cost of capital calculations for these purposes may be found in Bloxham's *Economic Value Management*, pp. 118–121.

ACTIVITY-BASED MANAGEMENT ENABLES THE DECOMPOSITION TREE

As Eleanor Bloxham outlines in her book, there is a great opportunity for ABM and its powerful cost-tracing techniques to provide more meaningful and accurate information than that available to most decision makers today. In particular, the cost of capital can now be traced as a capital charge to processes, products, and customers, using the same fundamentals that ABM already uses to assign other resource expenditures.[17]

In this framework, the cost of money is simply another resource cost that should be logically assigned, based on its causal consumption, similar to the way in which other expenses are assigned. The only difference for ABM cost tracing is that the general ledger does not specifically, separately, and directly identify the capital charge. It must be inferred (i.e., imputed) from the balance sheet accounts and an agreed-on rate assumption for the cost of capital. Any difficulties in gathering and computing this data should not prevent companies from proceeding and tracing capital costs. It is better to include capital cost thinking, even if it involves using approximations, than to leave it out of profitability analysis.[18] And as far as the cost of capital, sometimes simpler is better.[19]

Pick a Cost of Capital—Precision May Not Be Necessary

The determination of a specific cost of capital rate has become a separate debate among theoreticians, academics, and consultants, with elaborate weighted average cost of capital (WACC) formulas tied to risk levels. ABM is independent of these debates. At a basic level, ABM is a calculation engine that accepts whatever rate and/or charge is the outcome of the cost of capital rate debate. ABM applies that rate, often referred to as an imputed interest rate, and traces the capital costs to the costs of products, services, and customers to yield valuable information.

Rather than waste time in theoretical debates and excess digits to the right of the decimal point, companies may wish to select a commonly used rate calculation method, assume it is adequate, apply it, and start to observe the results in their own operations. They can later experiment with the sensitivity of the rate and debate which rate to apply for what types of decisions after managers and teams have started learning how to use the new data.

MAKING DECISIONS

Economic value management involves two major sets of analyses or decision processes:[20]

1. **Decision analysis** is the use of historical expenses, including traced cost of capital charges, and evaluative financial metrics to draw insights.
2. **Decision making** is the rational application of an ROI calculator to predict financial returns in order to judge them for "go or no-go" decisions or for "do more or do less" investment decisions.

"[Decision analyses] that use evaluative metrics assess how an organization has performed in a number of dimensions. . . . When we say evaluative, what we are measuring is not an expectation but rather what has been done and what has been achieved. . . . Often so-called financial evaluative measures are referred to as *backward looking*, and so-called nonfinancial evaluative measures, such as customer satisfaction, are considered *forward looking*. While it is true that current or past customer satisfaction will be a factor that *may* determine future financial results, this is true for every type of measure, including those labeled *financial*. The net income earned today or the cash flow for the month will influence how we will be able to run the business, what investments we will make, and our future cost of capital. In that sense, all measures, even financial ones, have a forward impact. Similarly, the term *nonfinancial* can be confusing. If customer satisfaction is *forward looking* in any sense, it is so called because it will be a factor that will determine future *financial* results. In that sense, customer satisfaction *is* a financial measure (although it is clearly not an accounting one).[21]

"Although so-called *backward-looking* (i.e., evaluative) measures are often disparaged, the right kind of evaluative measures—value-based ones—can provide extremely useful insights . . . [because] the seeds of the future are often hidden in the past."[22]

As described in Part Three, ABM yields a rich amount of profit margin layer data that provides insights as to where, on which products, and with whom the company is making or losing money. But this data is historical and hence limited to being descriptive. It does, however, communicate where previously committed money was spent, and it reports past spending in the form of outputs and outcomes. When output costs are considered as feedback, this data becomes very useful for taking corrective actions and making adjustments.

Decision making is about predictive testing for whether future spending opportunities (spending that will include investors' and lenders' precious capital) should be committed. Similar to the way in which ABM data is combined for what-if scenarios, "decisions to enhance value going forward use evaluative measures as the springboard and to that add predictive measures."[23] This involves classical investment justification and capital budgeting analysis. It applies return on investment (ROI) analysis with discounted cash flows (DCF methods)—all techniques that readers with MBAs learned in graduate school. This forward-looking logic aims to test whether all the money being spent now and going forward (which has gone into or will go into specific projects, products, service lines, and customers) will generate *economic* profits, not just accounting profits.

"Where value metrics improve on the DCF/NPV process is in the explicit linkage they provide between the evaluative and predictive measures. Unfortunately, although DCF/NPV provide the right answers, it is not easy to link them to typical evaluative measures. This issue, in fact, creates the disconnect in nonvalue-based systems between the typical performance measures and the basis for decisions! It is quite common for organizations to make decisions on one basis but never use those metrics to evaluate whether or not their predictions actually came to be."[24]

Given the expanse of literature on DCF, let's briefly discuss the way in which organizations may wish to use value metrics to analyze decisions after they have been made.

DECISION ANALYSIS: SEPARATING THE
WINNERS FROM THE LOSERS

Decision analysis leverages feedback information to indicate what to fix and change. ABM data plays a role here because it is all about tracing resource consumption (via activities performed) to products, service lines, channels, and customers. The tracing is based on cause-and-effect usage relationships, not on arbitrary volume-based cost allocations. Not all products are equally profitable; neither are all customers. As described in Part Three, ABM provides more accurate and visible pictures of the product and customer profit margins than do traditional accounting methods. In short, ABM traces the resources used by each and every customer. With the inclusion of the cost of capital into the resource consumption picture, ABM complements value creation objectives, and it provides more complete data for managers and employee teams to determine how to evaluate strategies and investments, and which next steps to take.[25]

As an example, a distillery's managers were of the belief that its scotch was more profitable than its vodka, but they were not sure this was a fact. They analyzed their liquor brands and, by including the capital charge, began to better understand the full financial impact of the lengthy time, storage, and handling required for aged scotch relative to their other liquors that required less aging time. By including the capital charge invested in both the assets used (e.g., kegs and cellar space) as well as the aging liquor inventory, ABM was able to prove that the aged scotch did not generate as much profit as the company thought it did relative to vodka. This was opposite to their beliefs. Vodka could be sold within weeks of being distilled. As a result, the company shifted its production and promotions toward selling the more profitable vodka.

Part Three discussed how the ABM cost assignment network enables calculation of profit margin statements for *each* customer. Figure 20.4 illustrates the expansion of the ABM cost assignment network to include the imputed cost of capital charges from the balance sheet. Similar to the role of activity drivers, *capital drivers* causally trace the cost of money to what is using it—to the specific assets, products, or customers.[26]

As described in Part Three, when the price and volume for a customer (i.e., each customer's total sales) are netted against that customer's costs, ABM reports how much profit, or loss, was left over—that is, how much profit was uniquely derived from that customer. Because profit translates into wealth creation for owners and stockholders, ABM has created an important intersection where the ultimate business drivers—customer demand and customer preferences—can be understood.

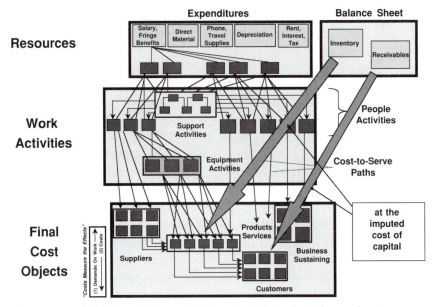

Figure 20.4   ABM Cost Assignment Network: Include the Balance Sheet

Revisit Figure 13.5 in Part Three, which shows a customer profit and loss statement. In that P&L statement, imagine that there is an extra profit margin line at the bottom to now include the *capital charge*. The capital charge is effectively traced from the balance sheet to the categories that consume capital investment and that reduce the profit margin below NOPAT. (In practice, this capital charge would be distributed, based on the capital drivers, among the costs of specific activities, products, and customers—not consolidated as a single line item.)

Tracing the capital costs via capital drivers adds the economic view to traditional profit reporting.[27] For example, a product with high traditional accounting profit may also require very high investments in inventory or expensive specialized equipment. Once the cost of these capital investments is also considered, this more complete view of a product's costs may then show a negative economic profit. By adding the capital charge, new impressions may be substantially different compared to the beliefs formed by the less complete, traditional reporting of only the accounting profit.

Key Sources to Impute the Capital Charge

The capital charge is made up of several components that reflect the imputed *cost of capital* charge for net assets and liabilities of the balance sheet. Here are examples of some of the balance sheet accounts for which costs of capital can be uniquely traced to activities, products, services, and customers:

- **Inventories.** The total inventory balance's imputed capital charge is traced to products. An appropriate measure may be based on the average balance (in monetary terms) of each inventory item during that period. This reflects the number of days of inventory turnover in the *cash gap* analysis. In this way, a customer who purchased a disproportionately high mix of products for which substantial inventory balances and costs were carried would reflect a relatively lower profit than would an identical customer buying products with lower levels and costs of work-in-process and finished goods inventories.

- **Receivables.** The total accounts receivable balance's imputed capital charge is traced directly to customers. This measure may be based on each customer's average balances carried. This is the days-sales-outstanding (DSO) in the cash gap metric. In this way, ABM serves somewhat like a billing system for a bank, charging for each customer's loan.

- **Payables.** With a reverse effect of inventories, products may be credited to benefit from favorable lengthy payment terms from suppliers (or penalized by fast-pay requirements of powerful, demanding suppliers).

- **Fixed assets.** Costs for purchased equipment are already traced to equipment work activities, but over a number of years as depreciation. However, the net asset value still represents an investment of capital. Therefore, the imputed capital charge can be traced to equipment activities similarly to how the depreciation is currently traced.

ECONOMIC VALUE MANAGEMENT: A MORE COMPLETE PICTURE

Economic value management, as defined in Eleanor Bloxham's book, provides a more complete picture. It can be driven down into the organization via ABM data and scorecards. With these tools in place, managers and employee teams can increase shareholder wealth by taking the following steps:

- Focusing on the more profitable customers, channels, and products.

- Addressing value-destroying customers, channels, products, and processes.

- Increasing revenue-related activities while holding invested funds constant.

- Reducing assets while holding revenue-related activities constant.

- Investing only in assets and projects whose projected return is higher than the firm's cost of capital.

ABM can assign capital charges to customers, products, and processes so that decisions to change any of them are based more on economics than on guesses or outdated and arbitrary cost allocations.[28] By tracing the cost of money, then the capital is equitably charged to the ultimate purchasing entity, the customer. With this more complete data, employee teams and managers can better see the intersection where customer value and stockholder value meet. Scorecards assist in managing profits by providing guidance in the form of score variance feedback that tells employees how they are doing on what is important—and where to improve. Performance management involves the methodologies discussed in Parts Two through Four—and now includes the cost of capital, too.

Economic value management helps companies determine how and where to allocate resources. ABM can provide the linkage of the capital charge to the economic profit statement. With this in place, employees and managers can become more aware of the importance of capital usage. Beyond that, they have a much better way of focusing where to place their efforts and what to change and adjust going forward.

NOTES

1. I would like to express my gratitude to Eleanor Bloxham, author of *Economic Value Management* (Hoboken, NJ: John Wiley & Sons, 2002) and president of the Value Alliance and Corporate Governance Alliance, for her assistance with this chapter.

2. Eleanor Bloxham, *Economic Value Management* (Hoboken, NJ: John Wiley & Sons, 2002), 148, 156.

3. Ibid., p. 24.

4. Ibid., p. 181.

5. The term *capital* implies financial and cash capital. Other forms of capi-

tal, such as intellectual capital, are relevant, but I assign their usage to the methodology of scorecards.

6. Bloxham, *Economic Value Management*, pp. 7, 19, 296, and Exhibit 9.19 on p. 298.

7. Frank Knight, *Risk, Uncertainty, and Profit* (Chicago: University of Chicago Press, 1921).

8. AOL Time Warner has since changed their company name to just Time Warner.

9. Robert A.G. Monks, quoted on back jacket of Bloxham's *Economic Value Management*.

10. Think of this *single* amount (i.e., the intrinsic economic value) as the amount of cash in a bank balance today that has the same cash-generating power of the business operating until the end of time.

11. Bloxham, *Economic Value Management*, 148–149

12. Merton Miller and Franco Modigliani, "Dividend Policy, Growth and the Valuation of Shares," *Journal of Business*, October 1961, 411–433.

13. See G. Bennett Stewart III, *The Quest for Value* (New York: Harper-Collins, 1991). Rather than the one-size-fits-all approach of the historical economic profit and economic value approaches, in *Economic Value Management* (referenced elsewhere in this chapter), Eleanor Bloxham sets out why and when to make these adjustments—and also how to better deal with cost of capital in situations that warrant more careful approaches. I recommend her book for those ready to make these processes relevant to their specific organization.

14. Bloxham, *Economic Value Management*, 296–297 and Exhibit 9.19.

15. Ronald Fink, "Forget the Float?" *CFO*, Vol. 17, No. 9 (Fall 2001), 54–58.

16. For examples of EVM decompositions and their use, see Bloxham, *Economic Value Management*, pp. 286–287 and Exhibits 9.12 and 10.6. See also p. 301.

17. Ibid., pp. 205–206, 211, 262–263, 280, 287.

18. Ibid., pp. 118–121.

19. Ibid., pp. 117–121.

20. Ibid., pp. 91–94.

21. Ibid., p. 92.

22. Ibid., p. 27.

23. Ibid., p. 93.

24. Ibid., p. 94

25. Ibid., pp. 211, 262–263.

26. Ibid.

27. Ibid.

28. Ibid.

21

EMPLOYEE INTELLIGENCE
Human Capital Management

"Failing to prepare is preparing to fail."
—Vince Lombardi, famous coach
of the Green Bay Packers,
U.S. National Football League

This chapter discusses two key elements of human capital management (HCM) systems: employee retention management and workforce planning. In the broader context of Performance Management (PM), HCM's purpose is to help an organization achieve the strategic objectives in its strategy map and balanced scorecard's *learning and growth perspective*. Remember that in the strategy map, an organization's learning and growth strategic objectives directly and indirectly influence all of the other strategic objectives. Organizations succeed through people.

As was stated in Chapter 1 regarding employees:

"The sources of value creation are in people's know-how and their passion to perform. You don't supervise a product development engineer or advertising editor to create a better product or ad copy. Rather, they do it, given the right environment. PM powers an organization as an economic engine by recognizing that social systems are the fuel. This is not to say that the organization's mission is not fundamental—it is. It simply means that performance requires cooperation, teamwork, and people giving effort for the benefit of the whole. Value creation is central to the purpose of an organization. . . .

Some publicly-traded corporations feel investor pressure to cut costs to meet earnings expectations, which usually translates into laying off employees. But right-sizing decisions based solely on head count and cost can rob an organization of its key talent. Human resource systems need to acknowledge employees as valued intangible assets, each with unique skills and experiences."

I have strong feelings about how much we underestimate the importance of understanding the needs and value of people. Despite the impression from this book that performance management is some form of autopilot that guides and drives an organization based on metrics and models, the reality is that PM is ultimately all done through people.

HUMAN CAPITAL: INTANGIBLE ASSET

In Chapter 1 I also described the importance of differentiating tangible assets from the intangible ones. With regard to employees I meant the following. *Tangible assets* are buildings, machines, and inventories. A simple definition of long-term tangible assets is things you purchase and *depreciate* as period expenses with time. However, employees are *human capital* who go home each night and return in the morning. People are intangible assets who produce value. *Intangible assets*, in contrast to tangible assets, are resources with potential that *grows* with time, rather than depreciates.

Human capital management systems can be thought of as a major advance across the stages of maturity of the personnel and payroll systems of the 1980s. They provide a better way to deal with these types of questions that managers struggle with:

- Some key employees unexpectedly quit, so how do we quickly fill the vacated positions without our organization skipping a beat?
- Our market and management's strategic direction has shifted overnight, and management wants instant traction. What do we change and who should do it? We can see a train wreck coming. Our current workforce members are aging and set in their ways, but does management see this impending problem? And will they give us the resources we need to fix it?
- *Succession planning* is not in our vocabulary yet. We know there are patterns in why employees leave us, and these profiles can be applied to predict our current employees most likely to leave. But how do we get started?

The heart of the HCM problem deals with retaining good employees and effective workforce planning to predict the needed number and types of skill sets of employees and expenses to meet future workload requirements. Let's first take a closer look at employee retention and workforce planning, and then finish this section by describing how employee relationship management (ERM) systems are a subset of HCM.

EMPLOYEE RETENTION: KNOWING
WHO WILL LEAVE BEFORE THEY LEAVE

Imagine if organizations had a much better understanding about who the current employees are that are most likely to leave, based upon the factors of why employees have left in the past. Once the organization begins to understand why people have left in the past and apply that understanding to the current employee population, then it can begin to implement effective retention policies for keeping good employees.

More specifically, imagine further that you could receive reports describing the following:

- Groups of employees most likely to leave within the next year.
- The numerous reasons why employees have left in the past—measured by type of reason.
- The exposure to the organization if the groups identified to leave actually leave.
- Categories of people leaving by job type.
- Scores[1] of individual employees (by name and employee ID number) in the high-risk category predicted to voluntarily leave.
- Current employees most likely to leave, broken down into categories, such as high, medium, or low risk, with the likely causes for their departure.
- Current top performers in the high-risk category and the percentages of reasons that historically caused separations of comparable positions and performers.

The knowledge that is lost when a valued, tenured employee leaves is costly to replace—and it requires substantial lead time to replace it. Ideally it is better to retain valued employees than to lose them. This is common sense. Many decisions are affected when employees leave, such as the following:

- **Succession planning**—identifying the next leaders of the organization.
- **Leadership development**—which other employees can provide leadership for the organization to increase revenue and generate greater shareholder value?.
- **Time to market**—the amount of time it takes to bring a product to market with experienced employees versus constantly hiring and training new employees.

Today's HCM systems help organizations understand the costs and impact associated with the acquisition, development, and retention of employees. HCM systems can identify employees most likely to leave. Of course, each location within the parent organization will see different reasons why people are likely to leave. Since each location is unique, it can tailor its own HCM system's parameters based on local, enterprise-wide, regional, and market factors.

Employee retention modeling and succession planning provides a statistically validated understanding for questions such as these:

- Which groups of employees are most and least likely to voluntarily leave or be involuntarily terminated?

- In which functions (e.g., sales, product development) would shortages most jeopardize the attainment of strategic objectives? For what reasons have different types of employees left the organization in the past?

  If the profiles of employees who have left in the past are applied to existing employees, which current employees are likely to depart? Names can be listed by high/medium/low risk and with information describing the possible impact to the organization. Examples of risk factors to include in such profiles are "reached x-year tenure mark," "less than $x\%$ salary increase within salary levels," and age at hire.

For example, if employees have been leaving at about the five-year tenure mark, they are probably just at the point where they have achieved a significant amount of experience and understanding of the organization's procedures. The knowledge that leaves with such an employee, at this point in their tenure, is difficult if not impossible to replace without significant costs.

Another example of a reason that employees may be likely to leave is their age at hire. Globally there is a shortage of workers between the ages of 35 and 44. This age range tends to include the experienced workers that are slated to take over management positions from the older, retiring workforce. Many workers in this age group are already in middle management. With the increased number of eligible retirees and the large number of younger workers, the middle-age work group can be of great importance to the success of many companies.

After evaluating all the reasons that an HCM model determined for why employees leave, management can focus on those employees in the high-risk category who are likely to voluntarily or involuntarily leave your organization.

There are ancillary benefits from *employee retention modeling*. Apart from the purpose of estimating workforce staffing requirements and understanding existing conditions of risk, a company can remedy the problems which have led to historical and recent employee turnover. That is, it can minimize future employee turnover.

It is possible that the management team and its policies have been responsible for much of the turnover of the past. New actions and policy adjustments can fix this. Identifying those employees with the highest risk for voluntary separation allows the organization to evaluate each employee's performance and implement training programs to help increase employee success and leadership capabilities.

Employee retention–increasing actions or policies include the following:

- Increased pay ranges
- Higher starting salaries
- Formalizing a management-by-objectives program (e.g., scorecards)
- More effective training and education
- Career path assistance

As changes for specific employees are made, such as a salary increase, the employee can be *rescored* to see how much the change will reduce the employee's probability of leaving the organization.

The obvious message here is, don't risk losing your top performers who possess the more critical skills—particularly to competitors!

WORKFORCE PLANNING: TRANSLATING FUTURE PLANS INTO THE HEAD COUNT REQUIREMENTS

In Part Three we learned how the descriptive (i.e., historical) activity-based costing data serves as a foundation for predicting future capacity requirements (e.g., cost estimating and budgets). That same forecasting methodology applies to workforce planning as well. It is superior to traditional budgeting approaches. The purpose of a budget is typically for managing short-term allocations of corporate spending. Budgets often start with a baseline of what level of head count and spending already exists at the end of the prior year and then incrementally adjusts that level. In contrast, activity-based planning starts with forecasts of the future workload coming at the organization, and then solves for the future periods' workforce and spending requirements.

Effective *workforce planning* needs:

● Planning for needed skills *beyond* a year.

● Knowledge of what capabilities currently exist, what will be needed, and the *gap* between that must be filled.

● Policies and programs for training, compensation, and diversity management.

In short, *workforce planning* needs a more systematic approach than a traditional budget to anticipate workforce level and skill set needs and to fill job positions in a timely manner.

Four Steps to Work Force Planning

A four-step program to workforce planning is straightforward, but it is challenging to do it well. Like all capacity planning exercises, resource planning begins with measuring where you are today, determines what you *will* need, measures the *gap* of shortages and excesses between today and the future, and finally identifies which resources should be added, shifted, or removed to close the gap.

The supply-and-demand equation is as follows:

New employee requirements = Existing employees + / − change in employees required (to meet the new planned workload) + voluntary and involuntary employee separations

The third element of the equation adds additional complexity, and I will discuss it later in this section.

These are the four steps to workforce planning:

1. **Know what you now have—the capacity to do work.** Workforce planning begins with collecting a skills inventory and profile of all existing employees. These are your treasured assets.

2. **Estimate the future demand load.** Ideally, do not start with a narrow capacity-requirements-planning view by simply estimating the future sales and order volume to determine capacity based on consumption and cost rates. This step hopefully also incorporates the plans from projects and programs documented from the strategy maps and scorecards discussed in Part Two that may require additional new employees.

Four Steps to Work Force Planning *(Continued)*

3. **Determine the gap—both shortages and excesses.** The projected deficiencies of skills and competencies will need to be filled to meet short-supply needs. Without filling these, service levels may decline or projects will not be completed as scheduled. There will also be cases of overly abundant, unnecessary, and/or obsolete skills that must be dealt with. A solution to this potentially sad situation of simultaneous shortages and excesses is to keep one step ahead by proactively cross-training your existing human capital. Training minimizes the awkward condition of forced layoffs while you concurrently recruit for open job positions. The investment in training can reduce overall long-term costs.

4. **Acquire, shift, and abandon.** Go do it. Close the gap determined in Step 3. But do it having the facts!

OTHER FACTORS AFFECTING WORKFORCE PLANNING

Activity-based planning (ABP) is a major advance over traditional budgeting, but it requires adjustments to make it a complete solution for workforce planning. In addition to demand-loaded resource calculations, a company's leaders must also predict and include internal and external factors such as the following:

- Changes in mission and strategy
- Economic conditions
- Big projects
- Market competition
- Union rules
- Government legislation

All of these factors can be at play at any given time. HCM software functionality allows what-if scenario planning to systematically evaluate interdependencies of multiple factors like these, plus other variables.

In addition, planning for man-hours and employee full time equivalents (FTEs) can be more complicated than just using activity-based planning. Why? ABP, being no different than standard Industrial Age methods of predicting resource requirements, assumes a near-zero transaction cost to acquire re-sources. ABP also assumes minimal learning curves and ramp-up time for new employees or for existing employees who change job positions. The transaction cost is in the form of recruiting fees, advertising expenses, and up-front employee training. There are also temporary inefficiencies incurred during the learning curve, which produces opportunity costs. (However, the usually hidden costs of a personnel function's recruiting efforts are included in the expense in an ABP model.)

The main point here is that with employee turnover, you have to add new employees even faster than what ABP calculates because you have to allow for the departure of employees.

EMPLOYEE RELATIONSHIP MANAGEMENT SYSTEMS: A SUBSET OF HCM

Employee relationship management (ERM) systems are typically what we might think of as 1990s systems. Figure 21.1 depicts ERM systems as intended for use

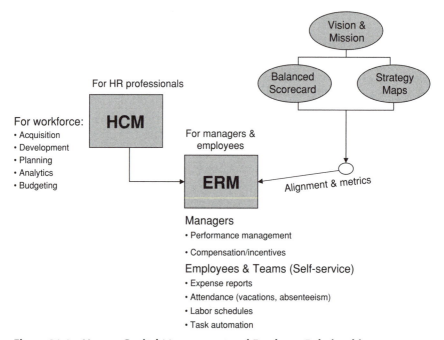

Figure 21.1 Human Capital Management and Employee Relationship Management Integrate with Performance Management Systems

by managers and employee teams. The new twist in modern ERM systems is that they provide *self-service* features. Today employees can personally submit their expense reports, time, or project reports, and maintain their attendance and vacation records. Managers can process employee reviews and compensation or job changes. All of this data is uploaded to a central database. There is substantial trust given to the employees.

HCM systems are designed for human resource managers. The enablers for the responsibilities that were just described here reside in the HCM system. HCM managers perform workforce planning, recruiting, and career pathing in the HCM system.

Note that strategy mapping and balanced scorecards are integrated with the ERM system. This provides for communicating the enterprise's strategy to employee teams and reports feedback on the key performance indicators.

BE PROACTIVE, NOT REACTIVE

A repeated theme in this book is that technology is no longer the impediment, the thinking is. This applies to HCM as well. However, armed with the proper analytical tools, workforce staffing can anticipate the probabilities. Continually align your organization's human capital with its mission and strategic objectives.

NOTE

1. *Scores* are calculated in HCM systems to measure the likelihood of an employee to voluntarily or involuntarily leave the organization.

PART FIVE

Performance Management, Business Intelligence, and Technology

"Type the field name Name in the Field Name field."
—An instruction in a software manual
awarded the worst-of-the-month[1]

In this Part, I will discuss why achieving business intelligence requires technology via data management and data warehousing coupled with data mining and analytic software in order to realize the maximum benefits of performance management. As I described at the outset of this book, organizations are increasingly requiring faster, fact-based, and more in-depth intelligence, combined with actionable decisions from employee teams, not solely from executives and managers. My concluding "Final Thoughts" (Chapter 23) describe a robust yet logical diagram that illustrates how all of the elements discussed in this book can link together.

NOTE

1. Winner by Corecomm, a Houston, Texas-based technical writing company, April 1996.

22

DATA MANAGEMENT AND MINING WITH PERFORMANCE MANAGEMENT

Organizations that are enlightened enough to recognize the importance and value of their data often have difficulty in actually *realizing* that value. Their data is often disconnected, inconsistent, and inaccessible. They have valuable, untapped raw data that is hidden in the reams of transactional data they collect daily. Information sharing among departments and functions is difficult. Unlocking the intelligence trapped in mountains of data has been, until recently, a relatively difficult task to accomplish effectively.

These organizations have been constructing their IT systems with nonintegrated single-point solutions. (For example, they have different departmental data warehouses built on different platforms using combinations of tools, some nonstandard, some with expired maintenance support, and some prebuilt in a tool purchased from a vendor no longer in business.) Implementing quick-fix solutions can become a software maintenance quagmire. With hindsight, even presumably researched software system purchases can still result in redundant tools, data inconsistencies, duplication of effort, and ultimately high IT operating expenses, with unintended barriers blocking systems from cleanly communicating among themselves. All organizations are reaching a point where it is important for computers to talk to other computers.

Innovation in data storage technology is now significantly outpacing progress in computer processing power, heralding a new era where creating vast pools of digital data is becoming the preferred solution.[1] As a result, some software vendors with superior tools offer a complete suite of analytic applications and data models that enable organizations to tap into the virtual treasure trove of information they already possess, and enable effective performance management on a scale broader than you can imagine. The tools provide easy access to corporate and enterprisewide data and also convert that data into useful and actionable information that is consistent across the organization—one coherent version of the truth.

These advanced software vendors' offerings are timely to solve today's problems in commerce and government. The market has been evolving from wanting just business intelligence tools to wanting *complete* solutions. This includes customizable *horizontal* solutions that apply across all markets (e.g., human capital management and scorecards), as well as industry-specific solutions for industries such as retail, banking, health care, or manufacturing. These are referred to as *vertical* solutions. Figure 22.1 illustrates the location of ABM in an information system and its more popular data outputs used in scorecarding systems. The figure also reveals how data from disparate sources can be extracted and stored to be retrieved for analysis.

In an example of a horizontal balanced scorecard application, data requirements for the popular four perspectives of the scorecard might be fed from Oracle Financials, Siebel CRM call center, SAP materials management, and PeopleSoft human resources. Bringing all of these pieces together can be challenging because of the different underlying data structure assumptions made by each. Direct access to source data is difficult due to the vast number of tables involved (tens of thousands in large systems). Data management tools by a vendor such as SAS integrates them and hides the complexity with an internal, logical

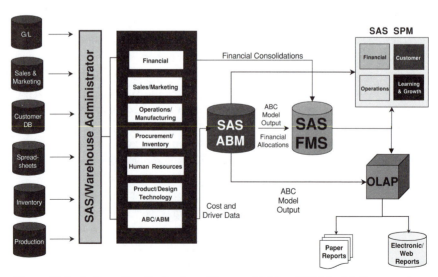

Figure 22.1   Information Technology Diagram Linking ABC/M with Scorecards

data model and metadata management. *Metadata* can be defined as information about the data, such as its origin, its processing, and its use.

EXTENDING DATA MINING AND BUSINESS INTELLIGENCE WITH ANALYTIC INTELLIGENCE

Analytic software applications extend the reach of data warehousing and mining tools to a wider user base, packaging these technologies in a business context for decision support. The information value chain is comprised of the following successive components, however, few organizations have added the last one:

- IT Architecture Planning—This component, often forgotten due to the rapid uncontrolled acquisition of IT tools, is the exercise of thinking ahead rather than starting the journey without a map. Many organizations skipped this step in the late 1990s during the Y2K scare.

- Extraction, Transform, and Load (ETL)—These tools provide prebuilt high performance capabilities to data manipulations, integration, and cleansing of quality before data is stored.

- Intelligent Data Storage—This component provides scalable and flexible data storage capabilities that ideally should be easy to administer and open to access by third party software from any commercial software vendor to exploit.

- Business Intelligence (BI)—This component, typically mistaken as the end of the information value chain, uses the stored historical data. A popular application is online analytical processing (OLAP) to view lists or multidimensional views of combination of data that can be rotated for ad hoc reporting and inquiries.

- Analytical Intelligence—This component, the true end of the information value chain, will differentiate superior performers from the inferior ones. The preceding business intelligence component provides managers and employee teams with previously unseen visibility, but this always begs new questions to be answered. Analytical intelligence, the jewel in the crown of the information value chain, is able to ask, analyze (with powerful statistical calculation engines), and answer the questions that are so critical to surfacing choices and making decisions.

The power of the last component, the robust analytical intelligence, is now available to business users in a compelling, easy-to-use format that is integrated with users' normal work flow. This component leverages the tools preceding it in this chain and is best considered as a set of solutions rather than more tools. Feedback from analytics leads to corrective actions that positively impact business operations. Feedback guides decision making, leading to actions that improve business performance. Rather than just reporting data, analytical intelligence software introduces forecasting, modeling, and optimization capabilities for decision support.

If you don't know where you are, then a map won't be of any use; if you don't know where you're going, then any road will do. The most advanced software vendors provide both the map and the road via the breadth and depth of their analytical intelligence applications and solutions. Many CIOs are cautious and believe that the goal of their IT strategy is to keep implementing automation technology of their standard processes, such as with customer sales order management or production systems. The fallacy is they believe improvement comes from streamlined operations, but in truth exceptional performance management comes from managers and employee teams understanding the business and situation they are in continuously better. Better understanding comes from leveraging analytical intelligence software to probe deeper, detect imperceptible trends, test hypothesis, and view the results of what-if scenarios combined with sensitivity analysis.

Analytics do not change the way people do business—they enhance how they do it. Analytic intelligence software applications are deployable across all levels of an enterprise, from top to bottom, and can be applied immediately to specific day-to-day business issues, such as with a customer call center, where information about each customer (e.g., account balance) should ideally not only be current in real time but also suggestive of what action to take and why. Analytics deliver key metrics and precisely tailored information directly to casual users and decision makers. While enterprises will increasingly require BI tools, complementing these capabilities with analytic intelligence applications substantially increases the overall value of their enterprise information and drives both sizeable productivity improvements across functional areas as well as profitable revenue enhancement.

The primary goal of analytic applications is to meld analytics with management functions so that analytics become an integral part of how managers and employee teams perform their job. Hence, successful implementation of analytical tools needs to focus first on specific business needs (i.e., supply chain management, customer churn detection and reduction, etc.).

According to IDC's study from October 2002, "The Financial Impact of Business Analytics,"[2] organizations that have successfully implemented and utilized analytic applications have realized returns ranging from seventeen percent to more than two-thousand percent with a median ROI of one-hundred and twelve percent. "The study has demonstrated that companies can derive significant ROI from analytics when they maintain a focus on a pressing business problem. Analytics positively impact the productivity of knowledge workers, across a range of industries and processes. The key is to continually apply the results of analytics in the form of corrective actions that improve a business process."[3]

EASE-OF-USE DATA MANAGEMENT

Data warehouses store transaction-based data and source records, such as customer transaction information, and summary information like account balances and time period totals. Data management technologies *extract* that data, *transform* it to serve decision making, and *load* it into analytical tools—the ETL tool set. Data management also includes the infrastructure technology (e.g., security, backup/recovery) required to regularly operate information processes involving large data volumes and generation of reports.

Most organizations have been purchasing software systems over the years as if they're dropping each system into a shopping basket in a grocery store. The problem is that all of the systems would have worked better if they were integrated, but that's no longer possible because they've already been purchased and implemented separately. One IT solution has been to try to store the data from all these disparate systems in a single data warehouse or operational data store, where multiple applications can share the data. A bet was made that common standards for databases would soon evolve, but the pace has been slow.

The next solution from the IT function has been to use data mining solutions to extract and synthesize the underlying knowledge from these massive data sources to enable their organization to gain a competitive advantage (or, if it is a public sector government or not-for-profit organization, to more effectively serve its constituents). Unfortunately, many data management tools do not integrate the diverse data sources well, might not be sufficiently scaleable, or are restricted in the scope of the problems they can solve. They are typically optimized around executing tasks for only specific business processes, such as customer management or supply chain management, and not all the necessary information resides in that particular system. Furthermore, data models optimized for *transaction processing* performance with literally thousands of tables are different from *analytical* data models optimized around subjects, metadata, and fast query responses on precalculated summary information.

As a result, organizations are increasingly demanding more powerful multipurpose data mining and analytic tools, characterized by a greater breadth and completeness of solution, that can be tailored to their needs. This provides all employees with one consistent version of the truth, rather than multiple versions that leave decision makers debating each other and doubting the quality of both their data sources and their resulting decisions.

In contrast to specialty software with closed, proprietary systems, tools that support open, standard architectures ensure that software application development environments are compatible with all forms of industry standards. Vendors with superior tools can directly access data in a wide range of source systems in each system's native format and provide platform independence that can be moved from platform to platform regardless of whether the target environment is a personal computer or a mainframe, or whatever the operating system. These superior tools make it easy to link information from individual solutions and leverage existing systems to produce reliable information with a holistic view that decision makers can act upon with confidence.

In short, the era of business intelligence for the masses has arrived. With these superior tools, now employees can also easily convert their business knowledge via the analytical intelligence tools to solve many business issues, such as these:

- Increase response rates from direct mail, telephone, e-mail, and Internet-delivered marketing campaigns.
- Identify their most profitable customers and the underlying reasons for those customers' loyalty, as well as identify future customers with comparable if not greater potential.
- Analyze click-stream data to improve e-commerce strategies.
- Quickly detect warranty-reported problems to minimize the impact of product design deficiencies.
- Uncover money-laundering criminal activities.
- Grow customer profitability and reduce risk exposure through more accurate financial credit scoring of their customers.
- Determine what combinations of products and service lines customers are likely to purchase and when.
- Analyze clinical trials for experimental drugs.
- Set more profitable rates for insurance premiums.
- Reduce equipment downtime by applying predictive maintenance.
- Determine with attrition and churn analysis why customers leave for competitors and/or become your customers.

- Detect and deter fraudulent behavior, such as from usage spikes when credit or phone cards are stolen.
- Identify promising new molecular drug compounds.

The list can be endless. What is common with all of these examples is to not stop at simply reporting, but to have the power to know the explanations behind the reported data.

EASE-OF-USE DATA MINING AND ANALYTICS

Data mining and analysis tools are designed to explore large quantities of data for comprehensive analysis to discover hidden relationships and uncover unknown patterns, trends, associations, or anomalies for the purpose of proactive or computer-automated decision making. These tools provide the ability to go beyond merely reporting *what has happened* in a business or organization to discovering *why it has happened*. They are also useful for deriving meaningful and accurate predictions. The superior data mining and analysis tools simplify and streamline both the data preparation time and the analysis process. The beauty of these tools is that they enable organizations to create unique value on top of an asset they already have: their raw data.

With these tools' rich suite of integrated data mining and analytic algorithms (e.g., classical statistics, outlier detection, neural networks, decision trees, regression analysis, a host of clustering methods, text mining) and unprecedented ease of use, nontechnical users can accomplish what only statisticians could do in the past. That is, the casual analyst is empowered with statistical and visualization techniques to extract the underlying business knowledge from vast deposits of data, exploit the data for predictive variables to yield validated findings and conclusions, possibly optimize their decisions, and finally present the results in actionable forms such as customer segmentation models.

Data mining tools provide a graphical user interface (GUI) that is designed such that analysts with only moderate statistical competencies can drive through the data mining and analysis process, while the quantitative expert can optionally go behind the scenes to fine-tune and tweak the analytical process. For example, nontechnical users can easily examine large amounts of data in multidimensional histograms to graphically compare their analyzed results derived from alternative scenarios and assumptions.

The benefit is that the time delay from data access to action is dramatically shortened—and the results can be deployed across the Internet. And all of this can be accomplished in a single computing environment. Organizations have made huge investments in their infrastructure—including operational software systems—and now they can leverage the value of these tangible assets by transforming them into true business intelligence. It will be the rate of organizational learning, not just the amount of learning, that will differentiate the advancing organizations from those that will fall behind.

USING THE TRANSFORMED DATA

For some industries, information *is* the competitive differentiator relative to the product or service line they sell (e.g., Amazon.com).

Organizations dream of having an elegant approach to *optimize* their decisions. However, you can't optimize everything because optimizing may not (yet) be feasible for a particular type of problem, or the economic costs to design and operate such an optimizing system may currently exceed the benefits of doing so (but in time, this cost versus benefit test will inevitably reverse). Regardless of today's trade-off economics, the potential to optimize business practices and their outcomes is immense—and there is already much evidence of business process optimization.

Short of sophisticated data mining–based capabilities, there are practical solutions to most problems that do not require optimization, but which nonetheless are fact-based decisions using analytic tools rather than being based on old rules of thumb, intuition, or gut-feel.

Figure 22.2 uses a staircase to show how information increases in value as it evolves. The steps represent the stages of maturity through which all organizations will eventually pass. These sequentially involve the following:

- **Capturing data.** It is increasingly economical to capture data from the entire range of business systems, organize that information, and store it, without knowing in advance every purpose that users will find for the data.

- **Accessing data.** What good is capturing data if people (or other computers) do not have appropriate access to that data or it is too painful to get to?

- **Using information.** Knowledge, wisdom, and intelligence are sources of competitive advantage.

As an organization ascends the staircase, underutilized data gets leveraged more fully as it is processed into managerial information.

Figure 22.2 broadly conveys, from left to right, how raw transactional and op-

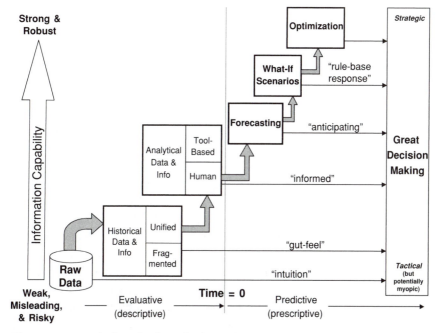

**Figure 22.2   Evolution of Value of Information
(On which step is your organization?)**

erating data are progressively converted into information, then into knowledge, and ultimately into intelligence—all used for decision making. The box to the right, labeled "Great Decision Making," is the ultimate destination and objective for converting the raw data.

DISTINCTION BETWEEN MANAGEMENT AND LEADERSHIP: TAKING RISKS

Leadership and communications are major pillars for any organization—and they are both innately human. By harnessing both leadership and communications to strategies and value creation (or mission accomplishment), performance management systems become the primary performance management tool that will likely blend into a successful organization's infrastructure—much like a phone system, but incredibly more valuable for fulfilling the organization's purpose.

The impact of the Internet, in all of its majesty, will play out for decades.

Web-deployed tools, like enterprise performance management systems, are sure to not only provide gains in efficiency and asset utilization, but also allow the sharp cornering at high speeds to assure that organizations apply and deploy capital and people to its highest returns.

As an organization proceeds up the staircase, its capability to make increasingly better decisions grows. That is, successive steps include and exceed previous steps. One of the key determinants of the rate at which organizations ascend this staircase of maturity is the leadership of its senior executives. There is a large distinction between managing and leading. Management is characterized as avoiding risks, whereas leadership is characterized as taking risks. Leaders must be decisive. Improved leadership can result from removing risks—or at least minimizing them into *calculated* risks.

Risks continue to exist even when accumulated data has been turned into usable information. In contrast, *calculated* risks are based not only on accumulations of past data but on calculations based on business-oriented mathematical models that can be used for predictive analysis. Predictive models analyze the risk, such as in giving customers credit, selecting one product or one market over another, predicting which higher-valued employees may likely resign, or consolidating vendors.

In the past, risk was only associated with the financials of the enterprise. Today's competitive business environment has redefined risk to encompass both financial and nonfinancial views. With the enactment of the Sarbanes-Oxley Act, managerial risk now incorporates personal risk, accountability, and personal consequence as well. As a result, corporations and executive officers must know the risk exposure of their enterprise at any point in time, combining risk analysis of not only financial information but people and process risk as well.

Reliable forecasts provide a much more accurate picture of the organization's risks. Make uncertainty your friend. You can't entirely remove risk, but you can reduce it. Analytical intelligence positioned on top of business intelligence opens the way for a bolder form of leadership.

STAGES OF MATURITY WITH INFORMATION SYSTEMS

Return to Figure 22.2. From left to right, progressively more important questions can be asked and answered:

- What happened?
- Why did it happen?

- What will happen if I act with varying alternatives?
- What is the best that could happen? (Which alternatives should I pursue?)

The centrally located, vertical dividing line in Figure 22.2 separates the future (on the right) from the past (on the left).

History

The left side of Figure 22.2 represents descriptive and evaluative information, rich in content if the intelligence in it can be mined. Using only historical data involves successive steps, each having two components.

1. **Historical data and information.** Raw data is converted into meaningful information for trend, correlation, anomalies, associations, and pattern analysis:

   - *Fragmented and disparate.* Despite their best intentions, IT's crystal ball just could not see into the future far enough. Data is there, but unfortunately not necessarily in locations that are easily accessible. Data management tools grab and store data in a common format. This data is centrally stored and managed, and, more importantly, is configured specific to the end goal.

   - *Unified.* Data is typically collected from different sources and requires normalization and standardization. For example, you may have three divisions from prior-year acquisitions, each with its own part-numbering scheme—for identical products. Normalizing this data provides that single version of the truth I keep referring to. State-of-the-art analytical companies rely on their data warehouses with data management based on extract, transform, and load (ETL) functions that make all data transparent and easy to consolidate, independent of the data source or platform. Cleansing, scrubbing, normalizing, standardizing, and reorganizing the data occurs here. Accurate and accessible data facilitates climbing up the stages-of-maturity staircase.

2. **Analytical information.** This is where the ability to interpret historical data enters in, perhaps spiced with some forecasts or plan information as well as optimization logic, in order to gain insights.

   - *Human analysis.* These include Excel, hand calculators, college 101-level course equations, and statistics courses. Some employees are pretty good at using these. Some organizations have been successful thanks to great leaders, out-of-the-box innovators, or luck.

- *Tool-based analysis.* Have you ever calculated the results of segmentation analysis that involve dozens of variables across hundreds of thousands of customers, part numbers, products, retail stores, routes and suppliers, and so on? Statistical analysis tools such as those from the software vendor SAS provide easy-to-use analytics to explore for the necessary findings that lead to hypothesis testing, conclusions, and ultimately actions.

Projections

The right side of Figure 22.2 represents prescriptive and predictive information for decision making by combining estimates of the future with descriptive information from the past. This is where uncertainty and risk intersect. With forecasting tools, predictions can be made with known degrees of uncertainty. Repeating myself, make uncertainty your friend. You can't entirely remove risk, but you can reduce it. There are three successive value-adding steps:

1. **Forecasting.** Some people estimate with straightedge projection using past data points on a scatter diagram. More progressive forecasters now use algorithmic tools and Internet-based sources of data that truly provide demand intelligence about future potential sales volume and mix. The reliability of forecasts improves every year.

2. **What-if scenarios.** Reliable forecasts of separate projections are great aids for making the best or right decisions, but in some cases there are so many interdependencies that you need the heavy-duty software ammunition of simulations, change sensitivity, and system dynamics tools.

3. **Optimization.** While everything cannot be optimized, some things can be. Constraints and conflicts are always present in optimization solutions, and performance management comprehensively considers the trade-offs for all of them. For those applications and processes that can be optimized (e.g., route selections and schedules), the outcome may likely separate the market leader from its competitors.

WHICH STEP IS YOUR ORGANIZATION ON?

Organizations have been doing many of the things described above (or at least striving to), but without the enabling technologies to move them up to the next levels of the staircase. Intuition, manual analysis with a number-two pencil, and spreadsheets can only take you so far. This discussion begs a question.

Which step of the staircase is your organization on? Often, an organization cannot easily label itself on a particular step since it typically straddles several steps. The epicenter for most organizations is located in Figure 22.2 approximately on the analytics step with human and tool-based analysis. For all organizations, employees will examine whatever data they can collect—primarily historical trends and correlations with some forecasts of future demand loads—and try to make the best judgments and decisions they can. This method can be satisfactory. After all, prehistoric humans figured out how to eat to survive, and trains and planes do make it from origin A to destination B (although not always on schedule).

The point is that there is nothing wrong with using historical data to support decision making. There are patterns, trends, and associations in history from which you can infer much about the future. For example, if a product has been unprofitable for years, and its unprofitable condition serves no other strategic purpose (such as being a loss leader), it makes sense to make decisions to improve the product's profit margins. The future often stems from seeds planted in the past. As another example, processing time and cost rates calibrated from past performance levels provide the foundation for profit-acceptance testing when price-quoting new sales orders and estimating schedule completion dates.

The superior software vendors can help organizations to proactively, rather than reactively, move up the staircase. Better decisions make a better organization—which means greater rewards.

In the next chapter, "Final Thoughts," I describe my vision of how an organization can operate as a single system using the performance management integrated suite of methodologies and tools.

NOTES

1. John Markoff, "In Computing, Weighing Sheer Power Against Vast Pools of Data," *New York Times*, June 2, 2003, C4.

2. Henry Morris, "The Financial Impact of Business Analytics," International Data Corporation (IDC), October 2002, at www.idc.com.

3. Henry Morris, Group VP of Applications and Information Access, IDC.

23

FINAL THOUGHTS
Linking Customers to Shareholders

"No facts that are in themselves complex can be represented in fewer elements than they naturally possess. While it is not denied that many exceedingly complex methods are in use that yield no good results, it must still be recognized that there is a minimum of possible simplicity that cannot be further reduced without destroying the value of the whole fabric. The snare of the 'simple system' is responsible for more inefficiency . . . than is generally recognized. . . ."

—Alexander H. Church, 1910[1]

There will always be skeptics. Are they a good check-and-balance to the enthusiasts whose vision may exceed reality? Perhaps. But I believe performance management will truly take hold because it can successfully pass the tests associated with the following four critical risks that arise with any big change in management style:

1. Technological risk. Does it work? Will it work? Any obsolescence issues?

Answer: Each component in the PM suite works stand-alone, and systems integration is now a proven and mature discipline. PM will work, and the sum of the combined parts will be much greater than each of them operating individually and unconnected.

2. Operational risk. Even if it works, will it work in my organization?

Answer: PM is mainly about principles that are universally applicable rather than rules that are case-specific. Principles apply to any organization in any industry.

3. Economic risk. Is it worth what you're going to pay for it

Answer: The cost versus benefits calculus will always work if you maintain low administrative effort by being industrious, smart, conscientious, and conserving in constructing a system. PM is not about intense effort but rather is facilitated by clever modeling, design, assumptions, and thinking.

4. Political risk. Will people be happy with the ultimately completed system?

Answer: If you help people solve problems in a reliable way, they are usually happy and appreciative.

PUTTING IT ALL ON A SINGLE SHEET OF PAPER

Some have said that the most dysfunctional part of an organization is its performance measurement system. The assumption is that if the measurements were more proper, aligned with strategies, and more tailored to the individuals and teams, then the organization would likely execute at a much better level of performance. Fixing the performance measurement system may very well be that holy grail that will wrench into place all of the improvement programs so that they work together in a coordinated way. That is why Part Two on *strategy maps* and *scorecards* is at the beginning of this book rather than near the end.

Others have described measuring shareholder value creation as the holy grail. They believe that if information systems were more linked to the actions needed to increase shareholder wealth, an organization would be more effective at achieving its ultimate goal. I described this in Chapter 20 as *economic value management*.[2]

My overall belief is that increasing shareholder wealth relates to satisfying, ideally delighting, customers via understanding derived from superior strategies. I further believe that all of this can be much better understood by using ABM data to view the linkages among customers, strategy, and economic wealth creation (or destruction). That is the mission of the performance management (PM) suite of tools described in this book: to translate strategic plans into results— profitably. PM is the process of managing the strategy.

ORGANIZATIONAL MODEL: A COST CONSUMPTION VIEW

Financial information is like the central nervous system, the means for organizations to communicate. Everyone seems to understand terms like *costs*, *profits*, *budgets*, *paychecks*, and *bills*. Financial data are simply a representation of cash and money. Cash and money are the common language of business and commerce. Commercial companies, not-for-profit organizations, and governments all speak the language of money.

The world is made up of thousands of businesses and organizations, but there are few basic principles that can be generalized to all of them. One is that if an organization continues to spend more money than it takes in, it will eventually disappear. The money flows through the organization like a circulatory system. If net cash back is constantly less than cash laid out, the organization suffers.

Business textbooks and magazine articles display many different exhibits of business models. They all convey how an organization operates. Figure 23.1 extends an ABM cross model developed by the professional organization CAM-I.[3] What I have added to the CAM-I cross are two important elements missing in the original: the organization's strategies and its performance measurements. The figure describes how an organization operates as a total system. It is a circulatory system based on the flow of money.

In one sense, the model begins and ends with customers, but it ultimately describes how the creation or destruction of wealth and economic value is a direct result of the organization's efforts. At the center of the model is the ABM cost assignment network described in Part Three that is considered the standard for

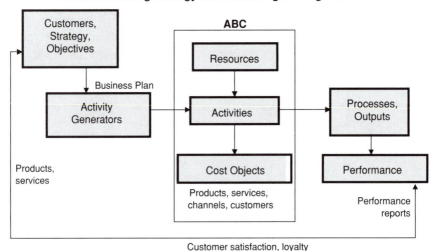

Beyond the scope of the ABC/M cross is a broader framework that includes defining strategy and measuring the alignment to it.

Figure 23.1   Strategic Management System

understanding cost management. The end game of this model is for the organization to continuously increase the financial wealth of its shareholders. In life, the organizations that excel in learning can win at this game—but there is no finish line.

EXPLORING THE MAP

Figure 23.2 is a decomposition and more detailed view of Figure 23.1. The money flow properties remain the same. Let's explore each of the major zones or regions of the map:

- Strategy and customers
- Profits and resource consumption
- Supply chain, cost drivers, processes, productivity, and value

This will not be unfamiliar territory because this book has already taken us along this journey traversing the routes on this map. The map is simply a bird's-eye

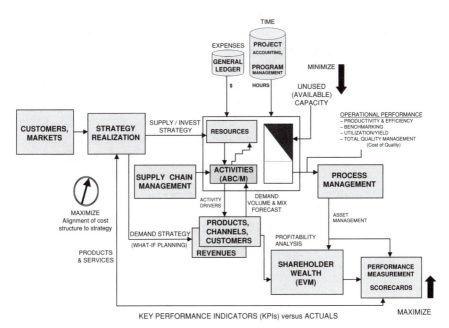

Figure 23.2   Performance Management

view of the whole mechanism of performance management, from the perspective of money flows.

Strategy and Customers

Examine the upper-left region of Figure 23.2. An accepted key to an organization's success is having a sound strategy with strategic objectives defined to guide employees to make the strategy realize its benefits. Customers are obviously essential. The strategy considers the customers' values, preferences, and needs. These provide the ideas for what products and services will satisfy customers so that they will exchange money for them. This in turn will produce customer satisfaction, loyalty, and retention—plus draw new customers. Chapter 17 discussed this as analytical customer intelligence and operational CRM.

There has been an evolution in strategy methodologies used to define and determine organization strategies. In the long run, strong leadership is a necessary ingredient to make the strategy work. Earlier I distinguished between managers and leaders according to their degree of taking calculated risks.

Once the strategy has been defined (and as it is continuously redefined), the strategy's outputs provide inputs to other elements of the business model:

- **Demand strategy and investment strategy.** A strategy has two components: how to generate customer interest and sales orders, and then how to provide the required resources and capacity to fulfill that demand. Usually the demand strategy comes first, and the supply strategy then matches it. This minimizes the amount of unused capacity, which if not minimized will detract from creating stakeholder wealth with costs of excess capacity.

- **Target measures.** These metrics, the key performance indicators (KPIs) from the balanced scorecard in Part Two, are used to communicate the strategy and test whether the organization is achieving the expected results. With that feedback, the organization can adjust its actions.

- **What-if scenarios.** These represent the many possibilities of what might result from alternative strategies and execution plans. Scenarios are used to simulate what-if analysis. As described at the end of Part Three, scenarios also provide some of the metrics needed to evaluate costs versus benefits and to quantify near-term target measures, spending plans, and budgeted resource costs.

If the demand strategy is successful and matched with the appropriate type and level of resources, then the correct products and services flow back to the customer and marketplace. If a long-term and healthy relationship with customers is maintained, then customers' satisfaction converts to loyalty and retention. The ideal goal for a supplying organization is a *customer for life*.

Profits and Resource Usage versus Spending

The middle region of the model expands on the ABM cost assignment network. In Figure 23.2, the work activities are located at the center of the map—work and processes are central to how an organization executes and creates results. Cost objects consume work activity costs, and activity costs consume resource expenses. There is tremendous variation in how diverse cost objects, such as products and customers, load demands on work activities. This is the location in Figure 23.2 that detects the different costs caused by diversity. Activity based costing, the math engine for ABM, has become accepted as the appropriate instrument to accurately measure these costs.

The resources are the economic expenses of people, supplies, equipment, buildings, and other items. Resources supply the expenses for activities. Then, as just stated, the cost objects consume the activities. If the work activities do not consume all the available resources, then there is some unused capacity remaining. (Synonyms for *unused capacity* are *idle capacity* and *excess capacity*.) In other words, the resource-spending expenses occur, but the resource usage costs are less than one-hundred percent of the expenses. The adjacent and partially shaded box spanning the resources and activities reflects the unused capacity. If the unused capacity is substantial, then its cost is probably displacing profits. Profits are calculated as a derivative of revenues net of the cost of the cost objects.

Near the center bottom of Figure 23.2 are the elements that determine profit. The revenues are a consequence of pricing and volume, where the volume is also governed by the customers' awareness, interest, and ability to afford the product or service line. In addition, competitors can eat into your sales volume. They can attract those same customers' money—remember that in the business-to-consumer (B2C) game it is a *share of wallet* contest. The costs of the cost objects are the combination of the costs-to-make (products), the costs-to-deliver (service lines), and the *costs-to-serve* (the customer). The resulting level of profit is an input to the performance measures (i.e., balanced scorecard). The profit performance is usually judged from the reported scores relative to the KPI targets (derived from the strategy maps) and relative to past months and years.

In the long run, the end game for organizations is to minimize unused capacity while maximizing cash flow returns and economic profit to increase shareholder wealth. This was discussed in Chapter 20 on economic value management. These two goals, capacity management and wealth creation, are noted in Figure 23.2 by the large up and down arrows labeled *minimize* and *maximize*. I think of this system as if it was a child's electronic Nintendo or Game-Boy for the executive management. They must push all the right buttons.

Cost Drivers, Processes, Productivity, and Value

The zone or region across the map's middle and ending at the right is where the business processes are located, including supplier relations. Supply chain and process management were described in Chapters 18 and 19. A business process can be defined as two or more logically related (or sequential) work activities with a common purpose. (The term *activity-based cost management* was coined a few years after activity-based costing was being applied. ABC/M, shortened to ABM in this book, stresses the importance of acting on the activity-based costing data to manage the organization through better decisions.) Cost drivers are an input to the work activities. A cost driver, such as a customer's order, is an event or factor that creates the need for and influences the type and amount of work activities.

Economic value management (EVM), described in Chapter 20, refers to maximizing cash flow returns and economic profit; however, in Figure 23.2 EVM is also associated with business processes and their outputs. The inputs to EVM are tools, such as benchmarking, related to execution and operational performance that were discussed as operational ABM, six sigma, and lean thinking.

FROM CUSTOMERS TO SHAREHOLDERS

There are many ways to diagram an enterprise-wide business model of how an organization determines strategy and then satisfies customer needs to create wealth for its stakeholders. Figure 23.2 is simply my diagram to visualize performance management as a system. But the figure does make, in terms of money, the critical link between minimizing unused capacity costs and maximizing stakeholder wealth, and it links the projected resource levels back to strategy and customers. Maximizing shareholder wealth using a method like economic value management (EVM) may be the ends, but ABM is logically one of the important means.

WHAT MATTERS MOST TO ME?

Admittedly, this book covered a broad landscape. However, to a computerized information system, it all connects. To such an inanimate system, the components of performance management represent a business model. Of course, the test of a business model like this is how well it not only represents an organization's behavior but also how well it can be used for predictive purposes.

My sense is that the primary usefulness of the performance management information is in repeatable and reliable reporting of the model framework, with secondary utility from its predictive power. Advancing to mastery with forecasting and estimating will come with time. But good performance results can come by just formulating and continuously adapting good customer-focused strategy using accurate, fact-based data, and linking the resulting strategic objectives (strategy maps), supported by properly budgeted projects and initiatives, to key performance indicators (scorecards). Customer and supplier relationship management as well as internal process control and human capital management can all benefit from scorecard, ABM, and budgeting systems because *behavior drives performance*. Misalignment of behavior is expensive in terms of misspent resources and missed revenue opportunities. That, in a nutshell, summarizes the powerful performance management framework described in this book.

However, if you were to ask me what one aspect of this book I am most intrigued by, I would be torn to choose between these three: (1) the calculated risks among trade-off decisions—specifically how to balance shareholder economic value creation to customer value; (2) managing capacity; and (3) forecasting.

Trade-Off Decisions to Balance Economic Value

When employees understand the strategy, and how what they do will impact the achievement of strategic objectives, marketlike behavior is motivated internally within the organization. It fosters a business-owner mentality with employees and makes strategy everyone's job.

However, there will always be conflict to be balanced. As I observed in the beginning of this book, conflicts result from different objectives for customers or processes or employees. This intensifies as organizations grow and become more complex. Managers and employee teams are constantly faced with conflicting objectives and with no way to resolve them. Work activities become more difficult to coordinate, and budget funding is not sourced to the managers needing it. By integrating the components of PM, a business can comprehensively consider and balance all objectives, such as strategic objectives with customer service needs and budgetary (profit) constraints

Maximizing everywhere is not equivalent to optimizing—it is suboptimizing. Trade-off decisions ideally balance value for all stakeholders—shareholders, customers, suppliers, partners, and employees alike. (And let's not leave out environmental and community interests.) No organizational function or silo should benefit at the expense of another.

Ever-changing customer preferences, needs, and demands cause constantly changing and competing priorities. Today's management systems, like financial budgeting, were not designed to balance conflict with value. They typically *control* things but do not *balance* things. *Cumbersome*, *inefficient*, and *ineffective* are words that come to mind.

Decisions are the intersecting points where economic value is either created or destroyed. Trade-offs must always be evaluated. Your eyes can now roll and you can take the opinion that the complexity and interdependencies are so overwhelming that performance management is a boiling-an-ocean endeavor. I conclude that it is about good modeling and reporting.

Capacity Management

Capacity management is one of the more informal disciplines, even in factories where you would think, with the massive amounts of data that production planners have, they would have this down pat. Capacity management fundamentally means matching the level of resources with the expected demand. It is actually code for *unused* capacity management, where the goal is either to juice up demand to fill it or to remove it as an unnecessary expense.

The airline industry is a role model for this discipline. In the short term, an empty seat at liftoff is a revenue opportunity lost forever. Hence their use of price optimization principles, with variable pricing tied to different customer segment price elasticity sensitivities. In the long term, too many aircraft for the gross passenger demand across all routes drags down profits.

Most organizations regulate head count levels and equipment purchases based on incremental sense-and-respond. For example, if the queue lines (i.e., customer wait time) get excessively long, customer service representatives are added. If good employees are still processing inbound workload after the dinner hour, you consider adding staff.

I will shorten a long diatribe. Quantitative analysis, permeating PM, has tremendous potential to improve the informal practices. Thin profit margins reduce help anywhere you can get it. My bet is capacity management will someday soon be in everyone's vocabulary.

Forecasting

If forecasts came true at every level of detail, many headaches would go away. Not only would the unnecessary extra costs be removed to staff and provide resources at higher buffer (i.e., insurance) levels due to uncertainty, but also customer service levels would improve. For example, if distributors and retailers knew the *exact* demand, hourly, of their consumption pipelines, then the velocity of material throughput (i.e. inventory turnover improving the cash-to-cash cycle) would shift from a Los Angeles–like traffic jam to Indianapolis 500 car racing speeds (well, you get the idea). That is, when future planned demand load has minimal uncertainty and therefore is likely to arrive as true, then scheduled replenishment and delivery for each item can become *just-in-time*, and fewer extra resources are needed.

For me, the intrigue of greater competency with forecasting relates to the massive power of today's computing systems to apply highly granular quantitative forecasts by customer, by item, and by day. All the data is there—somewhere. What is required is the will to harness it and transform it.

FINAL THOUGHTS

Several themes were repeated throughout this book, such as the need for managers and employees to understand the strategy, and why technology is no longer the impediment to implementing PM but, rather, it is the thinking. The theme I'd like to conclude with is why making trade-off decisions is the central message underlying this book.

Life, business, commerce, and government are a continuous process of making choices. Strategy, which I described as of paramount importance, is all about making choices. When making choices and decisions, conflicts are naturally competing, and they are weighed among options when the final decision is made. Computers, data management, quantitative analysis, and analytical theory have made huge strides that facilitate making performance management pay off. PM provides managers and employees clear direction and the computational horsepower to measure and weigh the trade-off decisions to always point to the highest value creation.

In Part One, a blending of the two basic managerial approaches and orientations was advocated: Newtonian quantitative and Darwinian behavioral. People are what it's all about, so I honor and respect the importance of applying the principles of behavioral change management. However, my love for quantitative analysis influences me to conclude with a short narration by the great Princeton University mathematician and Nobel Prize winner, John Nash. Nash introduced a theory describing how rational human beings should behave if there is a conflict of interests. In the Academy Award–winning movie about Nash's life, *A Beautiful Mind*, he said:

> "I like numbers because with numbers truth and beauty are the same thing. You know you are getting somewhere when the equations start looking beautiful. And you know that the numbers are taking you closer to the secret of how things are."

The executive management teams with the courage, will, caring attitude, and leadership trait to take calculated risks and be decisive will likely be the initial adopters of fully integrated performance management systems and will achieve its complete vision. Other executive management teams will follow them.

NOTES

1. Alexander H. Church, "Organization by Production Factors," *Engineering Magazine*, April 1910, 80.

2. If we use the term *stakeholder* rather than *shareholder*, we broaden the pool of who benefits when the organization takes in increasingly more money than it spends. For example, for government organizations, the stakeholder may be the service recipient or the governing board. Another example is a commercial company that can elect to selectively increase salaries, but this obviously reduces the after-tax profits that fall to the bottom line.

3. CAM-I is the Consortium for Advanced Manufacturing International at www.cam-i.org.

INDEX